TWAYNE'S WORLD AUTHORS SERIES

A Survey of the World's Literature

Sylvia E. Bowman, Indiana University

GENERAL EDITOR

FRANCISCO DE QUEVEDO

by

Donald W. Bleznick

Francisco de Quevedo (1580-1645) is one of Spain's foremost literary figures of all time. His nonpareil manneristic style is for some critics the key to his greatness. Endowed with a prodigious mastery of the Spanish language, he taxed words and phrases to the limits of their meaning, created new words and expressions, altered normal syntax, and indulged in every conceivable stylistic artifice. His reputation as Spain's most celebrated satirist derives chiefly from his *Buscón,* the masterpiece of picaresque novels, his allegorical *Visions,* and his burlesque poems, all of which ingeniously and incisively expose to public view the very souls of seventeenth-century Spaniards. His sonnets to Lisi are among the finest love poems ever written in Spain. He also wrote noteworthy books on politics, religion, and philosophy. A zealous love of Spain and a constant striving to halt his country's political, economic, and moral decay inform his literary work. Borges has compared Quevedo's extensive and complex writings to those of Joyce, Goethe, Shakespeare, and Dante.

TWAYNE'S WORLD AUTHORS SERIES (TWAS)

The purpose of TWAS is to survey the major writers —novelists, dramatists, historians, poets, philosophers, and critics—of the nations of the world. Among the national literatures covered are those of Australia, Canada, China, Eastern Europe, France, Germany, Greece, India, Italy, Japan, Latin America, New Zealand, Poland, Russia, Scandinavia, Spain, and the African nations, as well as Hebrew, Yiddish, and Latin Classical literatures. This survey is complemented by Twayne's United States Authors Series and English Authors Series.

The intent of each volume in these series is to present a critical-analytical study of the works of the writer; to include biographical and historical material that may be necessary for understanding, appreciation, and critical appraisal of the writer and to present all material in clear, concise English—but not to vitiate the scholarly content of the work by doing so.

To Rozlyn, Jordan, and Susan

Preface

rise to prominence under the Catholic Monarchs to the middle
of the seventeenth century. In Chapter 2, I have essayed to
use as much documented material as possible in sketching the
essential events in Quevedo's life. A good book-length biography
of Quevedo, based on fact rather than on legends and fanciful
assumptions, is still to be written. In Chapter 3, I examine the
Sueños and related satirical works; in Chapter 4, I analyze the
Buscón. In my interpretation of these prose works, the best
written by Quevedo, I also refer to some of his lesser-known
writings. Chapter 5 comprises a detailed analysis of Quevedo's
style in prose and poetry. In Chapter 6, I treat his satirical and
serious poetry. Chapter 7 delves into Quevedo's political works
with special emphasis on the *Política de Dios* (*Politics of God*)
and its relationship with other Golden Age works on the governance of rulers. Rather than devote an entire chapter to Quevedo's
religious ideas, I have discussed them throughout this book and
especially in Chapters 6 and 7. Chapter 8, which is devoted to
an analysis of Quevedo's theater, stresses his interludes, some
of which have recently been discovered.

DONALD W. BLEZNICK

University of Cincinnati

Acknowledgments

I wish to express my acknowledgment to the Research Council of the Pennsylvania State University for the grants that have aided me in my research. I owe a special debt of gratitude to James O. Crosby who has supplied me with much useful bibliography and aided me in obtaining pertinent materials. María Elisa Delgado has provided valuable assistance in preparing the index.

Contents

Chronology

1556- Reign of Philip II.
1598

1580 September 17: Francisco de Quevedo y Villegas was born in Madrid.

1588 Defeat of the Invincible Armada.

1596- Quevedo studied at University of Alcalá where he received
1600 his bachelor's degree.

1598- Reign of Philip III.
1621

1601- Quevedo a student of theology at the University of Valladolid.
1605 Achieves some renown as a poet: eighteen of his poems included in Pedro de Espinosa's anthology, *Flores de poetas ilustres* (1605).

1604- Corresponds in Latin with the Belgian humanist Justus Lipsius:
1605 Lipsius lauds Quevedo's erudition.

1605 First part of Cervantes' *Don Quijote.*

1606- Quevedo returns to Madrid and pursues an active literary
1612 career.

1606- Writes first three *Sueños* and the *Buscón.*
1608

1609 Expulsion of the Moors.

1613 Quevedo travels to Italy to join his friend Pedro Téllez Girón, Duke of Osuna, Viceroy of Sicily (1610-1615), and later of Naples (1616-1620).

1615 Second part of *Don Quijote.*

1615 Quevedo sent by the Sicilian Parliament to present contribution of 300,000 ducats to the King of Spain. Represents the Duke of Osuna in court intrigues.

1616 Death of Cervantes.

1616 Quevedo leaves Madrid for Naples to rejoin Duke of Osuna.

1617 Returns to Madrid.

1618 Officially becomes member of Order of Santiago. Duke of Osuna's abortive attempt to establish a strong Venetian state independent of Spain.

1620 Quevedo imprisoned in Torre de Juan Abad because of his association with the Duke of Osuna.

1621- Reign of Philip IV.
1665

1621 Philip IV ascends the throne. Spain is ruled by the new minister, the Count-Duke of Olivares. Quevedo, briefly in good graces of King and Olivares, is released from Torre de Juan Abad.

1622   Philip IV orders Quevedo's return to Torre de Juan Abad. Death of Duke of Osuna whom Quevedo eulogizes in poetry, and in the *Política de Dios* and *Marco Bruto*. Grave illness. Released from his imprisonment. Restored to good graces of King.

1626   Publication of the *Buscón*, and the first part of the *Política de Dios* (second part published in 1655).

1627   Publication of the *Sueños*.

1628   Quevedo exiled to Torre de Juan Abad because of his defense of Santiago as the sole patron saint of Spain.

1632   Named secretary of the King.

1634   Marries the widow Doña Esperanza de Mendoza. Marriage fails within three months. Publication of *La cuna y la sepultura*.

1635   Death of Lope de Vega.

1635-
1639   Quevedo spends most of his time in Torre de Juan Abad, writing and taking care of his estate.

1639-
1643   Imprisoned in San Marcos de León supposedly because he wrote the poem "Católica, sacra, real magestad" ("Catholic, Holy, Royal Majesty"), criticizing the King. Recent criticism has demonstrated that Quevedo probably did not author this poem and it is believed that other causes, as yet unknown, motivated his imprisonment. Extreme physical and mental suffering during his incarceration. He is finally released five months after the fall of Olivares.

1644   Back in the Torre de Juan Abad. Publication of *Marco Bruto*. Works on the second part of his *Marco Bruto* and the *Vida de San Pablo*.

1645   September 8: dies.

CHAPTER 1

The Historical Background

I The Catholic Monarchs

WHEN Quevedo was born, Spain's political power had achieved its zenith under the rule of Philip II. However, it is necessary to cast our attention to the preceding significant events in this country's history in order to comprehend more fully the Spain of Quevedo's time. The genesis of Spain's rise to greatness harks back to the late fifteenth century.

Ferdinand and Isabella, the Catholic Monarchs (1479-1517), established the basis for a strong, unified nation, the first modern state of Europe. Their political, religious, and economic reforms led to a well-ordered and peaceful federal union comprising the autonomous states of Castile, Aragón, Catalonia, and Valencia. Isabella's Castile achieved a political and cultural primacy which it never relinquished. The discovery of the New World promised untold wealth and power. And, finally, it was under the aegis of the Catholic Monarchs that Spain subdued and extirpated its religious minorities, the Moors and the Jews. The Inquisition was founded as the instrument to accomplish Spain's religious purification, a mission which went on unabated during the sixteenth and seventeenth centuries. The year 1492 saw the conquest of Granada signaling the complete subjugation of the Moors, and the expulsion of the Jews, a dynamic community which had played a key role in the political and economic life of Spain.

II Charles V

Spain was destined to control a potent world empire and become the bulwark of Christendom under its alien ruler, the Fleming Charles. In 1516 he ascended the Spanish throne as Charles I and two years later he was also elected Charles V of the Holy Roman Empire. Spaniards were adverse to accept the rule of a monarch who was a stranger to Spain, knew no

15

Spanish, seemed dominated by Flemish advisors, and granted important posts to foreigners. The revolt of the *comuneros,* commoners, of Castile (1520-1521) was a vehement expression of Spanish desire to preserve their national integrity which they saw threatened with dissolution in Charles's empire. After the defeat of the *comuneros* and of the separate rebellion (1519-1522) of the *Germanías,* Christian brotherhoods of Valencia and Mallorca, there were no more Castilian revolts against Charles. Castile became reconciled to the government of Charles, increasingly more Spaniards entered his service, the language of the monarch and his court became Castilian, and, after abdicating the throne in favor of his son Philip II, he chose to spend the final period of his life in a small palace adjoining the monastery of Yuste in Extremadura.

Charles's empire was essentially a confederation of diverse territories each of which retained its own laws and liberties. Furthermore, a well-integrated empire was not possible in view of Charles's particular interests and in the absence of an articulated imperial policy. Charles V was largely an absentee ruler for Spain; in the nearly forty years he was their king, less than sixteen years were spent in Spain. During the King's extended absences, the effective government of Spain was carried on by secretaries—this foreshadows the entrusting of the affairs of state to court favorites during the reigns of Philip III and IV—notably Francisco de los Cobos who ably organized and conducted the affairs of Castile, Portugal, the Indies, and Italy. Castile was expected to supply men and money for some of Charles's enterprises which were not in consonance with their own interests—the wars with France and the conflict with the Protestant princes of Germany. These and other adventures had few positive results but did succeed in damaging Spain economically.

The year Charles came to Spain, 1517, was the year Luther nailed his ninety-five theses on the cathedral door at Wittenberg. Like the Catholic Monarchs, Charles was wholly devoted to the mission of achieving the unity of Christendom in his domains and protecting it against heretics and Moslems. Deeply disturbed by Luther's statements, he wrote his own statement for the Diet of Worms (April, 1521) in which he pledged his kingdoms, dominions and friends, and his own body, blood, soul, and life to the defense of Christendom. This attitude obviously struck a responsive chord among Spaniards. Yet Charles's attack on

Lutheranism arose from secular as well as religious reasons. He feared that Lutheranism would bring further independence for the German princes and weaken his sovereignty. At first Charles apparently was victorious, especially with the defeat of the Germans at the battle of Mühlberg in 1547, but five years later the situation was completely reversed. Pressed by the French and Turks on other fronts, he was unable to muster enough troops to stem the onslaught of Maurice of Saxony near Innsbruck (May, 1552) and had to take flight across the Alps. By the Treaty of Passau (1552) and the Peace of Augsburg (1555), Protestantism was recognized as the equal of Catholicism in the Holy Roman Empire.

Charles's campaigns against the Turks won strong support from the Spaniards in whom the zeal of the Crusades still burned. Under Suleiman the Magnificent (1520-1566), the Turks had increased their strength and were exerting pressure upon Spain in the Mediterranean and were advancing up the Danube to the gates of Vienna. In 1535, Charles personally led the attack that recaptured Tunis from the Turks. But the Turks could not be held in check and the Turkish navy continued its raids on Spain and Italy. The emperor himself led a large expedition— the celebrated conqueror of Mexico, Hernán Cortés took part in this action—against the stronghold of Algiers in October, 1541. A winter storm destroyed 150 of his ships and the operation ended in disaster. After this, Charles abandoned the Mediterranean until the end of his reign.

Spanish trade and industry boomed after the revolt of the *comuneros*. Cargoes of gold and silver from the New World abundantly flowed into Spain and the products of Spanish industry were shipped in large quantities to America. A price revolution accompanied this prosperity so that by 1550 the commodity prices on the average doubled over what they had been in the preceding thirty years, and were to double once more by the turn of the century. Seville, with its *Casa de Contratación* ("Trades House"), had a virtual monopoly over the American trade and rapidly became one of the most important and prosperous cities of Europe. However, Charles's enterprises against the French, the Turks and the Protestants always kept his imperial coffers empty and he was obliged to borrow under unfavorable terms huge sums from German and Genoese bankers. By the time Philip II assumed Spanish rule in the mid 1550's, Spain was in a bankrupt state. Soaring prices caused a diminution in trade with Europe and the American trade declined because of the increasing self-sufficiency of the colonies; agriculture suffered because of the support of the Mesta, the feudal association of sheep owners, and the lack of farmers in view of the general Spanish disinclination to undertake menial labor which they deemed fit only for serfs and Moriscos; and Charles's unsound economic policy, which dictated exorbitant and debilitating taxation, destroyed many industries.

Charles liquidated his empire in a series of abdications that began with the transfer of the Netherlands to his son Philip in 1555. The following year, Philip assumed the Spanish crown that included the Italian dependencies. Finally, Charles resigned the German Empire to his brother Ferdinand in 1558. Charles's plan to bring England into the Empire ended in failure when Mary Tudor, whom Philip had married in 1554, died childless in 1558, less than two months after the demise of the Emperor. As we shall see, Philip's legacy was also to be a bankrupt Spain and the struggle against heresy.

III *Philip II*

Philip II (1556-1598) worked long hours and spurned personal pleasure in striving to fulfill his mission of serving God and his subjects. In 1543, Charles left written confidential instructions to his son to guide him during his reign. These precepts advised him to keep God uppermost in his mind, to dispense justice without corruption, to heed the advice of good counselors, and to foster the Inquisition. His father's admonition that he depend on none but himself impelled him to assume personal direction of the government. This meant ceaseless attention to matters of state, even to insignificant details, which, coupled with his indecisive nature, led to procrastination in decision making.

The first two decades of Philip's rule were beset with many problems. Financial troubles plagued him as they had his father from whom he had inherited a debt of at least twenty million ducats. One of his first acts was to repudiate interest payments to foreign bankers, but the threat of losing future financial support from these bankers forced him to abandon this policy. Philip estimated in 1560 that his indebtedness amounted to seven times the annual national revenue, and by 1574 the sums of interest he was paying to German and Genoese bankers exceeded his total income. Bankruptcy occurred in 1575 and

Spain emerged from this financial crisis by having the bankers agree to lower their rate of interest, by increased taxation, and by the sale of certain church lands.

Philip's financial plight in the 1560's arose mainly from his costly foreign policy as well as from the revolt (1568-1570) of the Moriscos, the Moors converted to Christianity after the Reconquest. The Turks still continued their incursions against Spain in the Mediterranean, and it was not until the Battle of Lepanto (October, 1571) that the Turkish menace receded. Spain was unsuccessful in subduing the revolt in the Netherlands which became more adamant in its rejection of orthodox Catholicism. The Moriscos rebelled because of Philip's decree in 1567 which curtailed Moslem practices among them. After their defeat they were deported from the province of Granada and scattered throughout Spain while twelve thousand peasant families from the north were brought in to replace them. The final solution to the Morisco problem came four decades later.

The year of Quevedo's birth, 1580, represents a high mark in Spain's political fortunes. When Philip's claim to the Portuguese throne met opposition, he decided to annex that country by force. Portugal was subdued without much difficulty in less than two months and Philip was crowned King of Portugal in April, 1581. The acquisition of Portugal unified the whole Iberian peninsula for the first time in nine centuries. It also brought new Atlantic harbors, a large Portuguese fleet manned by expert sailors, and an extensive colonial empire which was second only to that of Spain. Philip's capability of pursuing his imperial ambitions in the 1580's and 1590's was enhanced by the increased shipments of silver from the New World which began in the late 1570's. However, future attempts to expand his hegemony over the world met with failures. The defeat of the Spanish Invincible Armada (1588) signalled the beginning of Spain's decline.

The chief cause of the deterioration in Anglo-Spanish relations began in 1585 when Queen Elizabeth decided to intervene directly in the Low Countries by sending six thousand troops to aid the rebels who were resisting the Spanish. The Spaniards were also vexed by English privateering and the persecution of Roman Catholics in England. Philip's plan to overthrow Elizabeth was to invade England through the English Channel with a fleet of 130 ships and thirty thousand men. Inferior leadership,

poor preparations, and a storm combined to diminish the effec-
tiveness of the Armada which suffered disaster.

The final adventure of Philip was his intervention in France
for the purpose of securing the crown of that divided country.
However, when Henry of Navarre was converted to Catholicism
in 1593 and became a national king, Philip's hopes of occupying
the throne of France faded. Yet Philip could find consolation
in being largely responsible for retaining France within the
Catholic fold. The bankruptcy of 1596 forced Philip to seek
peace with some of his enemies. The ties between Spain and
the Netherlands were loosened in 1596 when Philip handed over
the Low Countries to his cousin the Archduke Albert and the
Infanta Isabella Clara Eugenia. According to the terms of the
agreement, Spanish troops were to remain in the Netherlands
and the land was to revert to Spain if the new rulers died
without leaving an heir. In May, 1598, about four months before
his death, Philip concluded the Franco-Spanish war in a peace
treaty with Henry IV at Vervins.

Our appreciation of Philip's reign must take into account the
vital role that religion played in many aspects of Spanish life.
We have already seen that the defense of Catholicism motivated
much of his foreign policy and caused the repression of the
Moriscos within Spain. The intense religious activity of the
second half of the sixteenth century was due in large measure
to the Council of Trent (1545-1563), an ecumenical council of
the Roman Catholic Church convoked to meet the crisis of
the Protestant Reformation. A significant number of well-
qualified Spanish theologians participated in formulating the
reform program that resulted from this Council. The beginning
of Philip's rule saw the expansion of the Inquisition's powers.
Not only were heretics persecuted in the continuing effort to
establish total racial and religious purity within the country,
but also measures were taken to prevent contagion with dangerous ideas from abroad. In 1558 a law was issued forbidding
the import of foreign books and ordering that all books printed
in Spain should be licensed by the Council of Castile. In the
following year another pragmatic forbade Spanish students from
studying abroad. The new Spanish Index of the Inquisitor
General Valdés, published in 1559, was more extensive than any
that had appeared previously; it banned the works of Erasmus
and many other religious works that had been popular. The
Inquisition relaxed its policy of not permitting the printing of

religious writings which at first it thought might contribute to the spread of heresy, and in the latter part of the sixteenth century mystical and ascetic writings achieved wide circulation.

Philip II's legacy was a unified Iberian Peninsula which still controlled a vast empire. Catholicism was triumphant within Spain and the spread of Protestantism abroad had been checked. Literature, art and science had flourished during his reign. On the other hand, his naval and military forces had not prevailed against the Dutch, English and French, and at his death he left Spain in dire economic straits. Industry and agriculture had declined, inflation was rampant, taxation became even more burdensome, and it was only the wealth from the mines of Peru's Potosí that staved off complete financial collapse. A feeling of national disillusionment beset the Spaniards who could not understand or cope with the paradoxes of their life.

IV   *Philip III and Lerma*

The death of Philip II marked an ill-fated new direction in the governance of the Spanish empire. The personal involvement of the Catholic Monarchs, Charles V, and Philip II in the affairs of state did not serve as a model for the kings who ruled in the seventeenth century. These monarchs' abdication of power gave rise to the new period of rule by favorites for whom the true interests of Spain were subservient to the desire for personal gain. During the seventeenth century, there was a constant decline in Spanish power and morality.

Philip III (1598-1621), a sickly youth of twenty when he ascended the throne, seems, of his father's virtues, to have inherited only his piety. Shortly before his death, Philip II is supposed to have confided to his experienced advisor, Don Cristóbal de Moura, his fears that his son would be unfit to govern his many kingdoms: "Alas, Don Cristóbal, I am afraid they will govern him." The new King, unable and unwilling to assume his responsibilities, promptly dismissed his father's ministers and entrusted the government to Don Francisco de Sandoval y Rojas, Marquis of Denia, who was later to become the Duke of Lerma.

Lerma was an affable and tactful man, but inexperienced in statecraft. His main ambition apparently was to retain his power and quickly improve his own financial condition as well as that of his relatives and friends. By 1602 he was deriving

an annual income of two hundred thousand ducats from his
offices and generous royal gifts, and it was said that he amassed
the huge sum of forty-four million ducats by the time he fell
from power. This covetous man was more readily swayed by
bribes than by persuasive words. His son-in-law, the Count of
Miranda, was elevated to the presidency of the Council of
Castile; his uncle, Cardinal Sandoval, became Archbishop of
Toledo with an annual revenue of three hundred thousand
ducats; his eldest son was named Marquis of Cea; a brother
received the post of Viceroy of Valencia; an uncle was appointed
President of the Council of Portugal; and a brother-in-law was
chosen Viceroy of Naples. His favored page, Rodrigo Calderón,
gained several prestigious titles and honors, as did also his
friend Pedro Franqueza, who was chosen Secretary of State
for Italy.

The Duke of Lerma ordered extravagant festivities to celebrate royal marriages, births and other Court events, and the
King's household increased appreciably in size and cost. He
achieved all this splendor despite the shrinking treasury and
the pall of poverty that spread over the land. One of the
ostensible reasons why Lerma had the Court moved to Valladolid
in 1601 was to cut down the King's expenditures, but this move
probably was influenced by bribes from the citizens of Valladolid.
Madrid suffered, royal finances did not improve, and the court
returned to Madrid in 1606 only because Philip accepted a
bribe of 250,000 ducats together with one-sixth of all house
rents for a period of ten years.

Lerma failed to redistribute the tax burden within the peninsula
as well as within Castile, and the poor became poorer while
the rich were sheltered by exemptions. The total bullion imports
from America had attained their high point in the period 1591-
1595, declined by about a third in 1601-1605, recovered in
1606-1610, and then began a downhill course in 1611. By 1631,
they were less than half of what they had been in the last
years of Philip II's reign. Lerma had to resort to such expedients
as selling offices and jurisdictions, extracting subsidies from
Portuguese Jews, and debasing the Castilian coinage, a measure
which Philip II had refused to sanction. Thus, the *vellón* coinage
—the material out of which this coinage was made was originally
an alloy of silver and copper—was appreciably reduced in value
in 1599 when it was minted from pure copper. This *vellón* was
doubled in face value in 1603. Despite the opposition of the

Cortes, Philip's perennially bankrupt regime was forced to resort in the period 1517-1526 to *vellón* currency which came to drive gold and silver out of circulation and at the same time created problems in the storage and transportation of this coinage. The debasement of Spanish coinage also put the last finishing touches to Spanish industry.

About the only favorable accomplishment in Lerma's regime was his successful effort to establish peace with Spain's foreign enemies, a condition which Spain badly needed in view of her internal weakness. Hostilities with England still remained at the beginning of Philip III's rule. In 1601, Lerma sent an armada of fifty ships to attack England, but this effort failed because of a storm. The following year, a Spanish armada launched an unsuccessful attack against the English in Ireland. With the death of Queen Elizabeth in 1603, and the accession of the peace-loving James I, peace was concluded with England in 1604. Philip II had assured peace with France at Vervins and Lerma fostered cordial relations with this country by arranging the double marriage between Louis XIII and Philip's daughter, Anne of Austria, and Louis' sister Isabella de Bourbon and the future Philip IV. A treaty of 1612 established a close alliance between the two countries.

After continued warring with the Dutch, a twelve-year truce was signed in 1609 in which Spain recognized the sovereignty of the United Provinces. Spain was able to defend its Italian interests with little difficulty. The celebrated "conspiracy of Venice" (1618), by which Don Pedro Téllez Girón, the Duke of Osuna, allegedly aided by Quevedo, plotted to overthrow the Venetian Republic, was probably a fiction invented by the Venetians to spread hatred of the Spaniards throughout Europe. The charge that Osuna planned to install himself as king of Naples caused his speedy recall to Spain.

Spain's awareness of its weakness was probably a major determining factor in Lerma's decision to expel the Moriscos, which he conceived as early as 1602. The date on which Philip formally approved the decree of expulsion, April 9, 1609, was the very same day on which Spain concluded the humiliating Twelve Years' Truce with the Dutch. It appears that Lerma astutely timed the definitive solution of the Morisco problem, which was enthusiastically welcomed by the Spaniards, with another event that diminished Spanish glory.

The Moriscos had been a problem to a Spain that had for

centuries zealously devoted itself to the establishment of a
single religion within its realms. The Spanish government abandoned any hope they might have had to effect a genuine conversion of this racial minority and assimilate them completely
into Spanish life. It is doubtful, however, that the Spaniards
sincerely desired the total absorption of the Moriscos since
they failed to provide them with ample instruction in the
Christian religion, constantly subjected them to ill treatment,
and denied them access to secular and ecclesiastic offices.
Spaniards also feared that Moriscos were potential fifth colum-
nists in league with the Turks and the French.

The expulsion began in Valencia where there were around
135,000 Moriscos in 1609, perhaps a third of the population
of this kingdom. Over the next two years it was extended to
Castile, Andalusia, Aragón, and Murcia. Veteran troops and
naval vessels were brought from Italy to protect and transport
the Moriscos to North Africa, where many died of starvation
and exhaustion, or were massacred on their arrival since they
were considered as Christian Spaniards in the land of exile.
The estimates of the total number of Moriscos expelled have
differed widely; a conservative figure is three hundred thousand.

The loss of the Moriscos intensified the economic depression
that Spain was undergoing under Lerma's regime. The industrious
Moriscos were skilled farmers, artisans, weavers and tradesmen,
and also performed menial but indispensable jobs such as
common laborers, muleteers, smiths, cobblers, porters, and steve-
dores. Keeping in mind the Spanish aversion to manual labor
and commerce, one readily can understand that the removal
of a large productive segment of the country's manpower caused
trade and industry to suffer.

Spain was in such dire financial and economic straits in the
early summer of 1618, and so overwhelming was the pressure
of the King's financial ministers and the Castilian Cortes, that
Lerma agreed to create a committee for reform. The Council
of Castile was ordered to make a detailed report on the state
of the country and propose remedies for its problems. Nevertheless, it was already too late for Lerma and he was deposed
on October 4, 1618, in a palace revolution headed by his son,
the Duke of Uceda. His favorite, Rodrigo Calderón, was imprisoned and tortured, but Lerma went scot free since he had
persuaded the Pope to make him a cardinal. On February 1,
1619, the Council of Castile submitted its report which essentially

proposed reforms that advisors and preceding Cortes had advanced previously: the reduction in taxes and a reform of fiscal policies, a cessation of the King's grants and pensions, a curb on extravagance in dress and customs, a moratorium on the establishment of new religious foundations, and a reduction in the number of existing convents. The Duke of Uceda was no better a prime minister than his father, and the report was ignored.

Two years later Philip III died, having served Spanish interests very little in his reign of twenty-two years. A superficial look at Spain showed that its Empire was still intact and that it was supreme in Europe. Literature and art flourished. Cervantes produced his great works during this period, Lope de Vega was writing his popular plays, Luis de Góngora was composing his superb poetry, and Quevedo wrote the masterful *Buscón* and the *Sueños*. Yet beneath this façade of apparent opulence, cultural splendor, and fervent religiousness lay poverty, corruption, hyprocrisy, and a laxity of morals. The proliferating religious orders of the Church provided food and shelter for many who were not suited to the religious life. The Church was wealthy and offered enticing opportunities for financial gain. It is estimated that there were two hundred thousand regular and secular clergy by the time Philip IV began his reign. The Court was flooded with aristocrats and their enormous households. Impoverished hidalgos flocked to the Court in hopes of restoring their fortunes. Parasites of all descriptions were attracted to the Court, seeking to climb the ladder of success through influence and recommendation rather than through scorned productive labor. Beggars and prostitutes plied their trades. And with it all came a deepening national disillusionment.

V *Philip IV and Olivares*

Spaniards hoped for a favorable turn in their fortunes with the accession of the promising lad of sixteen who succeeded to the throne on March 31, 1621. However, this intelligent and cultured new King was more interested in pursuing pleasure than in governing the affairs of state and, as a result, he followed his father's example of relegating regal authority to a favorite. The new favorite was Gaspar de Guzmán, Count-Duke of Olivares, who ruled Spain for twenty-two years. Olivares, who had helped plot the overthrow of Lerma, ruthlessly liquidated

the important ministers of the previous regime. Rodrigo Calderón was beheaded, and both Uceda and Osuna were thrown
into prison and left there to die. Although Olivares seems to
have been driven more by an ambition for supreme power
than by the avarice that motivated Lerma, he still managed to
achieve an annual income of around half a million ducats for
his service to the crown. More able and energetic than Lerma,
he worked tirelessly to revive Spain's imperial tradition which
had lain dormant during the reign of Philip III.

Seeking to establish an efficient, centralized regime that
would not bog down in the customary red tape of bureaucracy,
Olivares ignored the traditional councils for the different depart-
ments of government and set up a series of committees answer-
able to himself. Behind this attempt to streamline the government machinery lay the ultimate goal: the creation of a unified
and integrated Spain, an objective he was incapable of fulfilling.
The incompetent prosecution of this scheme eventually led to
his fall from power.

Olivares recognized the need for financial and other reforms
to stem Spain's decline and enable the country to carry on its
militaristic foreign policy. In 1622 he set up a Council for the
Reform of Customs whose purpose was to prevent politicians
from enriching themselves at the expense of the state. The
following year he issued a series of twenty-three articles of
reform that regulated abuses in economic practices and in
manners. The number of municipal offices was cut to one-third,
sumptuary laws were promulgated to curtail extravagance in
dress, financial gain from the administration of justice was
prohibited, lords were ordered to reduce their households so
that more workers would be available for farming and manu-
facturing, measures were taken to promote an increase in the
birth rate, emigration from Spain without royal permission
was forbidden, and the import of manufactured goods was
placed under tight control. The economy move also affected
the King. His expenses were cut in half and the number of
offices on the councils was cut to one-third. Unfortunately,
Olivares' excellent reform program was dissipated within three
years through public apathy and lack of support from the Court.
Of all the reforms proposed by Olivares, the most lasting and
important was the introduction of the *golilla,* a high spreading
collar of cardboard and silk invented by a Madrid tailor to
replace the much more extravagant ruff which was so costly

both in purchase price and upkeep. Olivares' scheme to establish a national banking system—originally proposed in 1622 and abandoned in 1626—might have helped the Crown to reduce its debts, and diminish Spain's reliance upon foreign money lenders. If this measure had been adopted, it would have permitted the abolition of the *millones,* an excise tax on essential consumer goods which was most burdensome to the poor.

Shortly after Olivares came to power, he embarked on a policy of foreign involvement. The archduke Albert died without leaving an heir and Flanders reverted to Spain. Although Albert had been in favor of a continuance of the truce with the Dutch, it came to an end since Spaniards were loath to recognize Dutch independence. Except for Spinola's capture of Breda (1625), immortalized in the famous painting by Velázquez, Spanish arms could not subdue the rebels. The Duke of Uceda had embroiled Spain (1620) in the Thirty Years' War (1618-1648) and, in view of Spain's Catholicism and traditional ties to the Holy Roman Empire, it was inevitable that Olivares should continue in this conflict which pitted the Hapsburgs and Catholic princes against the German Protestant princes and their allies—ultimately France, Sweden, Denmark, England, and the United Provinces were to participate in this war. At first Spanish forces managed to achieve some important victories but eventually disaster overtook them after Richelieu declared war on Spain in 1635. This Franco-Spanish confrontation was foreshadowed several years earlier when Richelieu sent troops across the Alps to support the claim of a Frenchman, the Duke of Nevers, to the duchy of Mantua. The Mantuan War (1628-1631) ended in the defeat of Olivares' efforts to oust the French, thus endangering Spain's hold over North Italy and Milan. The war with the French went on for a number of years until Spain, beaten militarily and financially, signed the Peace of the Pyrenees in 1659.

Olivares recognized the need for a strong, unitary monarchy if Spain was to be successful in its imperial policy. Castile was always burdened with supplying the major share of money and manpower required to sustain Spain's foreign policy, and it was Olivares' judicious intention to enlist the aid of other regions of the Empire in strengthening Spain's sinews of war. In a famous secret memorandum to Philip (1624), Olivares recommended that the laws of the various kingdoms be made to conform with those of Castile, but he also proposed that leaders of non-Castilian parts of the Empire should be allowed to participate more actively in the affairs of state. This was to be accomplished by employing these leaders in important posts and by more frequent royal visits to the provinces. An important feature of Olivares' plan was a union of the realm's arms whereby all the kingdoms would supply a stipulated force of men and an agreed tribute to the Crown for the defense of any of the states that went to war. Seeking to implement this program, Olivares and Philip set out in 1626 to visit the Cortes of Aragón, Valencia, and Catalonia. Aragón and Valencia refused to provide their troops for foreign service but did offer to send annual subsidies to the Crown. The most adamant and complete refusal to cooperate in the scheme came from Catalonia, the wealthiest and most powerful of the three regions, which feared that this was a Castilian attempt to usurp its liberties. In fact, the Catalans were so hostile to the proposal that the King and his prime minister secretly left Barcelona while the Catalan Cortes was still in session. The continuing strained relations between Castile and Catalonia were to cause serious damage to Spain's domestic and foreign policy.

In 1639, the Catalans joined Castilian forces in successfully repulsing the French on their border, but they balked at Olivares' subsequent plan to force the billeting of "foreign" troops on Catalan soil and send Catalan troops to serve in Italy. Civil unrest began in 1640, the viceroy was murdered, Castilians were massacred, and the Catalans at first proclaimed Catalonia a republic under French protection; later, through French insistence, Catalonia declared its allegiance to the King of France as in the time of Charlemagne. The Catalan revolt ended with the recapture of Barcelona in 1652, and was formally concluded at the Peace of the Pyrenees in 1659. Philip managed to recoup Catalan allegiance by guaranteeing the customs and privileges of Catalonia. Another determining factor in this return to the Spanish fold was Catalan dislike of the French.

Another revolt on the other side of the Iberian Peninsula dashed all hopes Olivares might have entertained for a unitary and integrated Empire. The Portuguese saw their opportunity to accomplish their long-nurtured desire to reestablish their national identity while Spain's troops were occupied in Catalonia. The spontaneous revolt successfully overthrew Spanish authority in Lisbon within a few hours on December 1, 1640, and the next day the Duke of Braganza came out of retirement to become King John IV. Portugal's total independence was finally recognized in 1668.

Spain's internal disintegration, the debilitating war against the French, and financial difficulties at home combined to undermine Olivares' influence. The King decided to dismiss his favorite in January, 1643, and the Count-Duke left Madrid for his estates where he died two years later. His grandiose plans never attained fruition and imperial Spain's fortunes, now at their lowest point since the reign of Charles V, would continue to deteriorate during the rest of the seventeenth and later centuries.

Unlike his two predecessors, who had been devoutly religious and spent time and money in support of the Church, Philip IV was virtually unconcerned with religious observance and Christian morality during most of his reign. His many extramarital affairs were public scandal and it is said that he had as many as thirty-two bastard children. Reports of the period reveal that licentiousness, ostentation, vice, and corruption were widespread in the Court and in the cities. However, literature and art still continued to flourish. Philip himself wrote plays and encouraged dramatists. During his rule, the Spanish theater attained its period of greatest splendor. Lope de Vega was still writing, and the last great dramatist of the Golden Age, Calderón de la Barca, composed his best plays. Quevedo authored many of his important political and religious works as well as his satires in prose and poetry. As an art patron, Philip handsomely favored Velázquez who painted innumerable pictures of the King, the royal family, and Olivares.

Shortly after the end of Philip IV's rule, Spanish literary decadence set in and now the deterioration of a great empire was complete in all aspects of its civilization.

CHAPTER 2

Quevedo's Life

FRANCISCO de Quevedo y Villegas was born in Madrid on September 17, 1580. He was the only son and the third of five children born to Pedro Gómez de Quevedo and his wife María de Santibáñez. His father, descended from notable ancestors, was private secretary to Princess María, the daughter of Charles V and wife of the Emperor Maximilian II, and later served in the same capacity with Queen Ana of Austria, the wife of Philip II. He married María de Santibáñez, who was a lady-in-waiting for Queen Ana. After her husband's death in 1586, María returned to serve in the Court, this time with Princess Isabel Clara Eugenia. She died shortly after the turn of the century and Francisco was placed under the protection of Agustín de Villanueva, the prothonotary of Aragón.

Little is known of Quevedo's childhood and youth. He apparently received his first formal education in the celebrated Colegio Imperial of Madrid run by the Jesuits. Like other great literary figures of the Golden Age—Cervantes, Góngora, Lope, and Calderón—Quevedo manifested his respect and liking for the Society of Jesus. We know that by 1596 he was enrolled as a student at the University of Alcalá in such courses as logic, physics, and mathematics, and he undoubtedly also studied classical languages, French, and Italian. In 1600 Quevedo obtained his bachelor's degree and, after taking courses in natural philosophy and metaphysics, the master's degree was conferred upon him. He apparently studied theology in Alcalá, but in 1601 he abandoned these studies for unknown reasons—some biographers ascribe this to an unfounded duel involving a lady's honor—and went to Valladolid. Quevedo felt very much at ease amidst the gay festivities and the stimulating literary environment of the Court, which was not to return to Madrid until five years later. In this period of his life, he apparently studied theology at first, but then dedicated himself to writing poetry, achieving some measure of success despite the fierce

30

competition of an array of splendid men of letters. Among the eighteen compositions of his included in Pedro de Espinosa's anthology, *Flores de poetas ilustres* (*Flowers of Illustrious Poets*), 1605, is the famous rondelet "Poderoso caballero es don Dinero" ("Powerful Knight is Sir Money"). He became friends with Cervantes, was praised by Lope de Vega, exchanged letters in Latin with the celebrated Belgian humanist Justus Lipsius, and began his corrosive polemic with Góngora that did not terminate until the latter's death.

When the King decided to return with his Court to Madrid in 1606, Quevedo felt obliged to follow since he was bent on continuing his literary career. In his ballad (probably written in 1606) ironically praising Valladolid on the occasion of the departure of the Court, he wrote that the poets would abandon this city now that the king was leaving. In 1606 he began to write the *Sueños* (*Visions*) and was planning or had started, to write the *Buscón*. He evidently established friendship with noble and influential people of the Court, such as Count Lemos to whom he dedicated the first of the *Sueños*, "El jucio final" ("The Final Judgment"); the Marquis Villanueva del Fresno, to whom he dedicated the second of the *Sueños*, "El alguacil endemoniado" ("The Bedevilled Constable"), 1608; and the Duke of Osuna, Pedro Téllez Girón, to whom he dedicated a translation in verse of Anacreon's poetry.

The period between 1609 and 1613 was a productive one in Quevedo's literary career. Besides continuing his work on the *Sueños*, he wrote several short satirical pieces, many original poems, and translated from Anacreon, Focilides, and Jeremiah. In 1609 he wrote the celebrated *España defendida* (*Spain Defended*), a panegyric stoutly championing the Spanish people and their culture. The Jesuit Juan de Mariana availed himself of Quevedo's humanistic background in the correction of Hebrew passages the censors required for the monumental edition of the Polyglot Bible which Benito Arias Montano had begun in 1569. He mingled in literary academies with Lope de Vega, Góngora, and the Argensola brothers. During a meeting of one of the literary academies he attended, there occurred a notable episode of his life, the quarrel with Luis Pacheco de Narváez, a famous celebrity on fencing. While trying to prove that Pacheco de Narváez was wrong in explaining a fencing maneuver, Quevedo demonstrated his objection with a sword and knocked the fencing master's hat off his head. The feud between them

endured for a long time. Quevedo satirized Pacheco de Narváez
in several works and the fencing expert retaliated by collaborating
in the well-known attack on Quevedo's works, *El Tribunal de
la justa venganza* (*Tribunal of Just Vengeance*).

In 1609 Quevedo began his embroilment in a number of
lawsuits against the small town of Torre de Juan Abad, located
south of Toledo in the province of Ciudad Real. Quevedo's
mother had invested a large sum of money to benefit the town
but, despite a number of litigations that went on beyond his
lifetime, Torre de Juan Abad refused to pay the debts it owed
Quevedo and his family. Although the lawsuits caused him
no small bit of anguish, there was a brighter side to the frequent visits he made to his estate there. It afforded him peace
and solace away from the intrigues of the Court and provided
him with an idoneous atmosphere in which to think and write.

In 1613 Quevedo went to Italy in response to the invitation
of his friend Pedro Téllez Girón, Duke of Osuna and Viceroy
of Sicily (1611-1616). The two men had probably met in Madrid
in 1608 when the ambitious Duke of Osuna had just returned
from a campaign in Flanders. Evidently the Duke wanted
Quevedo at his side to serve as a faithful advisor, confidant,
and agent. In the fall of 1615 the Duke sent Quevedo to Spain
with a dual mission: to deliver to the Spanish King the Sicilian
Parliament's biennial contribution of three hundred thousand
ducats, and to convince the King's ministers that the post of
Viceroy of Naples should be granted to the Duke. The first part of
his mission, the official one, was easily carried out. Through the
clever manipulation of his contacts and the judicious distribution
of bribes, Quevedo's mission was successful in having the Duke
named Viceroy of Naples in 1616, a post he held until 1620.
In his letters to the Duke, Quevedo's satirical assessments of
the corrupt officials in the Court resemble the corrosive lampooning of such types in the *Sueños* and other writings.

Before returning to Italy, in addition to having aided the
Duke of Osuna in obtaining the lucrative post of Viceroy of
Naples, Quevedo petitioned to secure an income of one thousand
escudos for his faithful service in Italy, or, as an alternate
reward, the income of five hundred ducats and entrance into
one of the three religious-military orders that had been established in the Middle Ages. He was granted admission to the
Order of Santiago but with an income of only four hundred

ducats. Quevedo always maintained staunch loyalty to this Order as we shall see below.

By the end of the summer of 1616 Quevedo had returned from Spain to rejoin the Duke of Osuna in Naples. Evidently the Viceroy relied heavily on Quevedo's counsel in governing the affairs of Naples, and the Italians had the highest respect for his diplomatic talents. On February 18, 1617, the Parliament of Naples convened to vote on the biennial contribution to the Spanish King. The contribution of 1,800,000 ducats was approved and Quevedo was chosen to deliver this money to the King. As a reward for this commission he was granted the sum of eight thousand ducats. Prior to undertaking this mission, Quevedo was sent by Osuna to have an audience with Pope Paul V in Rome. There is no documentary evidence to reveal the exact nature or the results of this meeting in April, 1617, but it is assumed that Quevedo was to seek the Pope's moral support and perhaps some naval assistance for Osuna's plan to destroy Venice's power in the Adriatic.

Quevedo left for Spain on May 28, 1617, and during his stay in Madrid properly executed his tasks as representative of the Duke of Osuna and the Neapolitan Parliament. He also satisfactorily arranged the marriage between the Marquis of Peñafiel, first-born son of the Duke of Osuna, with Isabel de Sandoval y Rojas, daughter of the Duke of Uceda, a Court favorite of Philip III. Quevedo stayed on in Madrid where in June, 1618, he defended Osuna before the Council of State against the charges that Osuna had been one of the chief architects in plotting the overthrow of the Venetian Republic on Ascension Day, 1618. There is no evidence to support the oft-repeated claim that Quevedo himself participated actively in this "conspiracy of Venice" since he was in Spain at the time this event took place. Despite Quevedo's valiant efforts to save his friend from the enemies in Madrid, Osuna was relieved of his viceroyalty and then imprisoned until his death in 1624. Quevedo himself was sent to jail at Uclés in 1620 because of his connection with the Duke of Osuna. Relations cooled between the two friends, but Quevedo always maintained his high regard for Pedro Téllez Girón, to whom he dedicated several sonnets and, especially, the beautiful one written shortly after the Duke's death.

After a period of six months in the prison at Uclés, Quevedo was exiled to Torre de Juan Abad. During this banishment

from Madrid, he kept abreast of Spain's political events and
immersed himself in writing more *sueños*, retouching and adding
to the *Política de Dios* (*Politics of God*), begun in 1617, and
composing the short *Mundo caduco* (*The Worn-Out World*),
Quevedo's version of what occurred in Italy in the years 1613-
1620. *Grandes anales de quince días* (*Great Annals of Two
Weeks*) is another political piece written at Torre de Juan
Abad when Quevedo got word of the death of Philip III. In
this account of the first events during the reign of Philip IV,
Quevedo obviously tried to get in the good graces of the
monarch and particularly of the new and powerful favorite,
Gaspar de Guzmán, Count-Duke of Olivares, who held his
power until 1643. This opuscule attacked the actions of the
favorites who controlled the government during the previous
reign—the ineffectual Duke of Lerma who held power until
1618, and his incompetent son, the Duke of Uceda, who was
the favorite until Philip III's death—and shared the optimistic
feelings of the Spanish people who expected that long-overdue
reforms would be accomplished under the new regime. In
March of 1623 Quevedo was free to leave Torre de Juan Abad
and return to Madrid. During the next twelve years, he was
generally on good terms with Olivares, and he wrote and published his most significant works.

In 1623 or 1624, Quevedo dedicated to Olivares his famous
"Epístola satírica y censoria" ("Satirical Letter of Censure"),
a long poem lauding the Count-Duke's austerity program and
prognosticating a glorious new era in Spain's political fortunes.
Quevedo was among the poets who helped celebrate the opulent
festivities which took place when Prince Charles of England
came to Madrid (1623) to woo Princess María, the sister of
Philip IV. In February of the following year, not only did he
accompany the King on a trip to inspect Andalusian coastal
defenses, but he also was host to the King at Torre de Juan
Abad. He collaborated with Antonio de Mendoza and Mateo
Montero to write a play—no record of it exists today—honoring
the saint's day of the Queen in 1625, and coauthored another
play—it is also lost—for the King and Queen in 1631. In 1626
he accompanied the King on a visit to Aragón, and in 1632 he
received the honorary title of Secretary to the King. Quevedo
continued to maintain his good relationship with Olivares. In
the earliest editions of *Política de Dios* there are two letters
eulogizing the great chancellor. Quevedo's edition of the poetic

works of Luis de León was dedicated to the Count-Duke, and Olivares' economic policies were defended in the opuscule *El chitón de las tarabillas* (*The Babblers' Stopper*), 1630.

The years 1626 and 1627 were particularly significant in Quevedo's literary career for it was at this time that his three greatest works were first published. The unusual number of nine editions that the first part of the *Política de Dios* had in 1626 gives evidence of Quevedo's renown at that time. (The second part of the *Política de Dios* was written between 1634 and 1639, but was first printed in 1655, ten years after Quevedo's death.) The same year saw the publication of four editions of Quevedo's extremely popular book, *El buscón* (*The Swindler*), a great picaresque novel whose only competitors are the anonymous *Lazarillo de Tormes* (1554) and Mateo Alemán's *Guzmán de Alfarache* (1599). In a short period of time this work was known in translation throughout western Europe. In 1627 the masterful *Sueños* were first published in four different Spanish editions and one French translation came out in Rouen.

In the years 1627-1628, Quevedo was embroiled in a controversy over whether Santa Teresa, the sixteenth-century mystic who was canonized in 1622, should share the patronage of Spain with Santiago (St. James), who had been Spain's sole patron saint since the Middle Ages. At this time, Quevedo had been a knight in the Order of Santiago for about a decade and strongly supported the position that St. James remain the one and only patron saint of Spain. In 1627 he wrote the *Memorial por el patronato de Santiago* (*Memorial for the Patronage of Santiago*), published early in 1628, a passionate justification of his posture. The attacks of the opposing forces compelled him to retreat to Torre de Juan Abad where he composed a longer exposition of his point of view that he sent off to Olivares. There is no doubt that Quevedo's active participation in the issue helped the backers of St. James to prevail. Pope Urban VIII made it official on January 8, 1630. Quevedo could return to Madrid after the dispute was settled. Olivares offered him the post of ambassador to Genoa but his devotion to his writing and the bitter memories of his previous experience in Italy probably dictated his refusal of this offer. The title of Royal Secretary conferred upon him in 1632 was an honorary one and he did not enter into the political affairs of the government.

Quevedo's frequent criticism of women and marriage seemed to indicate that he was a confirmed misogynist who considered

matrimony the worst of human tortures. It is astonishing and
incomprehensible that he finally decided to take a wife when
he was almost fifty-four. It was common gossip that he had
had affairs with different women. His enemies indulged in cruel
satire of his long liaison with his mistress, Ledesma, by whom
he had several children. His love sonnets dedicated to Lisi
indicate that he probably maintained a strong but unrequited
passion for a noble lady which lasted from around the time he
was thirty until the time he reached the age of fifty. He wrote
love songs to different women, but we still cannot determine
whether they express a real or a fictitious emotion. It has been
said that the women of the Court, irked by Quevedo's frequent
satirizing of women, hatched a plot to take vengeance on their
tormentor.

The chief promoters of the plan to find a suitable wife for
Quevedo were his friend, the Duke of Medinaceli, and Doña
Inés de Zúñiga y Fonseca, the Countess of Olivares. Evidently
the matchmaking game was already going on in 1633, and
Quevedo was cognizant of this. In that year, Quevedo sent to
Olivares' wife a letter in which he discussed in his usual witty
fashion the kind of wife he desired. He stated that he wanted
his wife to be noble, virtuous, and intelligent and that she should
not possess too little or too much of good looks, wealth, height,
weight, and age. His ideal woman also had to be of pleasant
disposition, thrifty, not too talkative, and desirous of pleasing
her husband rather than of seeking the admiration of others.
Above all, no *dueña* (duenna)—as we shall see in later chapters,
this type of person was the most maligned of all the women
satirized in Quevedo's writings—should ever step foot across the
threshold. The woman selected for Quevedo's "quietude, honor,
and salvation" was Doña Esperanza de Mendoza whom he
married on February 26, 1634.

Doña Esperanza came from the best families of Aragón and
Castile. Undoubtedly in her fifties when she married Quevedo,
she had been a widow for some twenty years and had three
children. The marriage foundered almost immediately and the
couple lived together for scarcely three months. By May 4
Quevedo was in Madrid and his wife remained in her native
town of Cetina where they had been married. The definitive
separation of Quevedo and Doña Esperanza took place in the
summer of 1636 and they never saw each other again after this
time. Quevedo never mentioned her in his works or his letters,

and from 1636 to December, 1641, the date of her demise, she signed her name officially as widow of her first husband. A disillusioned Quevedo returned to his literary pursuits.

Between 1635 and 1638 Quevedo spent most of his time in seclusion at Torre de Juan Abad. His letters of that period reveal that he felt lonely, lived in poverty, read religious and philosophical works, and wrote assiduously. By March of 1636 he finished *La hora de todos* (*The Hour of All Men*), a scathing satire not only of the Spaniards' enemies but also of Spanish mores, and, especially, of the Count-Duke of Olivares whose policies had by now disillusioned him. In 1635 Quevedo was also the butt of some of the harshest abuse levelled against him in his lifetime. Juan de Jáuregui launched two harsh lampoons against Quevedo: a memorial to the King attacking Quevedo's advice to Philip IV on foreign policy; and a dialogued essay criticizing Quevedo's *La cuna y la sepultura* (*The Cradle and the Grave*), 1634. In the same year was written that most acrimonious censure, *El tribunal de la justa venganza,* which labelled Quevedo "a master of errors, a doctor in impudence, a licentiate in buffoonery, a bachelor in filth, a professor of vice and the prototype of the devil."[1] The author of this work is listed as Arnaldo Franco-Furt, a pseudonym for one or more of his enemies. Evidently Quevedo learned that the author, or at least one of the authors, was his nemesis Luis Pacheco de Narváez, who was imprisoned after being denounced by Quevedo.

One December day in 1639, when King Philip IV sat down to eat, he found under his napkin a satirical memorial in verse which began with the verse "Católica, sacra, real magestad" ("Catholic, Sacred, Royal Majesty"). This celebrated poem criticized the King's conduct of affairs of state and urged him to alter his policies which were leading Spain to ruin. During the night of December 7 Quevedo was arrested at the home of the Duke of Medinaceli and was dragged off to prison before he could get fully dressed or put an overcoat around his shoulders. Some biographers of Quevedo have supported the belief that he was accorded such brutal treatment because he was the author of the poem. However, there is no documentary evidence to prove that Quevedo's imprisonment resulted from castigating the King right under his nose. The legend was born with contemporaries who were his enemies, and was perpetuated as other legends told about Quevedo's life and works. The true

reason that prompted Quevedo's incarceration during four miserable years has never been uncovered. He never wrote a single
word to shed light on why he had to languish in jail. In denying
Quevedo's authorship of this poem, Blecua has stated that this
composition does not evince Quevedo's usual very personal and
genius-like style.[2] It would appear that the usually astute Quevedo
would not be so foolhardy as to jeopardize himself at a time
when his enemies were defaming him.

In *La constancia y paciencia del Santo Job* (*The Constancy
and Patience of St. Job*), written in 1641, Quevedo reveals he
was rushed to prison in the royal convent of San Marcos in
León, and he recounts the suffering he endured during the first
two years of his internment.[3] He states that he was in solitary
confinement during the first six months of his detention, never
had sufficient money for basic necessities, underwent physical
and mental stress, lost his servants through death, and he affirms
he heard a rumor that he had been decapitated.

On October 7, 1641, he sent a memorial to Olivares suppli-
cating him to put an end to his long and miserable incarceration.
Four months later he addressed another letter to the Count-
Duke in which he maintains that he was unjustly accused by
some unknown person and desperately begs for clemency. He
reveals that his health is practically ruined: "Blind in the left
eye, crippled, and cancerous, my existence is no longer life but
the prolixity of death."[4]

His friends tried to intercede on his behalf but to no avail
until June, 1643, shortly after the Count-Duke of Olivares fell
from power. Quevedo complained bitterly, but also meditated
and wrote down his religious, philosophic, and political thoughts
during the four long years in San Marcos. *La vida de San Pablo*
(*The Life of St. Paul*), 1644, written in his last year of imprisonment, was dedicated to Don Juan de Chumacero, president of
the Council of Castile, who effected Quevedo's release.

La providencia de Dios (*The Providence of God*), another
ascetic work written in San Marcos, is one of the finest mani-
festations of Quevedo's Christian stoicism. After he was freed,
he went to Madrid where he supervised the publication of his
Marco Bruto (*Marcus Brutus*), a translation of, and a commentary on, one of the biographies in *The Parallel Lives* of
Plutarch, written originally in 1632.

Already considerably aged and infirm after his harrowing
experience, Quevedo remained for a short time in Madrid, com-

pletely ignored by the new ministers who had assumed power after Olivares was relieved from his position. At the end of 1644 he retreated to Torre de Juan Abad only to be tormented by a cold winter and physical afflictions. In January, 1645, he moved to the warmer climate of Villanueva de los Infantes, seeking relief for his tortured body and the solace of friends. He died September 8, 1645, not long after having rejoiced in the news that the Count-Duke of Olivares had preceded him in death.

Pablo Antonio de Tarsia, Quevedo's first biographer, is the source of two legends pertaining to Quevedo's physical remains.[5] One of Tarsia's stories takes place in Villanueva de los Infantes where Quevedo was interred. A few days after his demise, a gentleman, who wanted to bedeck himself when he entered the bullring to fight a bull, decided that the beautiful golden spurs with which Quevedo was buried should be the articles of dress to round out his ostentatious attire. Through the cooperation of a sacristan he was able to secure the spurs. Unfortunately for his plans, the first bull he faced attacked him viciously and put an end to his life. According to the second tale, ten years after Quevedo's death his coffin was opened by several curious gentlemen who wanted to view the body. They were astounded to observe that Quevedo's body inexplicably showed no sign of deterioration. Evidently, however, Quevedo's remains finally succumbed to the ravages of nature. Luis Astrana Marín uncovered a manuscript which reported that Quevedo's skeleton disintegrated a century and a half after his death and the remains were lost forever.[6]

There exist five portraits of Quevedo—one of them is by Murillo and the other is attributed to Velázquez—and a bust located in the National Library of Madrid. They all reveal his myopia, which the artists usually show by placing the famous *quevedos,* the pince-nez which were Quevedo's trademark, on a fleshy nose. Another distinguishing physical characteristic was his lameness to which attention was directed by himself, as also by his admirers and detractors. It is said that he generally wore a long garment to cover his deformed legs. A story has it that a brash girl made a funny remark about the appearance of one of Quevedo's legs which was the only one visible at the time. Quevedo told her that there was a worse leg among the people gathered in the room and then displayed his other leg, which was more twisted than the first.

It is obvious that he was an avid reader. Tarsia tells us that he read while travelling in a carriage, eating, and resting in bed. When he went on trips, he would take along leather bags filled with many pocket-sized books on different subjects. He had some five thousand volumes in his library and felt that every book had some value to it.

All sorts of legends about his exploits, mostly spurious, have been circulated throughout the centuries. Tarsia recounts what happened to Quevedo one night in Madrid after he had gone to bed. He was awakened by howling of dogs outside and, armed with his sword and shield, he went out to investigate. An escaped leopard-like feline that belonged to some ambassador pounced upon him in the darkness and, without knowing what it was, he killed it with his sword. Quevedo reportedly told his concerned friends that the wild animal would probably not have attacked him if it had known that Quevedo was the intended victim.

Many anecdotes are told to demonstrate his wit. When a young poet found it necessary to explain at length the meaning of one of his compositions, Quevedo supposedly told him: "Why didn't you say this in your poem?" Another poet asked Quevedo to judge two sonnets written on the same theme. After hearing the first sonnet, he said the other one was better. The puzzled poet wondered how Quevedo could make this assertion without having heard the second composition. Quevedo replied: "Sir, because no poem could be worse than the one I have just heard." While Quevedo was dictating his last will and testament, it was suggested to him that he have a lavish funeral with music. Quevedo supposedly voiced his objection by saying: "Let each one who hears the music pay for it."

CHAPTER 3

The Sueños

THE thought and style of Quevedo are admirably synthesized in his *Sueños* (*Visions*), which incorporate some of the finest and most popular satire of all Spanish literature. The compulsion to root out the truths about people, customs, and situations is a constant trait in his *Buscón,* his short satirical pieces, most of his poetry, his theater, and his political and religious works. In the *Visions* as in most of his other compositions, Quevedo echoes and reechoes his views on death, time, morality, the power of money and tyranny, in addition to excoriating deceiving women, hypocrites, physicians, constables, lawyers, heretics, bad poets, and a legion of other types. The *Visions* also illustrate admirably the richness and expressiveness of a style rarely achieved by other Spanish writers. Indeed, Quevedo's originality in style is perhaps the most fundamental ingredient that has enhanced his stature as a literary figure.

I *The Satirical Purpose of Dream Literature*

Quevedo could not have chosen a more suitable literary form than the dream to express the thoughts seething in his fertile mind. The dream permitted him to pursue his penchant for exaggerating, distorting, and reducing to absurdity the Spanish mores and people—both real and types—of his day. It allowed him full freedom to pile one fantasy upon another without being compelled to make logical transitions in time or space. He could indulge at will in stylistic gymnastics by extracting the greatest number of meanings from words, and by utilizing a wide range of grammatical and rhetorical devices.

Satire seems to be ineluctably fused with dream literature from its beginnings. The original Latin word *satura* means "medley" or "jumble," and the best satirists have known this or guessed it. The satirist keeps the reader off balance by introducing the unusual, the unexpected. He holds up to scorn, derision or ridicule the vices, abuses, and follies that he observes

41

in the society of his day. Uppermost in the satirist's mind is an attack designed to make the reader react unfavorably toward the victim or the absurd situation or custom that is the object of the attack. At the heart of the satire must be a recognizable truth which the undiscerning or insensitive reader is shocked into perceiving. Although a satirist may pretend to tell a story, such as in the picaresque novel, his main concern is not with plot and the development of characters, but with the forceful presentation of ideas. Thus, he prepares himself for the onslaught with a varied arsenal of weapons—irony, parody, distortion, colloquialisms, neologisms, obscenities, paradox, antithesis.

Quevedo's recourse to satirical dreams has abundant antecedents in European literature. An early prose satirist was the Greek Lucian (second century B.C.) whose wit and characterizations have been greatly admired and often imitated. The most important and characteristic of his writings are his dialogues which are satirical exposés of ancient mythology and contemporary philosophy. One of these dialogues is a well-known dream in which Sculpture and Education debate their merits in order to entice Lucian into following one or the other career. Education—in reality it represents a literary career—triumphs, and Lucian, after having awakened from the dream, states the lesson for himself and his readers: "So it was with me, and I told you this dream in order that those who are young may take the better direction and cleave to education...."[1] An expressed didactic message appears more than once in the conclusion of several of the *Visions*. A good example comes from "El sueño del infierno" ("Vision of Hell"); "*Sólo pido a quien las leyere, las lea de suerte que, el crédito que les diere le sea provechoso para no experimentar ni ver estos lugares...*" ("I only ask that he who reads them [the *Visions*] do so in such a way that any credence he gives to them will benefit him so that he will not have any experience with these places...")[2]

Lucian's influence is seen in sixteenth-century Erasmian literature such as Alfonso de Valdés' *Diálogo de Mercurio* (*Dialogue of Mercury*) and Cristóbal de Villalón's *El crotalón* (*The Rattlesnake*). In the latter work, the author states that he is imitating Lucian in using the dream device since he proposes to write on diverse matters without following any logical order, a characteristic of the dream.[3]

On several occasions Cervantes used the dream device to uncover reality. The realistic episodes in *El coloquio de los*

perros (*Dialogue of the Dogs*) are narrated within the framework of a dream as is the case in Quevedo's *Visions.* In the
Cave of Montesinos episode Don Quijote *descends* into the cave,
falls asleep, and has a dream which strips away the illusion that
has informed his world of chivalry. In Spanish literature of the
seventeenth century, disillusionment with worldly affairs was
a recurring theme. This led to speculation about the reality of
life which is so well captured in Segismundo's famous soliloquy
in which he called life a frenzy, an illusion, a shadow, a fiction,
a dream.[4]

Literary tours through hell have been a commonplace since
classical antiquity. Undoubtedly Quevedo was familiar with
Dante's *Divine Comedy* and the Italian imitations of this work.
The Middle Ages furnish us with allegorical literature in which
authors composed vivid, grotesque visions of what happens
to people in hell. The medieval dances of death appear to be
primitive versions of Quevedo's *Visions.* In them death is depicted as summoning the ecclesiastical and civil estates to a
wild dance. Death, the irresistible leveller of social classes,
shows all who participate in the dance how to follow the right
path. In the process, the various social classes are subjected to
a macabre satire. Other possible literary antecedents for the
Visions are the *End of the World and the Second Coming of
Christ* by St. Hippolytus (died around 236 A.D.); *The Praise of
Folly* by Erasmus (1466?-1536); and, the *Satira Menippea
Somnium* by Justus Lipsius (1547-1606).

Quevedo's *Visions* has a remarkable affinity with the works
of Hieronymus Bosch (c. 1450-1516), the Flemish painter,
some of whose finest creations were avidly collected by Philip II.
Bosch's grotesque and macabre paintings were familiar to
Quevedo, who referred to this painter several times in his
writings. Executed in brilliant color and with a mastery of
detail, Bosch's paintings abound with fantastic plants and
animals, monstrous figures, demons, and lewd acts. What confronts us is reminiscent of Quevedo's animated topsy-turvy world.
Both Bosch and Quevedo were motivated by a moralizing religious animus in times of spiritual licentiousness.[5]

Goya (1746-1828) would have been a fitting illustrator for
Quevedo's *Visions.* The *Visions,* widely read in Goya's time,
was reprinted in 1791, five or six years before Goya began to
work on the *Caprichos* (*Caprices*). The conniving, hypocritical
men and women, primping old hags, bawds, witches, quack

doctors, mercenary constables, merciless lawyers, charlatans, fops, misers, and fantastic creatures populate the worlds created by Quevedo and Goya. Caprice 43 reveals the sleeping artist leaning on a table, his head buried in his arms. Hovering over him are monstrous bats and owls, symbols of superstitious belief. An owl, symbolic of wisdom, is perched near the artist's head and is apparently offering him a pencil. The caption for this capricho reads *El sueño de la razón produce monstruos* ("The dream of reason produces monsters") and it epitomizes the whole series. In a preliminary sepia ink drawing of this caprice, the caption reads: "The artist dreaming. His only purpose is to banish harmful, vulgar beliefs, and to perpetuate in this work of caprices the solid testimony of truth."[6] It is pertinent to note that when the *Visions* was first published in 1627, the complete title was *Sueños y discursos de verdades descubridoras de abusos, vicios y engaños de todos los oficios y estados del mundo (Visions and Discourses of Truths Revealing Abuses, Vices and Deceits of all Occupations and Estates of the World)*. Although both artists pointed out man's absurd behavior with the hope that he might mend his ways, Goya did not have Quevedo's pre-occupation with man's eternal salvation or damnation.

II   *Early History of the Five Original* Visions

Quevedo began to write his five *Visions* in 1606 or 1607 and finished them by 1622. However, because of censorship and other reasons unknown, they were not published until 1627. Their popular appeal is manifested by the number of editions that followed the princeps of Barcelona. Two other Spanish editions appeared that same year (Valencia and Zaragoza), and the first French edition was published at Rouen. Another two came out in 1628, three were printed in 1629, four were issued in 1631 and since then, this work, on numerous occasions, has gone to press in Spanish, French, English, German, Dutch, and Italian versions.[7] In this chapter, I shall also include a discussion of the two well-known pieces, *Discurso de todos los diablos (Discourse of All Devils)*, 1628 and *La hora de todos y la fortuna con seso (The Hour of All Men and Fortune in Her Wits)*, written in 1635 but published in 1650, which, although not originally contained in the *Visions*, have traditionally been intimately associated with them in view of their form and content.

It is virtually impossible in a devout Catholic environment

to write a Catholic satire involving eschatological visions and final judgment. The sharp censure of his first vision, "El sueño del juicio final" ("The Vision of Final Judgment") made Quevedo realize the danger inherent in attempting this. The imprimatur for this *sueño* was denied in 1610 but finally granted in 1612. For unknown reasons, it was not published until 1627. The Inquisition warned Quevedo to disown this and the other *sueños* that appeared in 1627, and he was compelled to prepare a revised manuscript (1629) which was issued in Madrid in 1631. In the prologue to this edition that bore the new title *Juguetes de la niñez y travesuras del ingenio* (*Youthful Jokes and Witty Pranks*), Quevedo confessed that he had written his visions in the heat of youthful impulsiveness and that the titles of these pieces were more scandalous than fitting. "El sueño del juicio final" was now called "El sueño de las calaveras" ("The Vision of the Skulls").[8] A number of textual modifications are evident in this vision as well as the others. Now Quevedo falls asleep while reading Dante instead of St. Hippolytus, Jupiter becomes the judge instead of God, lawyers are the substitutes for angels, and executioners take the place of devils. There is no doubt that the titular and textual alterations considerably reduce the author's original satirical punch. The Spaniards living in the hotbed of the Counter-Reformation would surely be more profoundly affected by what occurs in the Christian hell and heaven and the Christian God's rendering of his final judgment than the less immediate, paganized view that had obtained since 1631. Consequently, in my analysis of the *Visions,* I shall use the 1627 princeps edition which represents Quevedo's authentic satire of the Spain of his day.

The causticity characteristic of the *Visions* also prevails in the sarcastic dedication that precedes the edition of 1631. This "antidedication," inscribed *a ninguna persona de todas cuantas Dios crió en el mundo* ("to not one person of all God created in the world"), is designed to burlesque a typical grandiose dedication. Quevedo informs the reader that he has written all the criticism of people that he wanted to and the reader can do what he pleases with his copy of the book.

III *Analysis of the* Visions

At the beginning of "The Vision of Final Judgment," Quevedo relies on Homeric authority in declaring that dreams

should be believed. He accepts Claudian's opinion that dreams
are a rehearsal of the events that occur during one's waking
hours. Quevedo believes this dream especially valid since it
descended upon him from heaven after falling asleep while
reading St. Hippolytus' *End of the World and the Second
Coming of Christ*. A youth towering in the air sounds a trumpet,
and Quevedo suddenly plunges the reader into the gruesome
parade of condemned sinners. In this vision we encounter the
general types and historical figures who appear throughout the
Visions: notaries, lawyers, physicians, pharmacists, tailors, wine
sellers, pastry cooks, whores, adulteresses, poets, barbers, Judas,
Mohammed, and Luther are some of the most frequently lampooned people.

"El alguacil endemoniado" ("The Bedevilled Constable") ridicules the Italian priest Genaro Andreini who was a notorious
exorciser in Madrid at the time this vision was written. In his
prologue to the "pious" reader, Quevedo states that this vision
is *una reprensión de malos ministros de justicia*, "a reprehension
of bad ministers of justice." (O.C. I, 133b) The portrayal of the
two characters that give the title to this *sueño* admirably disclose the hypocrisy prevalent in our author's topsy-turvy world.
The clergyman Calabrés is a "handsome sepulcher," (O.C. I,
134a) i.e., he is a dissolute libertine in his soul, but gives the
impression that he is the purest man of God. The person being
exorcised has the appearance of a man but he really is a
constable—the *alguacil* (constable) is one of the types most
frequently satirized in Quevedo's works—who, in pursuing his
job, cannot be distinguished from a devil. Many of the types
condemned in the previous vision are similarly excoriated in
this *sueño*. Allegorical figures, which abound in "El sueño de
la muerte" ("The Vision of Death"), are included for the first
time in this *sueño*. The abstractions personified are naked Truth,
who was obliged to take up quarters with a mute, and Justice
who, after much peregrination through the world, was banished
to heaven by mankind.

Longer than the first two *sueños* combined, "El sueño del
infierno" ("The Vision of Hell") presents to the "unappreciative"
anonymous reader a truculent depiction of the denizens of hell.
Quevedo terminates this vision with the plea that his readers
profit from his frightening experience. This is one of the most
vivid and appalling of all the *sueños* in its scathing social,
religious, and political incriminations. The reader is shocked

at the very beginning of the dispiriting narration. The author finds himself surrounded by the beauty and serenity of nature. (Quevedo is primarily concerned with man and, consequently, vegetation is generally absent from his hellish scenes. In fact, he states later on in this *sueño* that in hell there is no tree of any size. [O.C. I, 147a]) Then, of the two paths of life he paints —the traditional rough, narrow road to heaven and the primrose path—he finally manages to follow the vice-ridden travellers going down the broad, pleasurable avenue to the infernal pit. In addition to the usual types and vices satirized, we find derision of the commonplace attitudes toward nobility, honor, and valor; some treatment of the imminence-of-death theme; attacks against heretics, and particularly Luther; and criticism of the superstitions propounded by astrologers, alchemists, and other cultivators of the occult sciences.

"El mundo por de dentro" ("The World from Within") is probably the most acrimonious and, at the same time, the most cohesive of all the *sueños*. Couched in somber, pessimistic tones, this piece exposes the ubiquitous hypocrisy of the world turned inside out. Quevedo demeans himself as well as his readers in the prologue when he confesses he is among those who know nothing, do not want to know anything, and believe that nothing is known. (O.C. I, 164a) At the beginning of the vision we find our author wandering in a state of confusion through the labyrinth of the world. He encounters the Undeceiver, a venerable old man, bruised and in tatters, who has reached this pitiable state in return for the truths he has revealed to mankind. The Undeceiver takes Quevedo on a tour of the world's main street, Hypocrisy. Almost all mankind participates in perpetrating fraud. The appearances and actions of the people unmasked in this *sueño*—the deceit of women is highlighted—are diametrically opposed to the truth.

Quevedo's recurring eschatological preoccupation attains its climax in "The Vision of Death," the last of the original *sueños*. In his introductory remarks to the reader, he cogently states: "I have wanted death to finish my discourses as it does all other things." (O.C. I, 174a) The author falls asleep while contemplating the words of Lucretius and Job on man's self-torment and the brevity of life. Early in the vision he meets Death, a seemingly feminine creature, young on one side and old on the other, both elegantly and ordinarily bedecked. She mouths the Quevedesque commonplace that one begins to die at birth.

Death sits on her throne attended by a multitude of little Deaths. Among these are the abstractions love, cold, hunger, fear, and laughter. A long string of conventional and allegorical figures give an account of their actions. The World, the Devil, Flesh, and Money take part in the procession as well as a host of well-known historical and proverbial people. When the dream is over, Quevedo tells the reader that his vision should be believed since the disinterested dead are beyond jesting.

IV   The Discurso de todos los diablos and La hora de todos

The *Discurso de todos los diablos o infierno enmendado* (*The Discourse of All Devils or Hell Reformed*) was written in 1627 and first published the following year. It was roundly censured by Father Niseno (1629) mainly because of its sacrilegiousness. Niseno added an interesting criticism: naive people might consider Quevedo's depiction of hell as completely real since he did not even pretend, as in the five previous visions, that it was a vision. Quevedo had to change the title which became "El entremetido, la dueña y el soplón" ("The Meddler, the Duenna and the Informer") when included in *Juguetes de la niñez*. Allusions to God and his angels are suppressed from the beginning since Quevedo had had ample experience with the censors in connection with the first *sueños*. Lucifer and his demons deal with the types and historical figures satirized in this work. Quevedo's increasing interest in political matters is patent in this piece. Caesar and Brutus, Seneca and Nero, Solon, and several Roman rulers discuss their ideas on government and there is an attack made on the writers of books on kingship that abounded in the Golden Age. (Quevedo himself was one of these writers on the governance of rulers as we shall see in a later chapter.) Novel figures interspersed in this *sueño* are the poet of the rogues lampooned for his *cultismo*, "ornate style," the devils of Tobacco and Chocolate, and the devil of nuns. But it is the *dueña* who is most abused. So vile and terrifying is she that Lucifer and all the demons wish to flee from her. Lucifer decrees that all offending devils shall be delivered to the torture of the *dueña*.

La hora de todos y la fortuna con seso (*The Hour of All Men and Fortune in Her Wits*), a "moral fantasy," has much in common stylistically and thematically with the *Visions*. Valbuena Prat has aptly observed that this work and *The Discourse of*

All Devils or Hell Reformed correspond to "two analogous attitudes of the paradoxical Quevedo; if one is that of 'hell re-
formed,' the other is that of the world re-formed..."⁹ Again
we are confronted with Quevedo's *al revés* (topsy-turvy) world
in which the naked truth shocks the reader. Of the original five
visions, *The Hour of All Men* is probably the closest to "The
World from Within," in which our author does not utilize the
dream device but gives us the impression that what the Undeceiver exposes are the real occurrences in the world. When the
clock strikes four in *The Hour of All Men*, each type receives his
due; this is in reality another version of the final judgment rendered by God in the first vision. Fortune is particularly appropriate as the final arbiter for Quevedo's topsy-turvy, chaotic
world view since in Greco-Roman mythology she was a personification of the arbitrary, unforeseen and capricious nature of
things.

Written in 1635, *The Hour of All Men* was not published until
1650 (in Zaragoza) because of uncomplimentary allusions to
contemporary dignitaries. The opuscule "La isla de los Mono-
pantos" ("The Island of the Monopanti"), which Quevedo said
had been lost during his last stay in prison, was finally recovered
and around 1644 inserted near the end of *The Hour of All Men.*
This interpolated piece constitutes a thinly-veiled attack against
the Count-Duke of Olivares, advisers to the king, statesmen,
ecclesiastics, and Jews who were allegedly causing Spain's downfall. The Jews are portrayed in league with the Monopanti,[10]
whose prince, Pragas Chincollos, represents the Count-Duke of
Olivares. The Monopanti are characterized as "men of quadruple
slyness, complete hypocrisy, extreme dissimulation, and of such
deceitful appearance that all religions and nations take them
for their own." (O.C. I, 266b) The Jews and the Monopanti
have apparently formed their alliance to destroy Christianity;
their deity is money and their new sect is *dinerismo*, "moneyism."

Physicians, constables, notaries, lawyers, pharmacists, marriage
brokers, pedantic poets, deceiving women, flatterers, babblers,
and cheating tavern keepers are lampooned in the first part of
this work as in the *Visions.* However, new types appear and
political matters come to the fore. In addition to the harsh dis-
paragement of the Jews in "The Island of the Monopanti," there
is a severe vilification of the *moriscos,* Moors converted to
Christianity after the Reconquest, who are considered as treach-
erous among the Turks as they were among the Spaniards before

their expulsion from Spain in 1609. (O.C. I, 257b) Quevedo
evokes sympathy for the Chilean Indians who were mistreated
by the evangelizing Christians and for the Negroes about whose
slavery a spokesman of theirs comments: "For our slavery there
is no other cause but color, and color is an accident, not a
crime." (O.C. I, 262b)

Quevedo's chauvinism and staunch Catholicism are revealed
in his acrid observations on the politics and religion of the
English, French, Italians, Dutch, Danes, Germans, and Turks
as well as his fellow countrymen. The episode involving the
three French peddlers and the proud Spaniard discloses his
hatred for the French: *Y ahora veo que los franceses sois los
piojos que comen a España por todas partes, y que venís a ella
en figura de bocas abiertas, con dientes de peines y muelas de
aguzar, y creo que su comezón no se remedia con rascarse, sino
que antes crece, haciéndose pedazos con sus propios dedos* ("I am
now convinced you Frenchmen are the lice that devour all parts
of Spain; that you bite us with the teeth of your combs, and
grind us with your stones; nor do I think that scratching is any
remedy against this itching, but that it increases it, and makes
us tear ourselves to pieces with our own fingers"). O.C. I, 252a[11]
At the outset of the conversation between the Frenchmen and
the Spaniard, the latter relates that Spaniards have no trade but
war, and that those who are poor borrow or beg in their travels
and that those who have had some means resort to thievery.
(O.C. I, 251b)

V   *The Devil in the* Visions

Quevedo's notions of the devil and his abode are drawn from
the beliefs that flourished in the Middle Ages and still existed
so strongly during his day. We see that his inhabitants of hell
faithfully represent the original nature of the evil spirits whose
generic name *diablo* is derived from the Latin *diabolus* (Greek
diábolos) which signifies an "accuser" or "assailant." Indeed, the
Quevedesque demons pursue, attack, flay, and torture those who
are condemned to the infernal regions. There are, as usual, the
specialized devils in charge of the different moral and physical
evils which plagued mankind. Some of the devils in the *Visions*
are those of money, bribery, tobacco, chocolate, nuns, thievery,
and political embroilment. In the dedication to "El alguacil
endemoniado" ("The Bedevilled Constable"), Quevedo classifies

devils according to the medieval book on demonology written by the well-known Michael Psellus. Six types of devils are distinguished according to their different habitations: those of fire, air, earth, water, the underground, and the night.[12]

The devil also has many varied shapes and colors in Quevedo's *Visions* as well as in popular lore. Traditionally the devil is lame because of his fall from heaven, but Quevedo explains that a devil in the "Vision of Hell" is lame and hunchbacked because he had to carry so many hell-bound tailors on his back. Ugly, horned demons are depicted as giants, dwarfs, as bowlegged, bald, skin-chapped, pug-nosed, spotted with mud, and left-handed.[13] In addition to their customary blackness, which reflects the color of their dwelling place, we find devils of all hues in European and Oriental tradition.[14] Quevedo conceives a mulatto devil and also a yellow-complexioned devil who has achieved this color of infamy because of the concoctions of the druggists he watches over.

Quevedo follows traditional beliefs in other respects. His devils are legion in number and ubiquitous. They can appear in the form of either sex and in any guise. Hell is located below ground and purging fires burn throughout the nether region. Quevedo supposes frigid regions in hell, which is derived from Dante's descriptions and ultimately from classical mythology. He renews the legend of a person possessed by the devil in "The Bedevilled Constable." The imprisonment of Enrique de Villena in a glass phial in the "Vision of Death" continues the folklore brought to Spain from the East by the Moors. People isolated from the world in glass balls and globes is a frequent motif in Bosch's pictures.

VI *Women Lampooned*

Woman is the most frequently maligned of all the types that are lampooned in the *Visions*. All concepts of courtly love and the Renaissance neo-Platonic deification of woman are absent from the visions. Indeed, Quevedo leads us to the opposite pole in his denigrating portrayals of women who are ugly without and within. Woman is mercilessly satirized in "El mundo por de dentro" ("The World from Within") for masking her true physical appearance. (O.C. I, 172) Paint, powders, toilet waters, and wigs disguise her frightful imperfections and foul odors. Her bodily and moral repulsiveness are cogently revealed: *Si la besas,*

*te embarras los labios, si la abrazas, aprietas tablillas y abollas
cartones; si la acuestas contigo, la mitad dejas debajo de la cama
en los chapines; si la pretendes, te cansas; si la alcanzas, te
embarazas; si la sustentas, te empobreces; si la dejas, te persigue;
si la quieres, te deja* ("If you kiss her, you smear mud on your
lips; if you embrace her, you squeeze corset slats and bruise a
stuffing of cotton and canvas; if you go to sleep with her, half
of her remains in her shoes beneath the bed; if you court her,
you get worn out; if you win her, you assume troubles; if you
support her, you impoverish yourself; if you leave her, she
pursues you; if you love her, she leaves you"). O.C. I, 172

Deceitful, greedy wives, fake virgins, old hags, whores, bawds
and *dueñas* constantly scheme to cause man's suffering and
perdition. In the "Vision of Hell," an unhappily married man
is pictured as having in his wife all the implements necessary
to become a martyr and, at times, he discovers a portable hell
in her. (O.C. I, 144b) Quevedo perpetuates the medieval belief
that the devil takes the form of a beautiful girl to incite men
to sin until their souls are carried off to hell. (O.C. I, 155a) In
Discurso de todos los diablos (*Discourse of All Devils*),
a nun's devil recommends that if at any time hell should be in
danger of peace, there should be convened an assembly of nuns
to select an abbess since nuns are expert at provoking sedition,
mutiny, and confusion. (O.C. I, 224) In the same *sueño*, the
she-devil Prosperity is singled out by Lucifer as the demon who
has damned more souls than all the other devils together. It is
natural for Quevedo to personify death in the traditional garb of
a woman in "The Vision of Death." He says that this figure
seemed like a woman—*parecía mujer* (O.C. I, 177b)—since this
is in consonance with his repeated exposing of woman's fraudulent
appearance and behavior. His description makes Death represent
all women—the elegant and the plainly attired, the alert and the
dull, the young and the old—who deceive men with their
capriciousness.

However, it is the *dueña* among all the female types who
attains the utmost degree of hideousness and chicanery. The
dueñas are infernal frogs, skulls preserved in grease, the scourge
of devils, and death incarnate. The theme of the *dueña* as an
unfit guardian of a maiden's virtue was a commonplace in Spanish
literature even before Quevedo's time.[15] Thus, Quevedo's unremit-
ting assaults on the appearance and habits of this type are so
well known mainly because of his stylistic genius. Old women,

usually inculpated for resorting to trickery to recapture their youth, are often a target for Quevedo's barbs, but, for him, there does not exist on earth or in hell a woman so despised as an aging *dueña*. The frightful depiction of Dueña Quintañona— *quintañón* means one hundred years old—in "The Vision of Death" is a masterful caricature that rivals the description of Cabra in the *Buscón*:

Con una cara hecha de un orejón, los ojos en los cuévanos de ven-dimiar, la frente con tantas rayas y de tal color y hechura que parecía planta de pie; la nariz, en conversación con la barbilla que casi jun-tándose hacía garra, y una cara de la impresión del grifo; la boca, a la sombra de la nariz, de hechura de lamprea, sin diente ni muela, con sus pliegues de bolsa a lo jimio, y apuntándole ya el bozo de las calaveras en un mostacho erizado; la cabeza con temblor de sonajas y la habla danzante; unas tocas muy largas sobre el monjil negro; es-maltada de mortaja la tumba, con un rosario muy largo colgando, y ella corva, que parecía, con las muertecillas que colgaban dél, que venía pescando calaverillas chicas . . . Llegóse más cerca, y tenía los ojos haciendo aguas, y en el pico de la nariz columpiándose una moquita por donde echaba un tufo de cimenterio,

(Her face was wrinkled like the skin of a dried peach. Her eyes seemed to be sunk in two grape baskets. Her furrowed brow resembled the soles of her feet. Her nose came so close to her chin that the two together formed a claw. Her face was that of a griffin. Her mouth, shaded by her nose, was completely toothless like a lamprey's and above the ape-like baggy folds of flesh a downy moustache was sprout-ing. Her head was shaking like a rattle and her voice trembled. Very long veils covered her shroud-like black mourning dress. Little skulls were hanging on the lengthy rosary she wore and since she was so stooped she seemed to be fishing for small skulls . . . She came closer, her eyes watering and mucous swaying on the tip of her nose, which gave off a foul cemetery smell.) O.C. I, 189b-190a

This repugnant and malodorous prototype of *dueñas*, blamed for all plagues, calamities, and unpleasant occurrences, is abhor-rent to the dead and the living, and she herself desires to abandon her trade. The *dueña* as an anathema is epitomized in the tale that Doña Quintañona relates of a traveller who preferred to end his life on a gibbet rather than stay one night in a village near Valladolid called Dueñas, a town that still exists today. (O.C. I, 190b-191a) No type is more antipathetic than the *dueña* in the *Discourse of All Devils*. Lucifer himself is at a loss to decide what to do with them, and the devils dread a deluge of *dueñas* in their realm and the threat of being delivered to the eternal torture of the *dueña*.

The origin of Quevedo's apparent misogyny in the *Visions* and other satirical works in prose and poetry is obscured because of his contradictory nature. Critics have ascribed this hatred of women to an early-manifested inability to have any feeling for them, arising from his cold, intellectual appraisal of the opposite sex. Mas, taking a diametrically opposite view, asserts that Quevedo's misogyny really stems from his natural liking of women whom he cannot do without.[16]

Two combining factors help us understand Quevedo's attitude toward women. First, his volatile, contradictory vision of life did not preclude experiencing the whole gamut of human emotions. He was capable of tender feelings of love in his amatory poetry and particularly in the lyric poems to Lisi. Let us bear in mind that his satirical visions were written to reveal *abusos, vicios, y engaños en todos los oficios y estados del mundo* ("Abuses, Vices, and Deceits in all the Occupations and Classes of the World") as the title of the *Visions* informs us. The *alguacil* ("constable") is consistently execrable in Quevedo's works, but in his introductory remarks to "The Bedevilled Constable" he informs us that this vision reprehends only bad ministers of justice, for there are many who are virtuous and noble. Similarly, the censure of women is a poignant exposé of the defects and sins of those women who deserve castigation, but it is not necessarily a condemnation of all women. When Quevedo severely castigates the events, customs, and attitudes of the Spaniards of his own day, he does so largely out of love for his country and distress on viewing its decay.

Second, Quevedo's censure of women's affectations and immorality was an old tradition in European literature going back as far as the Roman writers Martial, Juvenal, Ovid, and Horace. Biblical writings also frequently were a guide for Quevedo in his serious works. In his *Homilía a la Santísima Trinidad* (*Homily to the Holy Trinity*), Quevedo recalls the episode of the original sin which shows that women follow the worst advice, desire what is forbidden them, persuade their husbands to do their bidding, believe gossip, and give credence to the superficial. (O.C. I, 1166b) The church fathers believed that Satan brought about the downfall of men through the enticements of women. St. Paul's fear of women's charms, exemplified by a young girl possessed by a devil, is recounted in Quevedo's *Vida de San*

Pablo Apóstol (*Life of the Apostle St. Paul*). (O.C. I, 1501a)
That woman was the instrument of the devil and the cause of
man's destruction was a popular belief in the Middle Ages and
still maintained its vigor in Quevedo's day. This is reflected in
medieval Spanish literature in which some authors considered
women as dangerous and false creatures who used hypocrisy and
cunning as their weapons. Antifeminist exposés are encountered
in such writings as *Libro de los engaños y assayamientos de las
mujeres* (*Book of the Deceits and Wiles of Women*), 13th
century; the Archpriest of Hita's *Libro de buen amor* (*Book of
Good Love*), 14th century; the Archpriest of Talavera's *Corbacho*
(*Whip*), 15th Century; Fernando de Rojas' *La Celestina* (1499)
and the imitations of this work; Francisco Delicado's *La lozana
andaluza* (*The Lusty Andalusian Woman*) (1528); and other
Golden Age works featuring the *pícara* (female rogue). Especially
germane to this discussion are the comments of Francisco de
Santos which reveal woman as an instrument of the devil:
"...*peores sois que el demonio, pues para meter el pecado en
el mundo se valió de vuestro rostro y nombró por su abogado,
siendo vosotras el principal instrumento para que entrase la
culpa por los puertos de la naturaleza.*"[17]

VII *Physicians Excoriated*

The physician is one of the types most frequently inveighed
against in Quevedo's satirical writings. And with good reason,
since in that time medicine was not yet a true science. Diagnostic
techniques were rudimentary and good physicians put their trust
in the healing powers of nature rather than in the pursuit of
the usual therapy of bloodletting and purging which often produced harmful effects. Physicians were helpless in checking the
serious epidemics of typhus, plague, and typhoid. Quevedo
himself suffered from a complicated phlebotomy and must have
had unpleasant experiences with doctors during his illnesses.[18]
Physicians are portrayed as ignorant, mercenary assassins who
finish off their patients before their time. It is recommended in
Libro de todas las cosas (*Book of All Things*) that a person pay
money to a physician when he is in good health—a form of
preventive medicine—and not when he is ill, since under this
circumstance a doctor will not cure him as long as the money
enters his pockets. (O.C. I, 111a) Physicians are the same as
devils since both wish to destroy what is good in man—his health

and morals respectively. (O.C. I, 176a) When one asks of what
disease or wounds someone died, the answer should be that
he died of the doctor. (O.C. I, 178b)

A physician is the first type on whom the tables are turned in
The Hour of All Men. When the hour surprises him he suddenly
finds himself as a hangman with his legs across the shoulders
of his patient. He is now shouting to his victim the Latin word
credo (I believe), the beginning of the prayer said by persons
about to be hanged, instead of his usual Latin word *récipe* (take),
with which a physician begins his medical prescription (O.C. I,
231b) The most cutting caricature of the physician heads the
parade of types satirized in "The Vision of Death":

*Fueron entrando unos médicos a caballo en unas mulas, que con
gualdrapas negras parecían tumbas con orejas. El paso era divertido,
torpe y desigual, de manera que los dueños iban encima en mareta y
algunos vaivenes de serradores; la vista asquerosa de puro pasear los
ojos por orinales y servicios; las bocas emboscadas en barbas que
apenas se las hallara un brazo; sayos con resabios de vaqueros; guantes
en infusión, doblados como los que curan; sortijón en el pulgar con
piedra tan grande, que cuando toma el pulso pronostica al enfermo la
losa. Eran éstos en gran número, y todos, rodeados de platicantes
que cursan en lacayos, y, tratando más con las mulas que con los
dotores, se graduaron de médicos.* (O.C. I, 175b)

(A number of physicians entered riding on their mules, which, since
they were wearing long black cloths on their haunches, seemed like
tombs with ears. They trooped by in a careless, clumsy and disorderly
manner so that their masters were swaying from side to side. The
nauseated look on their faces came from scrutinizing all kinds of
chamber pots. Their faces were so overgrown with hair that their
hands could hardly find their mouths. They wore long robes and
carried their gloves folded as doctors normally do. On their thumbs
they had huge rings with enormous stones and when they felt a
patient's pulse the prognosis was always death. There were many of
them and they were surrounded by assistants who become full-
fledged physicians by spending more time in the company of mules
than with the doctors.)

Other types related to medicine are severely castigated.
Pharmacists are depicted as providing death-dealing weapons
for the doctors in the form of valueless medicinal herbs called
by fancy Latin or Latinized Greek names. We know that in
Quevedo's day the Spanish Parliament was seriously troubled
by the poorly trained apothecaries and the spurious and harmful

drugs they dispensed. The deputies recommended to the King that stronger controls should be exercised and harsher penalties be meted out to those druggists guilty of vending fraudulent medicines.[19] Included also are the surgeons laden with their instruments of torture, the quacks who pretend to cure with incantations and unorthodox remedies, the dentists who depopulate mouths and hasten old age, and the barbers—they performed bloodletting and other minor surgery in Quevedo's time —whose plucking of lively tunes on their guitars symbolizes the scraping and pricking of a patient's flesh.

VIII *Satire of Constables, Notaries, Judges, and Lawyers*

Quevedo was sorely troubled by the venality of those people entrusted with law enforcement. He especially denounced *alguaciles* (constables) and *escribanos* (notaries), but petty judges and lawyers were also targets for criticism. Alfredo Berumen has studied the *Actas de las Cortes de Castilla* (*Transactions of the Cortes of Castile*), Madrid, 1869, to show that the Castilian Parliament debated the abuses of these administrators of justice and recommended a tighter control over their activities.[20]

The Cortes was aware of the excessive and ever increasing number of constables in Madrid. The keen competition among them evidently led to more corrupt practices. Quevedo's loathing of the constable is manifest in "The Bedevilled Constable" and other visions. He adjudges this type inhuman and worse than any devil. In fact, the devil inhabiting the body of the constable wishes to leave this abode quickly, since he fears his association with the constable will tarnish his reputation among his companions in hell. In the "Vision of Hell," a devil wittily exclaims that bad *alguaciles* are not in hell since all of hell is in each bad constable. (O.C. I, 155b) The constable excels all in thievery since he steals with his whole body: he spies with his eyes, pursues victims with his feet, seizes with his hands, and accuses with his tongue. (O.C. I, 139a) The *alguacil,* usually accompanied by *corchetes,* his assistants, is seen vigorously carrying out his base duties throughout the *Visions*.

The Castilian Cortes wrote frequently on the misfeasance of notaries who are supreme ogres in Quevedo's gallery of Spanish types. These notaries, although petty officials, could substantially affect the affairs of Spaniards by such activities as authenticating contracts, acknowledging deeds, taking affidavits and depositions.

Mas has shown that the Cortes, in its deliberations for the years 1592-1598, denounced the great excesses and evils perpetrated by the notaries.[21] There was an inordinate number of them by the beginning of the seventeenth century, and they were pictured as disturbing the peace with their machinations and preying on the livestock and other goods of Spaniards living in rural areas as well as in the cities. Lackeys, coachmen, shoemakers, and masons and other equally untrained people easily became notaries on the payment of a relatively small sum of money. Consequently, many notaries were guilty of malpractice by design or by sheer ignorance.

Quevedo portrays notaries as enemies of one's purse who resort to deceit in order to satisfy their greed. ("The Bedevilled Constable," O.C. I, 135b) Expert in mudslinging, they heap guilt upon the innocent. ("The World from Within," O.C. I, 170) They are likened to cats which slink through the filthy, ancient infernal regions in search of rats. The cat has been a representation of the devil in all Christian lands. López-Rey suggests that Quevedo might have inspired Goya's *Caprice* which portrays a constable in an erect pose before a full-length mirror; the image reflected is that of a feline animal standing on its hind legs.[22]

The notary is usually depicted with his feather pen, the indispensable writing implement of his trade which he wields so adroitly that he can write reams in a jiffy. Through a clever double pun Quevedo captures what he considers the salient characteristic of a notary—stealing. This is achieved first by associating feather with the flight of birds, and then by the play on the verb *volar* (to fly), which also meant "to take something away." ("The Vision of Death," O.C. I, 188b)

Judges and lawyers were censured by the deputies of the Cortes for their venality and corrupt practices. In his own affairs, Quevedo had a surfeit of unpleasant contacts with representatives of the legal profession in the litigations over the villa of Torre de Juan Abad which plagued him until his death from the time he inherited it in 1598. In the *Visions,* judges are the devils' pheasants, delicious dishes, and the most fertile seeds demons can sow since each judge harvested brings in a host of lawyers, notaries and litigants. (O.C. I, 138a) In the "Final Judgment" a judge is washing his hands over and over vainly attempting to cleanse them of the stains resulting from having had his palms "greased" during court actions. (O.C. I, 127a)

In *The Hour of All Men* judges are depicted as ignoramuses or corrupted by bribes if they possessed any intelligence. When the hour of justice arrives, they damn themselves and strip each other of their beards which are the real repositories of their judgment. (O.C. I, 232b-233a) Judges and lawyers are shown as manipulators of the law for their own gain. Lawyers are pictured as fleecing their clients so that these unfortunates come out poorly whether they win or lose a case. (O.C. I, 241a)

IX   *The* arbitristas

Quevedo harshly lampooned the *arbitristas* (projectors) in *The Hour of All Men.* (O.C. I, 237a-239a) These were public-spirited men who proposed schemes mainly designed to remedy Spain's economic crisis that was steadily worsening during the reigns of Philip III and Philip IV. Unfortunately, many of the panaceas they suggested to the Kings' ministers were incredibly absurd, and few sound nostrums were advanced to cure the country's ills. Elliott has weeded out several intelligent *arbitrios* from the plethora of proposals for reform: the slashing of government spending, the overhaul of the Castilian tax system, stepped-up contributions to the national treasury from all the kingdoms of the monarchy, a repopulation of Castile, irrigation of fields, making rivers navigable, and a fostering of agriculture and industry.[23] Unfortunately, such measures were not put into effect, and the decay of Spain's economy continued unabated till the end of Quevedo's days and beyond. Despairing of the fruitless schemes of the *arbitristas,* it is no wonder that he paints them as destroyers of a kingdom. Ending his tirade against the projectors, a Danish prince ruined by these men addresses them in these words: "Antichrist will be an *arbitrista,* and will burn you all alive. I ought to keep your ashes to cleanse the stains of all republics. Princes may be poor; but, in dealing with *arbitristas* so as to become rich, they cease being princes." (O.C. I, 238a)

X   *Parody of the Hidalgo and His Code of Honor*

The hidalgo—a man of the lower nobility—lampooned in "The Vision of Hell," is similar to the classic petty nobleman who appears in the third chapter of the *Lazarillo de Tormes* (1554). This parasitic, egoistic type shunned work even if he was im-pecunious and starving, and principally occupied himself in

demonstrating his nobility to the whole world. He was obliged
to use the mask of pretense partly because of the honor code
peculiar to Spaniards. Honor meant one's reputation which had
to be maintained unsullied at all cost. The extrinsic and the superficial were considered of greater import than one's authentic,
intrinsic value.

The attack on the hallowed honor code made by Quevedo
and other Spanish satirists of the seventeenth century is a manifestation of what Castro has termed the "radical duality in both
art and life . . . [which] has as its base the breaking up of the
compact unity of certain beliefs."[24] He sees this process as an
example of *vivir desviviéndose* (a kind of construction by destruction) which reaches its apogee during the baroque period.
Quevedo combatted this time-honored Spanish concept of honor,
saying that a person's worth should be determined by his acts
and not by the nobility he inherits. He declares that all blood
is red and the true hidalgo is the one whose customs are noble.
(O.C. I, 148b) He aptly expresses the vanity and waste inherent
in the honor code:

*Por la honra no come el que tiene gana donde le sabría bien. Por
la honra se muere la viuda entre dos paredes. Por la honra, sin saber
qué es hombre ni qué es gusto, se pasa la doncella treinta años casada
consigo misma. Por la honra la casada se quita a su deseo cuanto pide.
Por la honra pasan los hombres el mar. Por la honra mata un hombre
a otro. Por la honra gastan todos más de lo que tienen. Y es la honra
mundana, según esto, una necedad del cuerpo y alma, pues al uno
quita los gustos y al otro la gloria.* (O.C. I, 149a)

(For honor the one who is hungry does not eat. For honor the widow
pines away between two walls. For honor the maiden spends thirty
years alone without having known a man or pleasure. For honor the
married woman completely denies her desire. For honor men cross the
seas. For honor one man kills another. For honor everybody spends
more than he has. And worldly honor is accordingly an inanity related
to the body and the soul, since it takes away corporal pleasures and
the glory of the soul.)

Quevedo points out the perversion of the traditional honor
code in "The Vision of Death." Everybody talks of honor but
nobody puts it into effect. Every man sets up his own standards
of honor and deems honorable everything that suits his purposes.
In Quevedo's topsy-turveydom the Spaniards have succumbed to
lying, trickery, insolence, and drunkenness. The harmful effects

of honor are later similarly to be evinced in the second part of Gracián's *El criticón* (1653). Traditional honor was now considered rancid and inappropriate for the contemporary period; although many people suffered all sorts of mental, physical, and financial hardships to attain it, no one really managed to possess it in life.[25]

XI   *Quevedo's Xenophobia*

Quevedo's patent xenophobia represented firmly-rooted attitudes of traditional Spain. It was directed toward the people inhabiting foreign countries as well as the aliens that had lived within the confines of Spain. The purge of Arabs and Jews from Spanish soil attest to the Spaniards' zealous extirpation of foreign peoples. Spaniards also have generally striven to insulate themselves from all those elements which might corrupt their goal of *casticidad,* i.e., the protection of the *purity* of traditional Spanish beliefs, customs, and language. The eradication of religious heresies threatening their Catholicism motivated the Inquisition and the Counter-Reformation.

Genoese bankers are a favorite target for Quevedo's outbursts against foreigners, for these men were the principal bankers of the Spanish government. Quevedo's mordant criticism of these gentlemen reflects their fraudulent negotiations and usurious interest rates which contributed to the further weakening of an economy that had begun to falter in the sixteenth century. The Spanish kings were forced to rely on foreign banking firms to fill the void created when the Jews, who were the Spanish money-lenders of the Middle Ages, were expelled from Spain at the end of the fifteenth century. Quevedo sees the Genoese bankers stealing Spain's treasures and bankrupting the country. They are vividly portrayed as leeches sucking out the silver from the veins of the Potosí mines. (O.C. I, 183b) One of Quevedo's best-known satirical poems pungently reveals how the Genoese bankers wound up with the Spanish treasure shipped from the New World:

> *Nace en las Indias honrado,*
> *donde el mundo le acompaña;*
> *viene a morir en España*
> *y es en Génova enterrado.*[26]

(Honored [money] is born in the Indies
where everybody partakes of it;
it comes to Spain to die
and is buried in Genoa.)

Among the other Italians satirized, the Venetians suffer most
from Quevedo's sharp criticism. They are characterized as con-
scienceless, always subordinating their Catholicism and ethics
to their selfish interests. The most severe attack upon them is
made in *The Hour of All Men* in which they are accused of
bringing discord into the world through their malice, double
dealing, and dissimulation. The Doge of that Republic proclaims:
"The wars we have occasioned among our friends and not those
we have made with our enemies, have given us peace and victory.
We shall be free as long as we keep others busy in subduing
one another. Our light springs from dissension . . . The more
monarchs batter one another the more we shine splendorously."
(O.C. I, 253a)

As for the Dutch, it was natural for Quevedo to rail against
them as we see in two sections of *The Hour of All Men*. The
Dutch, since the last quarter of the sixteenth century, rebelled
against Spanish hegemony, and the drawn-out effects to pacify
them were costly in men and money. In addition, Spain felt itself
ineluctably impelled to eradicate the Protestantism which was
spreading in the Netherlands. A third reason for the hatred
directed toward the Dutch was the inroads their merchant fleets
had been making since the end of the sixteenth century against
Spain's mercantile monopoly in the Caribbean and South American waters. Quevedo expresses the fear that the Dutch might
wrest all the New World from Spanish control after having taken
Brazil from the Portuguese in 1630.

While Quevedo has Chilean Indians reveal the deceit and
treachery of the Dutch—the Dutch were naïvely condemned
for having rebelled against their Spanish rulers and for having stolen territory from them—influenced by his accustomed
penchant for the defense of the underdog, he points out the
Indians' desire to be free of the Spaniards. In his attack on
specious Christian motives justifying the conquering of the
Americas, an Indian chief rejects the Dutch captain's offer
of friendship and trade: "You must observe that America is a
rich beautiful harlot, and since she was false to her husbands,
she will never be true to her bullies. Christians say that heaven

punished the Indies because they adored idols, and we Indians say that heaven will punish the Christians because they adore the Indies." (O.C. I, 262b)

Quevedo assails the French for draining Spanish treasure and also for fostering Calvinism. (O.C. I, 252a) The Spaniard who meets the conniving French pedlars in *The Hour of All Men* achieves some measure of revenge by soundly thrashing them, something which the Spanish armies were unable to do during the war of 1635-1659 from which the French emerged victorious. Germans are maligned for their heresy and treachery, and the Turks, the feared enemy of Christendom, are described as barbarous infidels nurtured in the deceitful practices of Mohammed. (O.C. I, 256a)

XII *Quevedo's Attacks on Heretics*

Imbued with the fervent Catholicism that was the Spanish patrimony, Quevedo denounced all who espoused other beliefs. Following the broad concept that those who do not adhere to the dogma of Roman Catholicism are guilty of heresy, at the end of the "Vision of Hell" he commented on a host of heretics beginning with the misbelievers who lived *before* the coming of Christ and comprising those who existed up to his own time. His catalogue of heterodox persons prior to the Reformation is remarkably faithful in arrangement and observations to two heresiographies published in the sixteenth century.[27]

Among the enemies of Christianity, Judas is probably the person Quevedo most frequently vilifies. References to Judas' betrayal of Christ for thirty pieces of silver constantly crop up when Quevedo wishes to emphasize the venality of people. In Quevedo's unorthodox and topsy-turvy world, Judas attempts to defend his infamous treachery saying that he should be commended for being the agent of man's redemption. In addition, he claims that he is not the only Judas who ever existed, that there are other far more wicked traitors who buy, sell, scourge, and crucify Christ. In Quevedo's "Final Judgment" Judas claims that he is far better than Mohammed and Luther—both of them wish to be called Judas—since his betrayal was the salvation of the world, whereas these heretics have sold out mankind and have destroyed everything. (O.C. I, 131b)

Lutherans, Calvinists, and other contemporary Protestant sects were impugned regularly, but Quevedo was most condemnatory of the Moriscos and Jews with whom Spaniards had had more intimate contact. The Moriscos were the Moors converted to Christianity during and after the Reconquest. Many, however, continued secretly to practice Islam. Persecuted by the Spanish Inquisition and subjected to restrictive laws, they rebelled more than once, and the armies of Philip II fought arduously to suppress the Alpujarra revolt in Granada (1568-1571). Moreover, the Moriscos at times provided the Ottoman Turks with information facilitating Turkish raids on the Spanish coast. Thus it was on religious and political grounds that Philip III, on Lerma's insistence, decreed their expulsion in 1609. With this act Spain uprooted its last vestiges of religious impurity, but lost the services of a segment of their population who had labored energetically in agriculture and industry.

Quevedo mercilessly lampoons the Moriscos in the opuscule *Confesión de los moriscos* (*Confession of the Moriscos*) O.C. I, 101, a precious example of his stylistic virtuosity. Not only does he ridicule the Moriscos' use of Spanish, but also cleverly points out their distorted concept of Christianity and their heresy. By means of solecisms, St. Peter (*San Pedro*) becomes St. Dog (*San Perro*), and Jesus becomes a substitute for God. The Morisco is considered persona non grata in Spain for being a bad Moor and rebellious, and among the Turks for being a bad Christian seeking the destruction of the Turkish Empire. Mohammed, the founder of Islam, is often inculpated for leading so many people to hell with his irrational doctrines.

The Jews are perhaps the most detested and maligned among the heretics that appear in Quevedo's satirical writings. They are depicted as hypocritical, avaricious, usurious, and inimical to Christianity. In the *Discourse of All Devils,* Quevedo unmasks a false *converso* (convert) who points out Judaizers all over the place in order to distract people from recognizing him as a Jew. It is curious that Quevedo utilizes circumstantial evidence, often negative, as was the custom of the Inquisition in ferreting out nominal *conversos.* The man in question is revealed a Judaizer because of these "facts": his father died of disgust on seeing a piece of fried bacon, he does not celebrate Easter properly, he keeps his money, and he follows the law of Moses. (O.C. I, 203b)[28]

Even after extirpating its Jewish population by banishment or by compulsory conversion of those who remained, Spaniards retained their distrust of this group of people who, for centuries

prior to 1492, had been active in the fields of medicine, banking,
tax collecting, and industry. Guillermo Díaz Plaja has shown that
Spain feared that the Jews abroad were hatching plots to undermine its political edifice.[29] Chronicles of the period, like the
Avisos written by Quevedo's contemporary, Jerónimo de Barrio-
nuevo, demonstrate the fear Spaniards had of the alleged Jewish
conspiracies. Quevedo shares this attitude toward Jews in
"The Island of the Monopanti," an important chapter in *The
Hour of All Men*—the key work of the Spanish baroque period
according to Díaz Plaja.

International Jewry and Quevedo's enemy, the Count-Duke
of Olivares, are fiercely assailed in "The Island of the Monopanti." Olivares was suspected of being in league with the
Sephardic Jews, perhaps because of some secret blood affiliation.
A delegation under the leadership of their prince Pragas Chincollos—an anagram for Gaspar Conchillos, the Count-Duke's
name—convenes at Salonica with a number of rabbis—undoubtedly disguised merchants and bankers—from all over Europe.
A rabbinical spokesman states that the Monopanti are really
the Jews of the New Testament since, although they originally
believed Jesus was the Messiah, a belief completely denied by
the Jews, they have since forgotten Jesus so that it seems he
never came to or for them. (O.C. I, 269b) Rabbi Saadías
declares the object of the assembly is to take advantage of the
tumult in the world for self gain. The Jews and Monopanti are
portrayed as enemies of Christianity—the Jewish spokesman
claims that his people are even false to the law of Moses—for
their only deity is gold. Their money and deceit will lead them
to acquire power in order that they may control the rulers of
Europe. The Monopanti, inspired by the works of Machiavelli,
have fabricated an infernal trick by which they and their
partners can accomplish their ends. But when the hour comes
upon them, each begins to suspect the other, and they determine
to meet again, "like flint and steel, to batter, bruise and beat
each other to pieces until they struck fire against the whole
world, and founded the new sect of Moneyism, changing the
name of Atheists into that of Moneyists." (O.C. I, 271b)

XIII *Defense of the Underdog*

In the *Visions* and other satirical works that have been examined in this chapter, the attainment of absolute justice and
the setting to rights of the topsy-turvy world by a penetrating

exposé of the sins and sinners in it seem to be Quevedo's supreme aim. Ever preoccupied with Spain's welfare, he lashes out against those who willingly harm his beloved country through any abuse, be it financial, political, physical, moral, or religious. He defends or permits the self-defense of those who are unfairly maligned: the underdog, the hapless, the misunderstood, the innocent, and the real and proverbial people whose reputations are immutably tarnished through no fault of their own.

Juan del Encina, the founder of the modern Spanish theater, furnishes an important clue to this aspect of Quevedo in the "Vision of Death" when he attempts to dispel the commonplace belief that he is the author of absurdities. He claims himself innocent of any of the wrongdoing which Quevedo constantly criticizes, such as being hungry for power, feigning youth in his old age, enslaving himself to money, putting up a false front, consorting with heretics, and using the services of a physician—he preferred to die of an illness rather than be "cured." (O.C. I, 181b-182a) Enrique de Villena, a fifteenth-century literary figure, is the only other real person in the "Vision of Death." He seeks redress of the unjust popular reputation he has acquired as a sorcerer. Quevedo is in full sympathy with Villena since the latter manifests his concern for Spain's well-being by inquiring about the country's financial condition, the status of honor in the world, the machinations of lawyers, the political intrigues of Venice, and the activities of Philip IV. (O.C. I, 185b-186) Quevedo is so pleased with Villena's comments and leading questions relating to his favorite topics that he wishes to follow this legendary figure.

We have seen that even Judas defends himself against the slander he has suffered through the centuries. The attempt to lessen his bad public image rests on two central points: he was forced into his treachery by the Jews, and also there have been far worse sinners than he. Judas' betrayal of Christ does not have the immediacy of other "heinous" acts which were leading to the crumbling of the Spanish Empire and, therefore, Quevedo generally limits himself to taking pot shots at Judas while concentrating more on contemporaneous people and occurrences. Minimizing one's poor reputation by exposing greater malefactors is a dodge that the denizens of Quevedo's hell use at times. The devil who possesses the constable in "The Bedevilled Constable" fears that he will be discredited if word gets around in hell that he has been in the bad company of this morally inferior officer of the law. (O.C. I, 135a) The poor are absent from Quevedo's hell since they have nothing and people are only damned for what they possess. (O.C. I, 139b) Similarly, few ordinary soldiers, those who obediently offer their lives for the protection of their country, inhabit the infernal regions, but there is a whole slew of officers seeking power and glory. (O.C. I, 143b)

The oppressed Indians and Negroes evoke Quevedo's compassion in *The Hour of All Men*. Quevedo discloses the hypocritical colonizing policies of the Spaniards as well as the chicanery of the Dutch who wish to supplant Spanish enslavement of the Indians. We are struck by the Indians' intelligent assessment of the Dutch proposal to establish friendship and trade because it was not too long before that the Spaniards looked upon American Indians as animals. We have observed earlier that a Negro spokesman sees his color as the cause of his people's enslavement, but he asserts that color is an accident and not a crime. He further states that blacks may be physically ugly to whites and yet the physical characteristics of the whites may be just as repulsive to a black community. In concluding his defense of Negroes, Quevedo points out that they have also excelled in martial exploits, learning, virtue, and sanctity. (O.C. I, 263a)

The host of imaginary proverbial characters that parade through the "Vision of Death" clamoring for a mitigation of the low esteem in which they are publicly held are extrahistorical and do not affect Spain's fortunes so vitally as do the various types seriously maligned with regularity. These are insignificant, pitiable, will-less figures completely controlled by popular whim, and it appears that here Quevedo is indulging in a literary game largely devoid of the strict moral censure that characterizes the *Visions* as a whole. The very names of some of the proverbial figures Quevedo encounters in the "Vision of Death" reveal how inane and pathetic they are: Mateo Pico—*pico* (beak) is used colloquially for mouth—who "shoots his mouth off" so much that a good deal of what he says is nonsense; Arbalías, an incessant rapid talker; Chisgaravís, a small man of little substance; Pero Grullo, one who explains the obvious—*perogrullada* is used colloquially for "platitude"—and, Calaínos, a thing of little value. Other characters are boobs,

jokers, slovenly women, spineless people, and those who refuse
to accept responsibility for their actions.

It has been shown that at times Quevedo relaxes his criticism
of constantly-defamed types. This is justified only when the
impugned person can demonstrate that circumstances impel
him to behave the way he does, or there are others more guilty
of vicious or improper acts imputed to him. Such is Judas' case
and also the case of Diego Moreno and Dueña Quintañona.

The cuckold Diego Moreno objects to being considered the
exemplary complaisant husband since there are many more
married men than he who deserve to be the prototype of
cuckoldry. In addition, he places the blame for his reputation
on his wife who, like all women, manipulates her husband to
satisfy her own desires. However, Quevedo makes Diego Moreno
admit to having abetted and profited from his wife's infidelity.
In a spirited dialogue between the author and his "autonomous"
character, the latter evinces particular animosity toward Quevedo
for having added to his popular defamation by writing an
entremés—a one-act farce—of his life. A two-part *Entremés de
Diego Moreno*, written several years before the "Vision of
Death," dramatizes this character's complaisance, his death, and
the prompt remarriage of the widow Justa to a former lover
who gives all indications of zealously guarding his wife's fidelity.

The proverbial *dueña* feels that she unfairly shoulders the
blame for all *dueñas*, many of whom have occupied this position
far longer than she. She complains that maidens under her
wing are difficult to protect and resents being the scapegoat
for all that goes wrong. Tired of the abuse heaped upon her,
she wishes to escape once and for all from the eternal condemnation with which she is immutably saddled.

Quevedo's severe censure of women also momentarily vanishes
in *The Hour of All Men*. A horde of women descend upon
bearded lawyers to protest man's prejudice against them. They
complain of being denied education and the bearing of arms,
and object to the double standard by which man is permitted
all sorts of licentiousness at woman's expense. Yet the crack
is quickly repaired when the lawyer justifies, with Quevedo's
customary arguments, the perpetuation of woman's subservient
state. It is pertinent to note that this anomalous defense of
slandered women—as far as his satirical prose writings go—
was written precisely at the time when his short-lived marriage
was on the rocks and possibly before the definitive separation

from his wife in the summer of 1636. Perhaps this passage is
an echo of a dialogue with his wife or a debate within himself.

XIV   *Other Types Satirized*

Quevedo satirizes a legion of other common types of his
period. There are the tavern keepers who water down or "baptize"
the wine they sell; because they dilute their wine so much, a
customer who has imbibed too much should be described as
"drowned" rather than drunk. (O.C. I, 241b) Tailors are frequently assailed for their crime of purloining clothing material,
and stewards for thieving from their masters' larder. Pastry
cooks are condemned for their meat pies which contain horse
and dog meat, mice, flies, and other foreign flesh meats—the
meat of more animals than in Noah's ark. (O.C. I, 129a) They
are damned for the sin of flesh without having known a woman.
(O.C. I, 147) Coachmen, shoemakers, sycophants, booksellers,
indulgent fathers, people who realize too late the effects of
their actions, merchants, and busybodies also are the butt of
Quevedo's scathing satire.

Alchemists head the list of pseudoscientists lampooned in the
Visions and particularly in the "Vision of Hell." They are portrayed as laden with the tools and raw materials of their trade:
furnaces, crucibles, mud, minerals, slag, horns, dung, human
blood, powders, and alembics. Despite their frenzied activity to
make gold out of the base materials, they only succeed in con-
verting gold into dung. A devil finally decides that since
alchemists are the vilest matter, they are the best raw material
from which to make the philosopher's stone. They are burned
to death willingly since they will finally achieve their great
desire. (O.C. I, 158a)

Real and imaginary diviners and propagators of superstitions
are ridiculed. These are the astrologers, chiromancers, geo-
mancers, and seers who base their divinations on physiognomonic
signs and the analysis of handwriting.

CHAPTER 4

The Buscón

QUEVEDO'S famous picaresque novel, *El Buscón* (*The Swindler*), is an early work probably written by 1608, but it was first published in 1626.[1] The form of the popular picaresque novel allowed Quevedo to achieve a relatively more orderly and sustained satire of Spanish life than was possible in the scattered short pieces of prose—e.g. *Epístolas del Caballero de la Tenaza* (*The Letters of the Retentive Knight*), *Vida de Corte y oficios entretenidos en ella* (*Life in the Capital and the Types Who Inhabit It*) and the various *premáticas* or *pragmáticas* (imperial decrees) which, in criticizing types and customs, parody official decrees—and poetry which already contained much of the raw material for the novel. *The Swindler* has an intimate stylistic affiliation with the *Visions* and also incorporates a number of themes found in them. However, the novel obliges Quevedo to adopt a somewhat more cohesive and "realistic" manner in displaying his mordant satire of Spanish types, customs, and attitudes.

The Swindler was already known in manuscript form before it was first published in 1626. Four editions appeared in that year: the princeps of Zaragoza, a pirated edition which has Zaragoza as the place of publication but was actually printed in Madrid, one in Barcelona, and one in Valencia. Between 1626 and 1671 there were at least thirty-eight editions of this work published in Spanish and other languages. It became so popular in France beginning with the first French translation in 1633 that by 1671 nineteen French translations were made, while there were only fourteen editions in Spanish. Two Italian translations appeared in 1634, and the first two English translations were printed in 1657. *The Swindler* has enjoyed undiminished literary prominence in Europe and America down through the years. Besides the many Spanish editions and translations into English, French, Italian, German, and Dutch that have come out in the twentieth century, it has had appeal for Slavic people as demonstrated by the translations into Russian (1950), Serbo-Croatian (1951), and Ukranian (1956).

An examination of the picaresque and other types of novels popular from the middle of the fifteenth century to Quevedo's time will lead us to a deeper grasp of the significance of *The Swindler*. In the next section, we shall look at several kinds of novels other than the picaresque—the sentimental, the chivalric, the pastoral, and the Moorish—and another section will be devoted to the origin and characteristics of the picaresque genre.

I *Sentimental, Chivalric, Pastoral, and Moorish Novels*

The sentimental novel, which has love as its central theme, derives from the Provençal theories of courtly love and Italian prose fiction, especially the *Fiammetta* of Boccaccio. The characters in these novels devote an excessive amount of space to the analysis of the causes and effects of their idealistic love which usually has tragic consequences. Despite the artificiality in style and the seeming improbability of events, the sentimental novel contains passages of verisimilar passion which may indicate that they are autobiographical. The best-known example in this genre, which began around the middle of the fifteenth century, is Diego de San Pedro's *Cárcel de amor* (*Prison of Love*), first published in 1492. This is the story of the constant lover, Leriano, son of the Duke of Macedonia, who starves to death of his own volition because the Princess Laureola spurns his love. His complete self-destruction does not occur until he has had time to deliver a long speech in defense of women. The people in the Court avidly read this book, which went through twenty-five editions in Spanish and twenty in foreign languages.

The novel of chivalry also idealized love, but added the important ingredient of the knight errant, the heroic paladin who dauntlessly fights wicked knights and monstrous beings of all sorts all over the world. His fantastic exploits are motivated by the desire to prove his mettle in defense of just causes and by a burning urge to serve his lady fair. The ethical ideals of knighthood and chivalry, a fusion of Christian and military ideals that came about during the Crusades, originated in France and Spain and spread to the rest of the continent. The main virtues which governed a knight's comportment were piety, honor, valor, and loyalty. The virtue of loyalty was due to the spiritual and temporal lords, God and the suzerain, as well as one's sworn love. These chivalrous virtues were demonstrated on the field of battle and in tournaments or jousts. The French medieval romances in verse of Alexander the Great, The Trojan

War, and King Arthur preceded the development of the Spanish novel of chivalry.

Although there are some examples of the novel of chivalry in the fourteenth century, it was not until near the end of the fifteenth that they became widespread, and their popularity continued until the middle of the sixteenth century. *Don Quixote,* that celebrated parody of chivalresque novels, delivered the coup de grâce to this type of fiction which was, however, already moribund by the time Cervantes published the first part of his immortal novel in 1605. The finest example of Spain's novel of chivalry is *Amadís de Gaula,* whose extant version was written around 1492 and published in 1508 by Garci Rodríguez de Montalvo. Its genesis is obscure; critics have variously pointed to French, Portuguese, and Spanish origins of this work which may date back to the thirteenth century. This most successful of all novels of chivalry in Spain had many imitators and was translated into French (1540) and other languages, and served as literary source material for European writers. In the famous examination of books that takes place after Don Quixote returns ingloriously from his first adventure, *Amadís de Gaula* is one of the few books saved from the flames since Cervantes judged it to be the best of the books of this genre.

This long novel concerns the marvelous and incredible adventures of Amadís, born illegitimately from the union of King Perión of Gaula and Princess Elisena, daughter of King Garínter of Britain. In order to keep the birth of the child secret, his mother sets him adrift in an ark. Amadís is rescued from the sea by the Scottish gentleman Gandales who raises him with the assistance of his wife. At the age of ten, Amadís falls madly in love with the beautiful Oriana, the ten-year-old daughter of Lisuarte, King of Great Britain. There follows a series of fantastic adventures in which Amadís triumphs over knights, giants, monstrous creatures and enchanters, and along the way he unravels the secret of his birth. This paragon of faithful love and heroism, this model of virtue in all its forms, is finally rewarded with marriage to the peerless Oriana. The artificiality of its prose, and the tedium that accompanies the reader as he wades through the long series of extraordinary and improbable adventures combined to end the fad of reading chivalric novels by the time the second half of the sixteenth century was under way. The novel which came into vogue during the time of

Philip II was the pastoral, in which concern for the emotions replaced the action that dominated the novel of chivalry.

The pastoral novel idealized chivalric love as did the two previous types, but the complicated love affairs that informed the pastoral occurred among simple shepherds who were really disguised aristocrats inhabiting a bucolic environment. Nature is introduced in a limited sense; it only provides the setting and does not play the significant role it did with the romanticists in the nineteenth century. The pastoral novel, which presents shepherd life in a conventionalized manner, is just as false and absurd as the chivalresque. It has an artificial setting, lacks true emotion, contrives complex love plots, and often resorts to narrating fabulous events. The action and the rhythm of the prose is soothingly slow in consonance with the peacefulness of the rustic environment and the languid development of the shepherds' speeches.

The pastoral genre had a long tradition in European literature beginning with the poetry of Theocritus and Virgil in classical antiquity. Antecedents of the Spanish pastoral novel were the pastoral eclogues of Dante, Petrarch, and Boccaccio. The most direct influence on the development of this genre in Spain was the popular *Arcadia* (1504) by the Italian Jacopo Sannazaro, an elaborate pastoral romance in prose and poetry which was known to Garcilaso and other Spanish poets years before its translation into Spanish in 1547. Of the novels of this genre which were prevalent in Golden Age Spain—Cervantes wrote *La Galatea* (1585) and Lope de Vega the *Arcadia* (1598) using the pastoral form—the most famous are Jorge de Montemayor's *Diana* (1559?), in seven books, and one of the many sequels to this book, the *Diana enamorada* (*Diana in Love*) by Gaspar Gil Polo, which first appeared in 1564.

Montemayor's *Diana* relates the love adventures of the extremely beautiful shepherdess Diana who loves and is loved by the shepherd Sireno. The shepherd Silvano passionately loves Diana, but she abhors him more than anything else in life. Sireno must leave his sweetheart for reasons beyond his control, Diana's love for him fades, and she marries the shepherd Delio. The wise Felicia entertains all the lovesick shepherds in the palace of nymphs and causes them to forget their amatory problems by administering the enchanted water of forgetfulness. In Gil Polo's continuation, Diana and Sireno are finally united in marriage after Delio conveniently dies. Both novels recount in prose and poetry the love trials and tribulations of other shepherds and shepherdesses who live in an unreal, magical world.

The historical Moorish novel achieved wide success during the second half of the sixteenth century. It is ironic that the Moor, distrusted and hated by the Spaniards in real life, was idealized in this genre. He is portrayed as a brave knight who possesses the most sterling moral qualities. The first example of this type of novel—the gallant Moor had already figured in medieval ballads— is the anonymous *Historia del Abencerraje y de la hermosa Jarifa* (*Story of the Abencerraje and the Beauteous Jarifa*) which was inserted in the fourth book of Montemayor's *Diana* and also published in Antonio de Villegas' *Inventario* (1565). In this delightfully short prose work, the Spanish nobleman Rodrigo de Narváez captures the Moor Abindarráez who is on his way to marry the beautiful Jarifa. The Spaniard grants the Moor a parole of three days to visit his betrothed. When Abindarráez keeps his promise and returns within the allotted time, accompanied by Jarifa, Rodrigo de Narváez nobly frees the captive and showers the couple with gifts.

The most extensive and characteristic manifestation of the Moorish novel is the *Guerras civiles de Granada* (*Civil Wars of Granada*) by Ginés Pérez de Hita, which was published in two parts (1595 and 1619). The first part recounts the power struggle between two Moorish factions, the Zegríes and the Abencerrajes, prior to the fall of Granada. Fantasy and fact intermingle in the first part of this novel which draws freely from the frontier ballads. The fanciful depiction of the exotic and chivalresque life of the Moors appealed to writers well into the period of Romanticism—in the works of Chateaubriand, Martínez de la Rosa, and Washington Irving, etc. The Moorish tale *Historia de Ozmín y Daraja* was inserted in the picaresque novel *Guzmán de Alfarache,* and the *Historia del cautivo* (*The Captive's Tale*), included in the *Quijote,* belongs in this genre. The second part, more historical than fictional, is based on the revolt of the Alpujarra Moors (1568-1570), in which the author had participated as a soldier.

II *The Picaresque Novel*

The picaresque novel radically differs in form and content from the other types of novels discussed in the previous section. The

Lazarillo de Tormes (1554) represents the initial counter to the sentimental and chivalric novels then in vogue, but the full-blown reaction of the realistic picaresque genre to the idealized types of fiction that flourished in the sixteenth century dates from the *Guzmán de Alfarache* (1599) by Mateo Alemán. Before the first decade of the seventeenth century ended, the picaresque novel had supplanted the chivalric and pastoral novels. *Guzmán de Alfarache* was more popular and more influential in determining the development of the seventeenth-century Spanish novel than *Don Quixote*, the last of the chivalric novels.

The term picaresque (Sp. *picaresca*) that designates this new kind of novel born in Spain is derived from *pícaro* (rogue, thief), the label for its protagonist. The origin of *pícaro* is still debated. The first documented use of the word dates from 1525 when it meant "kitchen boy" and twenty years later it came to signify "a base person who leads an evil life."[2] The word *pícaro* is not mentioned in *Lazarillo de Tormes*, but by the beginning of the seventeenth century the public referred to *Guzmán de Alfarache* as *el pícaro*. One of the most widely supported theories regarding the origin of *pícaro* relates it to some of the various meanings of the verb *picar*: to nibble on food (as in the case of kitchen boys who worked without pay and were only able to nourish themselves by eating the food they were preparing); to make forcible entry with a *pico* (pickax), as in the case of thieves; to pique; and to attack with a sharp tongue. Another interpretation holds that *pícaro* comes from the French word *picard,* an inhabitant of Picardy, who had the reputation of being lazy, poor, and filthy. More important than these and other speculations about the origin of *pícaro* is the fact that the word was generally associated with menial laborers, vulgar characters of the low classes, beggars, and petty thieves.

The life of the low-born, antiheroic rogue of the picaresque novel sharply contrasts with that of the now outmoded noble and chivalrous knight. Gone are the beautiful princesses and shepherdesses and their handsome, dashing suitors and protectors, the self-sacrifice and valor to prove one's faithfulness in love through thick and thin, the fabulous and magical adventures in exotic settings, the beautiful and lofty speeches, and devotion to the highest ethical ideals. In their stead, the picaresque novel presents the self-centered rogue whose basic goal is to survive by hook or crook in a cruel world. He is incapable of love, compassion or loyalty, resorts to trickery, shuns work, and is beaten, deceived, robbed in the many and varied adventures into which he haphazardly wanders. The picaresque novel deals with the real world, the everyday world that encompasses the language, the noises and odors, and the morality of a milieu familiar to the reader.

Most of the picaresque novels are told in the first person to lend more reliability to the narration and to make the reader identify himself sympathetically with the *pícaro*. Their structure is loosely knit and the figure of the *pícaro* supplies the only unifying element in the rapid succession of desultory episodes which seem to reflect the chaotic nature of the world. The absence of order and the complete openness of the framework—whole chapters could be excised or new ones added without greatly affecting the rogue's autobiography—permit the author maximum freedom in pursuing the activities of his protagonist. Even after reading the final lines of many picaresque novels, the reader has the impression that the story could go on endlessly. The first part of *Guzmán de Alfarache* proved so popular that it had two sequels, a spurious one by Juan José Martí (1602) and an authentic one by Mateo Alemán (1604), at the end of which the author claims to have written a third part of which we have no record. Quevedo promised a continuation of *The Swindler* which he never wrote, and Juan de Luna, a teacher of Spanish in Paris, published for his students' use a reader (1620) in which he modernized *Lazarillo de Tormes* and added some of his own material.

As the *pícaro* meanders through the hostile world, at times in the service of a master—the *pícara*, the female rogue, has a series of lovers in place of masters—his encounters with people from all walks of life give rise to a satirical attack on the corruption and hypocrisy that seems to infest Spanish society. Frequently the types lampooned are the dregs of humanity, such as beggars, thieves, parasites, improverished noblemen, sheriffs, and avaricious priests. Beginning with *Guzmán de Alfarache*, the authors indulge in moral appraisal of the *pícaro's* conduct. The tendency to expand the moralizing aspect of the picaresque novel led to the deterioration of this genre toward the middle of the seventeenth century.

The first picaresque novel was *Lazarillo de Tormes,* an anonymous work that came out in three separate editions in 1554. It was read widely, translated into several languages, and many imitations and continuations of this short novel were made. It was placed on the Index in 1559 because of its anticlerical satire, and Philip II ordered the printing of an expurgated edition that appeared under the title *Lazarillo castigado* (*Lazarillo Chastized*) in 1573. The basic ingredients of the picaresque genre are already present in this novel: autobiographical narration; the humble beginnings of the protagonist—his father was a thief and his mother was not the purest of women; the social satire (which is still not so acrimonious as in later novels); the realism, arising from attention to quotidian life, descriptive technique, and psychological probing of the characters; the stringing together of independent episodes; the use of direct and spontaneous language which still avoids the crudities of the seventeenth-century novels; the open-ended finish; the rapid shifts from one milieu to another; and the variety of tasks the versatile and astute *pícaro* performs in the service of different masters. Lazarillo's seven masters are a blind beggar, an avaricious priest, an impoverished man of the lower nobility, a friar, a pardoner, a chaplain, and a constable. He finally achieves independence as a town crier—one of the lowest of vocations—and marries the maid of an archpriest. Despite Lazarillo's strong protestations to the contrary, the reader assumes that the protagonist's good fortune was the archpriest's invention to cover up his affair with the servant girl.

Guzmán de Alfarache was the second great picaresque novel and achieved extraordinary popularity both at home and abroad. It is considerably longer and more ambitious than *Lazarillo de Tormes*. Mateo Alemán's novel includes adventures that span Guzmán's life from the age of fifteen. This *pícaro* undertakes more extensive and varied travels than Lazarillo and concomitantly furnishes us with the total spectrum of the social classes of the time. After leaving his home to begin his picaresque life in Madrid, Guzmán serves several masters, but also pursues many adventures on his own in Spain and Italy. In Madrid, he is a kitchen boy and a street porter, and after committing a theft is forced to flee. He sets out for Toledo where he lives in high style pretending to be an hidalgo. Then he enlists in the army and lands in Italy where he indulges in many deceits as a beggar, becomes a servant to a cardinal, and acts as a go-between for the French ambassador. In succeeding episodes, he steals and is stolen from, spends some time in jail, loses two wives (the first dies and the second runs away), unsuccessfully tries to become a priest, and is condemned to the galleys for stealing. While serving as a galley slave, he corrects his moral behavior, and is freed. If Mateo Alemán had written a sequel based on the adventures of a spiritually redeemed Guzmán de Alfarache, it could not really belong to the picaresque genre.

The moralizing digressions that abound in *Guzmán de Alfarache,* a new feature of the picaresque novel, were to become a customary part of future novels of this kind. It is likely that this moral edification of the reader, a prevalent tendency during the seventeenth century, stemmed from the religious thought that characterized the Counter-Reformation. From *Guzmán de Alfarache* on, the satire becomes more corrosive, and the glimmer of optimism, such as found in *Lazarillo de Tormes,* yields to bitter pessimism. The *pícaros* in the seventeenth century are generally resentful people defending themselves from the harsh cruelties of the world. They struggle constantly but vainly against the ambient of a decaying Spain.

The Spanish picaresque novel attained its zenith with Quevedo's *Swindler,* the analysis of which occupies the remaining sections of this chapter. Other noteworthy seventeenth-century Spanish examples of this type of novel are: *La pícara Justina* (1605), generally attributed to Francisco López de Úbeda, the first to have a female protagonist; *La hija de Celestina (Celestina's Daughter),* known also as *La ingeniosa Elena (Ingenious Helen),* published in 1612 by Alonso Jerónimo de Salas Barbadillo, in which the female protagonist dies on the gallows; *La vida del escudero Marcos de Obregón (The Life of the Gentleman Marcos de Obregón),* published by Vicente Espinel in 1618, appreciably less harsh than most of the picaresque novels; and, *Vida y hechos de Estebanillo González (Life and Deeds of Estebanillo González),* published anonymously in 1646, which marks the end of this genre in Spain. Readers in western Europe avidly read these novels in translation, and German, French, and English novelists wrote their own picaresque novels: *Simplicissimus* (1699) by Grimmelshausen, *Gil Blas* (1715, 1724, 1735) by Lesage, *Moll Flanders* (1722) by Defoe, *Roderick Random* (1748) by Smollett, and *Tom Jones* by Fielding. These picaresque novels have a definite importance in the development of the modern European novel. In Spain, their influence can be observed in José Francisco de Isla's *Fray Gerundio* and the memoirs of Torres Villarroel, in the eighteenth century; in nineteenth-century realism, and especially the novels of Galdós; and, in such twentieth-century novelists as Baroja, Cela, and Darío Fernández Flórez.

III *The Plot of* The Swindler

The usual characteristics of the picaresque novel are observed
in *The Swindler*. The meager unity that we encounter in this work
is provided by the figure of the protagonist, an antiheroic type,
who goes from one adventure to another. Pablos himself recounts
his life's experiences as is the custom in picaresque novels. As
one would expect in this type of novel, his parents belong to the
low class of society and operate on the margin of the law: his
father is ostensibly a barber in Segovia but also indulges in
thievery; his mother is a Celestina type who apparently conceived
her son in an adulterous episode. Pablos leaves home and becomes
a servant to the rich youth Don Diego at Cabra's notorious
boarding school where hunger reigns. Later Pablos accompanies
Don Diego to the University of Alcalá, and the reader witnesses
the hazing, the stealing and cheating that characterize the milieu.
When Pablos receives the news that his father has died, he
returns to Segovia to collect his small inheritance. During this
journey, Pablos encounters a number of types that are frequently
the butt of Quevedo's criticism in other satirical works: a mad
schemer; an odd fencing master who is really Quevedo's enemy
Luis Pachecho de Narváez; an empty-headed priest who is also
a poet; a lieutenant who boasts of his heroic participation in
important Spanish campaigns; a gambling hermit; and a Genoese
usurer. After spending some time in Segovia with his uncle, the
hangman, and the latter's roguish companions, Pablos pockets the
ducats inherited from his father and sets out for Madrid. He
meets a poor hidalgo who, well versed in ignoble deeds, instructs
Pablos in the deceitful practices of the rogues of Madrid. He con-
sorts with the hidalgo and his underworld pals until they all land
in jail. Having bribed his way out of prison, Pablos unsuccessfully
seeks to marry his landlady's daughter. He continues on his
amorous path, but is once more foiled in a cleverly engineered
attempt to marry a rich girl. The scheme is discovered by his
former master, Don Diego, and Pablos suffers a sound thrashing
as a result. He becomes expert at begging and, after saving a
good sum of money from this trade, he leaves Madrid for Toledo.
There he enjoys a short but successful career as actor and poet in
an itinerant troupe of actors. He becomes a wooer of a nun and,
after tiring of this frustrating activity, he leaves for Seville. He
joins a gang of thugs and one night, as they roam the streets
hunting for policemen, they come across a night watch and

accidentally kill two officers of the law. The gang seeks refuge
in a cathedral where they are helped by several prostitutes.
Finally, Pablos chooses one of these women, La Grajal, to be
his companion on a trip to the New World where he hopes to
improve his lot. A continuation of Pablos' adventures is promised,
but it never appeared.[3]

In *The Swindler* as in the *Visions,* Quevedo's primordial aim is
to reveal the contemporary Spanish world in its harshest realities.
These works are two sides of the same coin. The *Visions* exhibit
the shocking truth of the society's mores by contrasting what
transpires in another world with what occurs in the "real" world.
On the other hand, *The Swindler* purports to tell the whole
unvarnished truth by presenting an apparently factual but
debased portrayal of society. Both works are model satirical
exposés since they successfully sustain the reader's interest
despite their negative and destructive elements. Although they
are replete with jokes and amusing situations, they differ greatly
from comedies and entertaining adventure stories for they leave
the reader with bitter, disturbed thoughts.

IV *Pablos Inescapably Drawn to Roguery*

In the tradition of the first picaresque novel, the *Lazarillo
de Tormes* (1554), Pablos starts out his life's adventures in the
service of a master, Don Diego. However, unlike Lazarillo,
Pablos serves only one master and then sets out on his own to
better his lot. The turning point in his career is reached in
Chapter 7 when Don Diego's father forces him to dismiss Pablos
at the very time when Pablos receives a letter from Alonso
Ramplón, his hangman uncle, informing him that his father
has been hanged—Alonso Ramplón himself was the executioner
—and that his mother, imprisoned by the Inquisition for witch-
craft, sodomy and other crimes, would shortly burn at the stake.
This is heady news for Pablos since he now can seize the opportunity to become the virtuous gentleman he has yearned to
be from early childhood. Now he can be rid of the shame he
felt as the son of base parents. Thus, when Don Diego offers
Pablos the chance to serve a young gentleman friend of his,
Pablos declines: "Sir, I have changed and so has my thinking.
I aim to have a higher and more influential post. If up until
now I have been at the bottom of the ladder like anybody
else, I now have my father's example." (BAC, pp. 89-90)

The determination to break loose from hereditary and environmental ties is finally realized when Pablos, in Chapter 11,
sneaks out of his uncle's lodgings, making sure to *lock the door
on the outside,* and then throws the key away. The letter Pablos
leaves his uncle neatly consummates his severance from all
familial ties and points the way to a new life: "Since God has
been so merciful in depriving me of my worthy father and in
keeping my mother in Toledo where I know she will certainly
go up in smoke, to top it off, I would be pleased to see done
to you what you have done to others [i.e. that he should wind
up on the gallows]. I intend to be the only one of my lineage
[i.e. he is the first one of a new family line] unless I fall into
your hands and you carve me into pieces, thus destroying my
oneness as you do in the case of others. Do not inquire after
me, or even utter my name, since I must deny our blood relationship. Serve God and the King." (BAC, pp. 141-42)

Having achieved some small measure of financial independence, and now his own master, Pablos changes his student's
garb for short, fashionable garments. He undergoes a marked
change in his attitude toward life. His strong feeling of shame
which had burdened him previously did not affect him in the
least, judging from his actions after he has achieved his emanci-
pation. In fact, the word *vergüenza* (shame) seems to have
disappeared from his vocabulary. After this point, the only
episode in which he experiences shame is the one in which he
unsuccessfully courts Doña Ana in Chapter 20. Pablos feels
very ashamed when a lawyer, whose horse he has surreptitiously
borrowed—the lawyer's lackey had "rented" the horse to Pablos
while the master was hearing mass—gives him a tongue lashing
and forces him to dismount in front of Doña Ana and his former
master, Don Diego. This feeling of shame does not arise from
an awareness of having committed some dishonorable act, but
rather it is a humiliation that he suffers because he has lost
face or tarnished his reputation in the eyes of the woman he
wishes to impress. At no time is Pablos truly concerned with
the morality of his actions. It is therefore ironical that, although
Pablos had nurtured from childhood the desire to escape from
the sordid milieu into which he was born so as to undertake
the virtuous life of a gentleman, when he had the opportunity
to pursue this path, he completely forgot his past ambitions
and undertook the life of an exemplary rogue. He lied, cheated,
and deceived. He consorted with underworld characters and

disreputable women, never once expressing any pangs of conscience, let alone any desire to alter his mode of conduct. *The Swindler* is an additional revelation of Quevedo's attitude of despair and hopelessness vis-à-vis the vice-ridden society of his day.

V *Pablo's Egoism*

Pablos is never really moved by his emotions. This is egregious in his relations with women in which pleasure, self-gain, whim, and need for solace preclude any feelings of love. The first girl that takes his fancy is the pert, blond daughter of the landlady in Chapter 18. This girl, eager to get married, unwittingly serves to provide Pablos with experience in wooing. In carrying out his desire to toy with her—"I thought the girl might be good for some fun..." (BAC, p. 195)—he pretends to be wealthy in order to derive the utmost comfort from his stay in the boarding house. After this brief initiation in the courting game, he feels that he can now earnestly seek a wife. Urged by his friends, he determines to snare a wealthy mate. The target is Doña Ana and the plan he contrives is to feign affluence and nobility. She appeals to him only because she apparently will make a good bed companion: "I don't want women for their advice or wit but to go to bed with them..." (BAC, p. 213) When his friends Brandalagas and Pero López vanish with most of Pablos' money, the only thought that consoles him is the marriage to Doña Ana since this will bring him a handsome dowry. The upshot of the whole affair is that he is badly beaten up and is left penniless; the opportunity to marry well has eluded him. He suddenly and completely forgets Doña Ana, and the recovery of his health is his only concern.

When Pablos abandons the acting troupe, he tells us that he has saved sufficient money and his goal is to have a good time. He undertakes the inane wooing of a nun, more out of desire to exercise wit than to satisfy amorous feelings. Evidently courting a nun was a popular activity, judging by the hordes of nuns' suitors: "It was necessary to reserve a spot [in the courtyard] by twelve o'clock, as at the opening of a play. (BAC, 250)[4] He finally tires of the futile wooing of a nun and, in order to placate his frustrated feelings, he steals goods from her. At last, Pablos meets La Grajal, a prostitute, who comforts him in his hideout in a church. Pablos evinces no feelings of love for this pleasing wench whom he will take to the New

World as a suitable moll. We can only suspect the motives of
Pablos, now a fully established rogue, when he promises to
remain with La Grajal until death.

VI *Distortion and Exaggeration in* The Swindler

The reader's shock at the disgusting and degrading episodes
found in *The Swindler* is mitigated by the author's superb use
of distortion and exaggeration. Being flogged almost to the
point of death, causing the starvation of innocent children, and
learning about one's father's execution at the hands of one's
uncle are ghastly occurrences, and would certainly have been
unpalatable to the reader of the novel if Quevedo had not
written these potentially nightmarish episodes in a ridiculous
vein. The classic caricature of Cabra in Chapter 3 is an excellent
illustration of Quevedo's gift for distortion and exaggeration.
Cabra—his name means "goat"—specializes in the education of
sons of wealthy families. In order to profit as much as he can,
he is parsimonious in everything and particularly in regard to
the feeding of the children. Cabra's physical appearance personifies this dominant characteristic: he is tall and excruciatingly
thin, his beard has turned white out of fear that the neighboring
mouth may swallow it to satisfy its hunger, a number of teeth
have been exiled from his mouth because of lack of use, and
his Adam's apple protrudes so much it is apparently searching
for food. He never has his beard trimmed so as to avoid spending
money, and one of the students usually serves as his barber.
His long hair and his shabby cloak make him look like the
servant of death. Even Cabra's room reflects the miserliness of
this man. Spiders never enter it, and he puts spells on rats out
of fear that they may gnaw at some crumbs he has there. His
bed is on the floor, and he always sleeps only on one side of it
in order not to wear out the sheets. Quevedo sums up the
attributes of this man by informing us that he is *archipobre*,
"the personification of poverty," and *protomiseria*, "the quintessence of stinginess."

Since food is so scarce in Cabra's establishment, no one has
the need to excrete bodily wastes and, therefore, chamber
pots are absent. One boy is so unaccustomed to eating that
when he has the chance to take a morsel of food he has difficulty
in locating his mouth with his hand. At one point Pablos asks
Don Diego whether they are still alive, for he feels that their

souls are in purgatory. On another occasion, Cabra's servant tells Pablos that two big work horses once entered the establishment and two days later, having lost so much weight, they were able to fly off through the air. It was only after Don Diego's father heard that one of the boys in Cabra's school had died of starvation that Pablos and his master are rescued from that ghoulish place. They are so emaciated that Don Diego's father does not recognize them. It takes them about three months to recover from their ordeal.

The utter absurdity surrounding the circumstances of the death of Pablos' father, as related by Alonso Ramplón, minimizes the tragedy that normally would be associated with such an event. To begin with, Alonso himself performed the hanging. The father went bravely and even eagerly to the gallows. As he neared his demise, he seemed quite unconcerned and bowed to the bystanders. He nimbly climbed up the ladder that led to the gallows and when he saw that one of the rungs of the ladder was broken he told the officials it should be fixed. At the top of the ladder, he smoothed out the wrinkles in his clothes, took hold of the rope, and made the noose himself. When he saw that a monk wished to say a prayer for his soul, he turned to him and told him not to bother, that he should just recite a bit of the Creed and finish quickly for he did not want to waste the monk's time. He swung freely without doubling up his legs or even twitching, and seemed so serious that nothing better could be desired for such a situation. Alonso quartered him and made the highway his tomb. The narration of these events ends with the expression of Alonso's grief at seeing that the remains of Pablos' father are providing free meals for the crows. Quevedo sees fit to have him add that the pastry cooks of that vicinity will use the leftovers in their meat pies.

VII   *The Excremental Vision*[5]

The actions of Pablos and those with whom he associates, especially prior to his attainment of freedom from his parents and his uncle, are determined by the alimentary canal and its functions. On the one hand, the *pícaro* is faced with the necessity of satisfying the basic drive of hunger. On the other hand, we find the manifestation of an "excremental vision" which is a calculated attack against the sordidness, the decadence, and the futility of the environment in which the rogue is trapped. Food and drink are basic to survival, and we find that the satisfaction of the hunger drive is vital to the *pícaro* ever since *El Lazarillo*. It has already been observed that the devilish machinations perpetrated by Cabra to deny children food was the motive that informs what occurs in his boarding school. (It is interesting to note that Pablos finds out subsequently that Cabra died of starvation.)

When Pablos and his master are on their way to Alcalá de Henares, they stop at the inn of Viveros where several young rascals and a priest cleverly contrive to eat most of the supper Don Diego has ordered for himself and Pablos. When Pablos shows up at his uncle's place to collect his inheritance, he is famished; however, he cannot eat much because of the feelings of disgust he feels on witnessing the gastronomical orgy in which his uncle and friends participate. While in the company of the hidalgo Don Toribio, Pablos learns of the stratagems employed by the impoverished noblemen to wangle food from others. He learns his lesson well and astutely invites himself to supper at the house of a former school chum, Flechilla. (Chapter 15) The ravenous Pablos rapidly and savagely stuffs himself with the food and he even lines his pockets with leftover bread. This scene is reminiscent of the episode at the inn of Viveros, but now Pablos performs a hoax which he had disparaged when Don Diego was the victim. Even when Pablos has risen above destitution and has the wherewithal to avoid being plagued by the necessity to satiate the hunger drive in order to survive, the need to gratify the alimentary canal remains strong. The drunken revelry, in which the full-fledged *pícaro* Pablos actively indulges prior to the killing of two policemen in the last chapter of the novel, is a repetition of the carousal in Alonso Ramplón's house which disgusted Pablos so much.

The use of the "excremental vision" as a protest against societal injustice is epitomized in the Cabra episode. Immediately after Cabra's seventy-year-old aunt pumps an enema into Pablos, he discharges it straight in her face. The offended alimentary canal is thus avenged through an act of poetic justice. In Chapter 2, during Shrovetide, observed as a season of merrymaking before Lent, Pablos is chosen "king" of a child's game called *rey de gallos,* "king of roosters." His task in the game is to sever the head of a rooster suspended from a rope, charging the prey on horseback. Gaily · attired on the sorriest nag that only a Quevedo could conjure up, Pablos is frustrated in his attempt to perform his regal task. He is pelted with all varieties of vegetables, and finally he and his horse collapse into a *privada,* a pile of garbage and excrement.

At the inn of Viveros, a student plays a practical joke on a miserly old merchant who is so stingy that he does not want to spend money for food, or share his provisions. The "food" he takes from his knapsack and places in his mouth, making sure to hide it from the eyes of the guests at the inn, turns out to be a piece of plaster smeared with excrement. The schoolboys at Alcalá initiate Pablos into their society with a severe hazing. He is furiously assaulted with a variety of bodily excretions. At first, they cover his face with spittle and with mucous from their noses. These hostile actions arise from the schoolboys' need to rid themselves of pent-up frustrations. He is later soundly beaten and is then forced into remaining for a protracted period of time in a bed covered with excrement. Having thus purged themselves of their aggressions, the schoolboys finally accept Pablos into their society. The manipulation of excrement to express defiance, mastery, and will to power in an adolescent's world is largely absent during Pablos' adventures as an adult.

The excremental vision in *The Swindler* not only symbolizes rebelliousness and a striving to dominate, but also serves to shock Pablos as well as the reader into an awareness of the illusion and the vanity of life. It is normal, according to Freudian psychology, to find this fascination over fecal matter restricted to the early years of one's life and, indeed, this is true in *The Swindler.* When Pablos finally reaches adulthood, there is only one occasion in which the excremental vision reappears. This is the episode in Chapter 17 in which Pablos bribes his way into better jail quarters than the dungeon into which his comrades have been placed. Ironically, his new cell proves to be much worse than the dungeon. It turns out that the prisoners' chamber pot is adjacent to the head of his bed, and the sounds and stench made by those who made nocturnal visits to the pot finally force him to rejoin his friends in the dungeon. In this manner, Quevedo rudely reminds his *pícaro* that, despite his desire to be a more "aristocratic" rogue, he is of the same calibre as his associates.

In Pablos' adult life, money substitutes for excrement as a weapon and as the symbol of independence and the quest for power.[6] More sophisticated now, his ambitions transcend the appeasing of hunger pangs and struggling just to survive. With money from his father's inheritance, he bribes the jailer to have more comfortable quarters in prison and then, by suborning a notary, he escapes the six years' exile meted out to his companions. (Chapter 18) In the next adventure, he feigns wealth in order to impress Doña Berenguela de Rebolledo. As soon as she and her mother learn that Pablos has money, they have implicit faith in all that he does and says, and desire to have him marry into the family. In order to emphasize his riches, he closets himself in his room and counts the same fifty gold coins over and over until he reaches the sum of six thousand. This so delights the mother and daughter that they spare no effort to please his every whim. Money is the instrument by which Pablos strives to win the hand of Doña Ana, whom he wants to marry mainly for the fine dowry she will bring. When he is short of cash, he resorts to gambling to obtain funds which in turn would give him the opportunity to increase his capital.

The episode in which Pablos secures money as a professional beggar patently illustrates his craving to free himself from a hand-to-mouth existence. At first he follows the example of a competing beggar to improve his earnings, and then forms a partnership with this fellow. Their most successful money-raising technique is to abduct small children and then return them to their parents for a reward with the story that they have saved the little ones from great harm. He continues this lucrative enterprise in order to amass a goodly sum of money. Before abandoning this occupation he has already completely recovered from the beating he received at the house of María de la Guía and, if he were to follow the psychology of a neophyte *pícaro*, he would certainly have passed on to a new adventure much sooner.

Money as the instrument to influence people's actions is once more exemplified at the beginning of Chapter 23. Pablos himself remarks that it was because of his money that an actor befriended him and got him into a travelling troupe. Later in this same chapter, after having prospered as an actor, Pablos becomes a wooer of a nun. Consequently, when he wheedles from the nun fifty *escudos* worth of her needlework, he does not act out of a need to acquire the property of others in order to survive. This deed symbolizes rather the venting of his spleen over the frustrations he has experienced in the effete pursuit of the nun. We have a clear demonstration of the entrenchment of money as the substitute for excrement if we compare Pablos' expression of his exasperated feelings in this chapter with what

occurred in Cabra's boarding school when his despair is epitomized in the discharge of his bowels in the face of the old woman.

VIII   *Moral Intent*

In the brief introductory remarks in *Al lector,* "To the Reader,"
Quevedo overtly posits the moral purpose he has in writing
The Swindler:

> *Aquí hallarás en todo género de picardía—de que pienso que los más
> gustan—sutilezas, engaños, invenciones y modos, nacidos del ocio, para
> vivir a la droga, y no poco fruto podrás sacar dél si tienes atención al
> escarmiento; y, cuando no lo hagas, aprovéchate de los sermones, que
> dudo nadie compre libro de burlas para apartarse de los incentivos de
> su natural depravado.* (BAC, 9)

(Here you will find every kind of knavery—which, I believe, is pleasing
to most—cunning, deceit, schemes and other ways, arising from idle-
ness, to live a fraudulent life, and you will derive no small amount of
benefit from this book if you pay attention to the admonition; but, if
you do not do so, at least profit from the sermons, for I doubt that anybody buys a humorous book to escape the stimuli of his wicked
nature).

In the next sentence, he informs the reader that he proposes to
write his hilarious life of a rogue in a style marked by *gallardía*
("elegance"), realizing full well that this is the way the reader
would want it. Quevedo, then, is telling us that *The Swindler* will
be a palatable, moralizing work in which the moral reflections
must not obscure the novel's artistic merits. Behind this is Quevedo's desire to avoid composing a picaresque novel like the long,
rambling, and over-sermonizing *Guzmán de Alfarache* (1599) by
Mateo Alemán.

Direct moral reflections are infrequently interpolated by the
author, and when they do appear, they are exceedingly brief.
Conscious moralizing is concentrated toward the end of Pablos'
adventures when he arrives at the point of no return in his
life as a rogue. Thus, while recuperating in the house of the
bawd María de la Guía (Mary the Guide), he enumerates her
many wanton talents *para que se me tenga lástima de ver a las
manos que vine, y se ponderen mejor las razones que me dijo...*
("so that the readers may pity me on learning into whose hands I
had fallen and consider more carefully the stories she told
me...") (BAC, 227) The didactic import of these words is quite

clear. In addition, they reveal Pablos' awareness of being a complete *pícaro*. The feelings of shame, expressed in his early adventures, at least offer some hope that he will alter his life's course. He ascribes the sad events that befall him to external forces: his bad luck and the machinations of the devil. But, the great irony of his association with María de la Guía stems from the realization that she is a type remarkably similar to his mother. Although he would have struggled to disassociate himself from contact with such women in the past, he now accepts such an affiliation without qualms.

In the last chapter of the book, Pablos finally becomes the *príncipe de la vida buscona* ("prince of the picaresque life"), as Quevedo calls him in the foreword. Now a rogue at the height of his career, Pablos can give professional advice to the reader. He exposes the gambler's tricks as a warning to the innocent: *mas quizá declarando yo algunas chanzas y modo de hablar, estarán más avisados los ignorantes, y los que leyeren este mi discurso serán engañados por su culpa...* ("but perhaps by my explanations of some tricks and gambler's language, the uninitiated will be forewarned and those who read my discourse will only have themselves to blame if they are cheated...."). (BAC, 258) He decides to renew his life in the New World but really is pessimistic about the possibility of changing his mode of existence. He feels that he cannot escape the bad fortune that constantly harasses him and confesses that he is a stubborn sinner who does not learn from experience. Pablos' comment that he is tired of the life he has been leading probably is an echo of Quevedo's desire to terminate the novel. We are promised a second part of the novel—such promises by authors were often made but not always kept; however, it is not surprising that this sequel never materialized since Quevedo generally eschewed prolixity in his early works. Also, Pablos tells us that his later life in the New World was even worse than what has been narrated in the first part. The reason for this, we are told, is that a man will never better his lot if he only changes the locale of his activities and not his mode of conduct.

IX *The Futility of Life*

The Swindler, as the *Visions,* exhibits the baroque writers' obsession with the artificiality and illusions of their world which induce desolate feelings of frustrations and futility. Pablos'

zealous striving to attain a noble life is perverted by the overwhelming immorality and deceit of the people he encounters, and
his resolve to escape the morass of wickedness that envelopes
him is unavailing. Despite his activism, he is tamed physically
and mentally, and resigns himself to a meaningless, hopeless
existence that characterizes the lives of his compatriots.

Pablos is a victim of failure in his adventures taken as a whole,
and also usually in the different episodes. We have seen that he
is denied the virtuous life for which he avowedly yearned in his
youth. He is starved, beaten, robbed, and imprisoned. He is foiled
in his attempt to marry well. His friends deceive him. Finally, he
loses the struggle to rise above his environment and becomes a
pícaro indistinguishable from the mass of rogues that infested
Spain in the seventeenth century. He lacked the superhuman qualities necessary to counteract the influence of the absurd types he
met at every step: Cabra, his uncle, the cruel students, the mad
schemer who would remove the water around Ostend by means
of large sponges, the crazy fencing master, the clergyman-poet
who composed verses commissioned by blind beggars, the spurious hidalgos, the charlatan healer, the corrupt jailers and notaries,
the plagiarizing dramatists, the girl who connives to marry a rich
husband, the bawd María de la Guía, the enterprising beggar, and
the nuns' suitors. The shamming hidalgos and the foolish wooers
of nuns poignantly emphasize the vanity of life.

By his words and behavior, the hidalgo Don Toribio Rodríguez
Vallejo Gómez de Ampuero y Jordán, a model of pretentiousness,
instructs Pablos in the parasitic and artifical life of the penurious
nobleman in the Court. Quevedo, always impatient to reveal
the truth, almost immediately exposes the false show that ear-
marks this petty nobleman. At a distance, he is ostensibly a
fashionably dressed gentleman jauntily walking ahead of his
coach servants. When Pablos asks him about his coach, he turns
around, thus breaking the single suspender that holds up his
breeches, and these promptly fall to his ankles. Pablos further
discovers that the man's shirt is tattered, and when his trousers
return to their normal position, they insufficiently cover his
buttocks. It turns out that he has no coach or servants: all that
this proverty-stricken man owns is his inherited nobility, and
this is useless when it comes to obtaining sustenance. He is
travelling to the capital to join his companions who, like him,
ingeniously manage to live from hand to mouth.

Although Don Toribio is of the same cloth as the *escudero*

("squire") of the *Lazarillo de Tormes,* they are presented in
different ways. The anonymous author of the *Lazarillo* reveals his
nobleman only through this character's actions. Quevedo goes
beyond this and has his hidalgo disclose his intimate thoughts.
(We recall how frequently Quevedo obliges the different types
in the *Visions* to confess the truth about themselves no matter
how damaging it may be.) Don Toribio divulges that his fancy
clothes and imposing figure mask a sorrowful, disillusioned
person. He has lost his father's estate, his letters patent of nobility
are worthless despite being written in gold letters, and he has
even been forced to sell the land for his grave. There are no
buyers for the vainglorious title of *Don* that he uses since no
material benefits accrue to its user. Even noble blood needs
bread and meat. He realizes that the person who has nothing
cannot be a somebody (...*no puede ser hijo de algo el que no
tiene nada*). (BAC, 144)[7]

The pretentious hidalgos thrive in the capital where evil goes
unnoticed and virtue is unrecognized. They must always mas-
querade their ingenious efforts to obtain their sustenance without
resorting to honest work in order to protect their public image.
Don Toribio manifests the pains these predacious men take to
make acceptable garments out of ancient, tattered pieces of
clothing. Once a month they must ride in public places, even
if the only mount they can find is a donkey; and once a year
they must ride in a coach to make a public display, even though
they have to sit near the driver or the footman. The truth never
crosses their lips. These affected leeches lead empty, aimless
lives, thus contributing to Spain's moral decay.

However, the chapter in which Pablos is a nun's wooer
epitomizes Quevedo's vision of the futility of life. Evidently the
courting of nuns was no uncommon activity during the sixteenth
and seventeenth centuries and even back into the Middle Ages.[8]
Pablos demonstrates the apparent popularity of this custom by
telling us that the fairly large courtyard of his nun's convent was
seething with the "devout" who even brought the vilest rogues
to witness the proceedings. The description of the different,
strange postures assumed by the suitors presents a weird spectacle: of the two wooers who stare without batting an eye, one
has his hand on his sword, and the other, holding his rosary,
seems like a stone statue on a tomb; another has his arms
stretched out like an angel; another has his mouth open wider
than that of a nagging woman, but is speechless because he has

his heart in his mouth; another is leaning full weight against a wall; another walks back and forth as if he were a stallion being judged on his pacing; and another, holding a love letter in his hand, is like a hunter summoning his falcon. (BAC, 250-51) Each suitor thus is frozen in the pose that reveals his essential nature. The baroque unreality of the scene symbolizes the utter futility in pursuing a goal which is unrealizable. This illusory quest exemplifies Castro's well-known expression *vivir desvivién-dose*, that is, the Spaniards' tendency to live self-destructively.[9]

At the beginning of the episode, Quevedo affirms the ineluctable failure that confronts the wooers: *... nunca salen de vísperas del contento, porque no les llega el día jamás* ("...they never go beyond the happiness of their expectation because their day never dawns.") (BAC, 250) Yet, oblivious of the outcome of their labors, they persist in their Sisyphean task in every season and in all kinds of weather. The disillusioned Pablos discloses how chimerical and impossible this love-making is with this observation: *... es como enamorarse de un tordo si [la monja] habla; y si calla, de un retrato* ("... it is like falling in love with a thrush in a cage, if [the nun] talks; and if she is silent, like courting a portrait.") (BAC, 254) He further wonders how worthwhile it is to continue a vicarious love affair that is leading him to hell at a great expense, since hell can be gained more easily along well-trodden paths. All illusion vanishes when he realizes that Bautista nuns are insincere in their prayers, filthy, dress in rags, and treat their suitors indecently.

As a reaction to this disenchanting episode, Pablos promptly immerses himself in the authentic life of a *pícaro*, and begins his association with the prostitute La Grajal. Any additional adventures, if they had materialized, would only be anticlimactic. Quevedo has effectively demonstrated that in seventeenth-century Spain a person born of the lower classes cannot fulfill his yearning to escape environmental influences and must finally accept this fact. He imparts to us also a pessimistic vision of a decadent Spain whose future is as vain and as hopeless as that of Pablos.

CHAPTER 5

Quevedo's Style

I His Striving to Convince the Reader

QUEVEDO's rich, dynamic style effectively impresses on the reader's mind the full import of the ideas he feels compelled to pour forth. Life's seemingly irreconcilable inconsistencies and man's omnipresent duplicity are exposed in a unique style achieved by ingenious manipulation of words and unusual syntax. Quevedo's stylistic acrobatism is most frequently encountered in his satirical writings and, to a lesser extent, in his serious prose and poetry. In this chapter, we shall see how Quevedo stylistically convinces the reader that the world is topsy-turvy. I shall focus mainly on the *Visions, The Swindler,* and the satirical prose and poetry, but will also allude to the serious writings in which Quevedo strives forcefully to bring home his thought.

The mannerism that pervades Quevedo's works is in tune with the literary mode of his time, characterized by the desire of poets and prose writers to attain a "newness" of style. Yet, a Quevedo living in almost any epoch would have been certainly spurred to utilizing a vast arsenal of verbal devices.[1] Possessed with a combative nature that generally induces him to spirited attack or defense—he is not a man of halfway measures—he needs a style that captures the reader's attention. Thus, the dazzling display of wit, and the surprises and shocks that constantly occur, mainly in his satirical works, are motivated by Quevedo's obsession to convince us of his point of view. Indeed, his message bursts forth stridently and unmistakably.

II Quevedo's Stylistic Dualism

Quevedo's shifts from one extreme to another are constantly operating in his works. In exposing his world view, his writings may be burlesque or serious. This is strikingly evident in his attitude toward women whom he frequently maligns, yet he has written beautiful love sonnets extolling their charms. He alter-

93

nately attacks his country's detractors and spiritedly defends
Spanish glories. In politics, only one of two types of government
may exist: the authentic one that completely adheres to God's
ways, or one that reflects the tyranny of Satan. Only Catholicism
can be considered man's true religion. Góngora is often excoriated
for his affected style, yet Quevedo at times employs a technique
that involves *gongorismo*. We have already seen the violent
opposition between reality and fantasy throughout the *Visions*
and *The Hour of All Men,* and the dualism that resides in Pablos'
abortive struggle to escape his environment. The title of René
Bouvier's study, *Quevedo, homme du diable, homme de Dieu*
(Paris, 1929), felicitously captures the dualism of a writer who
so vividly portrayed hell and also lauded God and Christianity.

While endeavoring to oppose *desengaño* ("disillusionment")
to the ubiquitous *engaño* ("deceit") that besieges man, Quevedo
avails himself of such techniques as antithesis, contrast, paradox,
ambiguity, creation of new words, enumerations, puns, sensorial
effects, and surprise turn of events. Generally speaking, the
intensity of Quevedo's satire governs the frequency of such
stratagems. I find that the *Visions* and *The Hour of All Men,*
the works in which Quevedo achieves the summit of his satirical
genius, reveal most pointedly the essence of his unique style
and, accordingly, I shall use these works as the basis of much
of my discussion. A number of examples will also be taken from
The Swindler and other compositions in prose and poetry.

III   *Antithesis*

Constantly pursuing the task of revealing the truth, Quevedo
is usually preoccupied with stripping away fallacious, superficial
appearances. Women are shown as morally and physically ugly
beneath their cosmetics and adornments; those officials who are
ostensible guardians of justice are really attempting to pervert
it; the hidalgos and men and women of the church, supposedly
models of virtuous conduct, are shown to be hypocritical by
their deeds and words.

Quevedo shatters false appearances in his relentless efforts
to expose the *mundo al revés,* "the topsy-turvy world," in other
words, the absolutely true nature of people and events. In "The
Bedevilled Constable" we witness a contest between two antag-
onists, the bedevilled constable and the exorciser Calabrés. In
addition, both contestants incorporate dualities within them-

selves. Thus, the devil inhabiting the constable's body discloses that, in reality, one should consider him as possessed by the constable who is non-human, has characteristics like those of a devil, and is worse than the devil. On the other hand, Calabrés is pictured as a dissolute soul and a complete hypocrite beneath his holy appearance. By turning apparent reality inside out, Quevedo leads the reader to the startling realization that the devil reveals the truth about man's morals and the exorciser is a lying sinner.

The "Vision of Hell" abundantly exemplifies the omnipresent antitheses and contrasts in Quevedo which shock the reader into heeding his message. Quevedo radically alters the usual function of a prologue by insulting the reader. He calls him an ingrate and a pervert, and further declares that he does not care in the least if the reader likes his discourse or not. The vision opens in a beautiful pastoral setting: the brooks are murmuring, the leaves of the trees are rustling in the breeze, and the birds are singing melodiously. But Quevedo does not find peace in this bucolic paradise. Suddenly he is confronted with two paths of which the one on the right contrasts markedly with the opening scene. It is the straight and narrow road so overgrown with thorns and brambles that the few naked and barefooted people who travel it leave pieces of skin, heads, arms, legs, and feet strewn about. After spending a brief period of time on this little-frequented path, he takes one step backwards and immediately finds himself on the easy road of the elegantly attired sinners who parade to hell singing, laughing, and dancing.

Quevedo later becomes confused as to which road he is on, but a close observation of the travellers dispels doubts. The dreamer of the vision is also confused; at times he identifies himself with the hell-bound sinners, and at other times he is a detached observer. Finally, one of Lucifer's assistants tells Quevedo that his mission is to report to the world all that he has witnessed. Popular attitudes and beliefs are completely inverted in Quevedo's upside-down view: tailors are fearful lest they be denied hell; cold-hearted buffoons and jesters are isolated in a frigid region in hell so that their chilly nature may not dampen the fires; devils speak the truth; life is death; Judas claims that he should be commended as the redeemer of mankind and, he adds that there have been many more wicked people than he; the idea that all of hell is found in a bad constable is a repetition of what has been stated in "The Bedevilled Constable"; seemingly pious devotees are unmasked as perpetrators of impiety; alchemists turn gold into dung; and Mohammed and Luther are obliged to confess their own heresies.

"The World from Within" represents an inversion of the usual structure of the *Visions* and especially in the editions of *Juguetes de la niñez* (*Jokes of Childhood*).[2] Not as in its companion pieces, the author is wide awake as he takes a tour of the hypocritical world. The types and customs he excoriates in this world-inside-out are the same as in the other visions; but, in keeping with the pretense that the world reviewed is real and not infernal, we do not find the chaotic fantasies that abound in the other four *sueños*. In the other visions Quevedo awakes from his nightmares, but in "The World from Within," his mind becomes exhausted from so much disillusion that he falls alseep.

In *The Hour of All Men* Quevedo attempts to give each sinner his due. The tables are turned and, in general, each offender is made to be the recipient of the sins that he has committed against others. However, Quevedo realizes that all this is useless since only the roles of the types have been interchanged: the wicked have become good but the good have become wicked. Resigned to the fact that corruption and evil will eternally plague mankind, Jupiter makes Fortune reverse what he has wrought. The mutability of fortune was a commonplace with Quevedo and his contemporaries, and he at times reveals how fortune's fickleness affects man's life. The ballad "Fortunilla, Fortunilla" ("Dear Fortune, Dear Fortune"),[3] written around the time of *The Hour of All Men,* clearly evinces Fortune's capriciousness. In this case, she is a blind beast chained to a *noria*—a device consisting of a series of buckets on a wheel used for raising water—which, as it endlessly goes round and round into and out of the well, alternately fills and empties the water buckets. We also see in this metaphor Quevedo's wont to unite opposites, fusing them into a whole characterized by extreme tension.

A superb illustration of this coexistence of antithetical elements is Quevedo's description of the female figure that personifies death in "The Vision of Death." To the slumbering author this figure *seemed* to be a woman. She appeared to be regal, with her crowns and scepters, but she also carried sickles that revealed her peasant nature. The adornments she wore indicated that she was noble and base at the same time: rustic leather footgear

and elegant shoes; papal mitre and paper hood like those put on
convicts prior to their execution; fancy headdress and peasants'
caps; brocades, silks and tattered garments; jewelry made of gold,
diamonds and pearls as well as trinkets of worthless stones. One
of her eyes was open and the other closed; dressed up and naked
at the same time, she displayed all the colors of the rainbow. She
appeared young on one side and old on the other. At times she
seemed to move slowly, and at other times quickly. It seemed
that she was both far off and near so that when Quevedo thought
she was about to enter his bedroom she was already at the head
of his bed. In assembling all these diverse traits in one female
figure, Quevedo apparently attempts to demonstrate the illogical
and ubiquitous nature of death, which inexorably claims all
people.

The affinity of life and death is a frequent theme in Quevedo.
We recall that in the *Visions* death constantly stalks life and that,
in essence, one begins to die as soon as he is born. The figure
of Death sums this up in "The Vision of Death": *Y lo que
llamáis morir, y lo que llamáis nacer es empezar a morir, y lo que
llamáis vivir es morir viviendo* ("And what you call death is
really the culmination of the dying process [which goes on
throughout life], and what you call birth is the beginning of one's
death, and what you call life is a dying while one is alive.")
(O.C. I, 178) The oxymoron *muerte viva,* "live death," recurs in
Quevedo's prose and poetry. The preoccupation with death and
the welcoming of death as the harbinger of final supreme peace
that terminates life's cruel struggle is especially noted in his
metaphysical poems. His life constitutes his own tomb. (Blecua,
13) He places life's brevity in sharp focus by juxtaposing the
opposing symbols *pañales,* "swadding clothes," and *mortaja,*
"shroud." (Blecua, 4) He so compresses the span of life that
only its start and end have relevance; what transpires between
those two poles is ephemeral and vain. What he desires is to
cease being burdened with life, to liberate his soul from its
prison of fears and suffering. *Nací muriendo y he vivido ciego,/
y nunca al cabo de mi muerte llego* ("I was born dying and I
have lived blind,/ and never do I arrive at the end of my death.")
(Blecua, 15)

This life-death motif also permeates Quevedo's love poetry.
The sensual sonnet *¡Ay Floralba! Soñé que te . . . ¿Dirélo?* ("Alas,
Floralba, I dreamed that I . . . Shall I say it?") (Blecua, 363-64)
is a capsulated version of a *sueño* in that the poet dreams that he

possessed his beloved. Prior to his rude awakening to the cruel reality of life, he asks Love to grant him everlasting wakefulness if this happening is real and to let him sleep eternally if this is a dream. Fully awake and disillusioned, he exclaims: *y vi que estuve vivo con la muerte,/ y vi que con la vida estaba muerto* ("and I saw that I was alive with death,/ and I saw that with life I was dead.") There are other poems in which the poet suffers a living death when his beloved does not favor him as he desires. (Blecua, 400 and 403) His poetic epitaphs, too, are naturally replete with the life-death theme.

Money is another potent force capable of unifying diverse elements. This is exemplified in the famous satirical poem "Poderoso caballero es don Dinero" ("A Powerful Knight is Sir Money."), Blecua, 734-36. Gold has value to Christian and Moor alike, it gives and takes away appearances and breaks any law, it makes equal the duke and the cattleman, it softens the severest judge, it gives quality to a nobleman and a beggar, women do anything to obtain it, gold coins are worth more in time of peace than shields in time of war, and gold buries the poor man and naturalizes the foreigner.

The burlesque "Poema hercico de las necedades y locuras de Orlando ("Heroic Poem of the Silly Deeds and Madness of Orlando") presents a further example of a synthesis comprising antithetical ingredients. Angélica's beauty is of such magnitude that it turns day into the blackest night, the haughtiest people turn into slaves, company becomes solitude, greatness becomes vassalage, valor is conquered with a glance, and even Moors and Christians join forces to idolize the lady's snow-white hands.

In order to impress the reader with the full import of the contemporary state of affairs, Quevedo likes to contrast the past with the present. This technique is typically applied to the appearance of a woman whose jaded looks are diametrically opposite to her former beauty. Sometimes we witness the spectacle of a woman vainly attempting to recapture her bloom of youth. The ephemeral nature of beauty, especially in the case of conceited ladies, is clearly illustrated in the love poem "Cuando tuvo, Floralba, tu hermosura" ("When you your beauty had, Floralba"), Blecua, 364. Here Floralba, once pretty and vain, is now a despised old lady.

The past-present polarity is particularly manifest in three poems. Quevedo's celebrated psalm XVII, "Miré los muros de la patria mía" ("I looked at the walls of my country"), Blecua, 31-32, reveals the poet's anguished vision of a deteriorating Spain. The once strong walls of his native land are now crumbling; his house is now tarnished and despoiled; his cane is more bent and weaker than ever; his sword has been conquered by age; and, wherever he looks he sees signs of death. Quite similar is the sonnet "Buscas en Roma a Roma, ¡oh, peregrino!" ("You seek Rome in Rome, oh pilgrim"), Blecua, 258-59. The Rome that a pilgrim seeks is gone. Its sturdy walls are now in ruins and the Aventine is a tomb for itself. The eroded medallions are more the victims of the ages' battles than the glory of Rome's valor. Only the Tiber remains and its current, which formerly brought water to the city, now mourns the city with a dolorous dirge. That which sustained Rome's grandeur and beauty has fled, and only that which is fleeting remains.

Ancient Rome is contrasted with its modern condition in "Esta que miras grande Roma agora" ("This great Rome that you see now"), Blecua, 112-17, but in this *silva* Quevedo appraises this city's metamorphosis from a spiritual, and not a physical, point of view. He recalls its humble beginnings and its rise to greatness as the hub of the Roman Empire. Then its decline is described, and once more we encounter the image of the Tiber sorrowfully coursing through a ruined city previously known for its might and beauty. But Rome was destined to be queen and mistress of all cities. After the Empire and its monarchs disappeared, Rome again achieved its greatness as the center of Christianity and the home of the popes. Rome attained life from the defunct Roman Empire whose tomb became the cradle of the Christian Church. Now it is the glorious Court of faith on earth.

The dualities heat-cold and fire-snow occur often in Quevedo's works. In the "Vision of Hell," Quevedo wanders into an intensely cold region ringed by the fires of hell. The Swedish king Gustavus Adolphus (1594-1632) is a "burning ray born of the frozen, cold sea" and also the "venerable fire of the icy region." (Blecua, 303) In "Ostentas, de prodigios coronado" ("You [Mt. Aetna], crowned with marvels, show"), Blecua, 334, the poet's burning love for his sweetheart is contrasted with the icy disdain with which she rebuffs him. Thus, the suffering poet can say to Lisi that she causes his soul to burn in snow and freeze while being inflamed with love for her. (Blecua, 507)[4]

Quevedo's split psyche is glimpsed in several poems in which he analyzes his feelings in such a way that he appears to be aloof from himself. In the metaphysical poem "¡Ah de la vida!...¿Nadie me responde?" ("Ahoy life! ... No one answers me?"), he sums up his life: *soy un fue, y un será, y un es cansado* ("I am a has-been, a will-be, and a weary soul"). Blecua, 4. It is as if his soul, already separated from his body, were assessing the futility of the existence of a person named Francisco de Quevedo. When he says *desnúdame de mí,* "strip me of myself," in psalm I of the "Heráclito Cristiano" ("Christian Heraclitus"), Blecua, 20, he expresses his surfeit of life and he supplicates God to divest him of worldly cares. In the love sonnet "Más solitario pájaro ¿en cuál techo?" ("Lonelier bird, on which roof?"), Blecua, 378, the poet exclaims *desierto estoy de mí* ("I am desolate") to express his separation from his beloved. He begins a love sonnet to Lisi with the words *cargado voy de mí* ("I am burdened with myself"), a condensed description of the bitter memories of his unfortunate love for his sweetheart.

IV *Oxymoron and Paradox*

As we have seen in the previous section, Quevedo effectively uses oxymoron—the use of mutually contradictory terms in the same phrase—to point out the absurdity of a situation in order to demonstrate the truth he visualizes in it. Other examples of oxymoron different from the ones previously given will now be provided. Gold is so omnipotent that it causes *descolorida paz, preciosa guerra,* "colorless peace, precious war." (Blecua, 96) In order to reveal the contradictory emotions which harass him during a period in which he is madly in love, the poet uses a series of oxymorons in a love sonnet: *velo soñando,* "I am dreaming while awake"; *escucho sordo,* "I listen though I am deaf"; *descanso trabajando,* "I rest while working"; and *hablo mudo,* "I speak although mute." (Blecua, 374) Defining love in another sonnet, he describes it with the following oxymorons: *hielo abrasador,* "scorching ice"; *fuego helado,* "icy fire"; *breve descanso muy cansado,* "short but very tiring respite"; *libertad encarcelada,* "imprisoned freedom"; and *enfermedad que crece si es curada,* "sickness which grows if it is cured." (Blecua, 387-88)

Related to oxymoron is paradox, which is often used in Quevedo's poetry and prose. Referring to cross-eyed women, Quevedo says in a poem: *lo que no miran ven,* "they see what they don't look at." (Blecua, 349) The beautiful girl who disdains a lover's wooing and whose face gives no indication of her feelings possesses *la voz del silencio, que prudente/ pronuncia majestad honestamente,* "the prudent voice of silence/ which properly declares her majesty." (Blecua, 361) Quevedo continues to adore the girl whom he calls an executioner because she has caused him to suffer a living death. (Blecua, 386) When the poet says at the end of a love song *vengo a matarme yo, por no morirme,* "I come to kill myself in order not to die," (Blecua, 403), he means that he is resigned to endure the agony of being spurned by the woman he loves. If he were deprived of this futile love, he might as well be dead.

In *The Swindler* we find an excellent example of paradox: *Cenaron, y cenamos todos, y no cenó ninguno,* "They ate supper, and all of us ate supper, and nobody ate supper." (BAC, 40) This short sentence keenly reveals the meager diet of the boys in Cabra's boarding house; their rations were so miniscule and so devoid of nourishment that they might as well not have eaten at all. Quevedo sets forth several paradoxical statements in his *Libro de todas las cosas,* (*Book of All Things*), and then provides ingenious solutions for them (O.C. I, 190-91): if one wants to make himself invisible even in a crowd, all he has to do is be a busybody, gossiper, liar, and cheat so that nobody except the devil will want to see him; to avoid getting gray and aging, it is recommended that a person die early; in order to have men and women comply with all that one requests of them, all one has to do is to ask women to take all that you have and ask men not to give you anything; and, finally, if one wants to guarantee that his falcon will not fly off even if he is set loose, he should simply remove all its feathers. Lucifer surprisingly orders all the devils to establish peace in the world in the *Discourse of All Devils* (O.C. I, 225) but his motive is far from noble. He reasons that peace will induce laxity in behavior and cause an increase in the vices which condemn people to hell. In the "Vision of Hell" we learn that hypocrites work hard to attain hell since all their activities ineluctably lead them to that region. (O.C. I, 143)

V *Punning*

Quevedo is one of Spain's greatest masters in the art of punning. It is probably impossible to find a work of his, in any genre, which is devoid of word plays. His frequent linguistic ambiguities serve to arrest the reader's attention and impress him with Quevedo's point of view. Through his clever puns he isolates, in condensed form, the nucleus of his thinking. It is natural that puns are most frequent in *The Swindler, The Visions,* and his satirical poetry.

A play on the word *cardenal* ("welt," "cardinal") occurs twice in *The Swindler.* When Pablos' father, who had been flogged in prison, was freed *con tanta honra, que le acompañaron doscientos cardenales, sino que a ninguno llamaban eminencia* ("with so much honor, that two hundred cardinals [welts] accompanied him although nobody could call any of them eminence"). (BAC, 17) When Pablos received his inheritance from his uncle, we learn that the latter wanted him to study to be a cardinal, and this would be fairly easy to accomplish since the uncle was handy in administering *cardenales* to prisoners. (BAC, 140) Another religiously oriented equivoque revolves about the word *pío* that means "pious," is the name of a number of popes, and also is the sound that represents the peeping of chickens. Pablos plays a trick on the ingenuous housekeeper who summons the chickens with the repetition of the word *pío.* (BAC, 75-77) He bamboozles her into believing that she invites the persecution of the Inquisition by profanely using this word which should be reserved only for the popes. (In the development of this scene, there is another pun relating to the word *papa,* "pope"; Pablos uses the verb *papar,* that colloquially means "to swallow," when he tells her to recant her peccadillo.) A similar pun, devoid of religious intent, appears in the "Vision of Death." The play is on *pío:* Martha the chicken breeder is seen running after chickens; at first, Quevedo thought this woman was Queen Dido in search of the "pious" Aeneas. (O.C. I, 193)

Quevedo's excoriation of Jewish converts and *moriscos,* which appears with some degree of frequency in several of his works, occurs also in *The Swindler.* In order to poke fun at the *converso* Pontius de Aguirre, Pablos calls him Pontius Pilate. Not only did Pontius de Aguirre pursue Pablos with a knife in order to vent his spleen, albeit unsuccessfully, but also Pablos' teacher whipped him and made him promise that he would never say Pontius Pilate again. The next day, when asked under whom Christ suffered, Pablos answered that he suffered under Pontius de Aguirre. (BAC, 25-27)[5] Cabra added bacon to his stew only to give evidence that his lineage was not tarnished with Jewish blood. (BAC, 41)

The *morisco* innkeeper at Viveros in Chapter 4 of *The Swindler* is portrayed as combining the characteristics of a dog and a cat. (BAC, 50) In Quevedo's time, the word "dog" was synonymous with *morisco* and "cat" meant "thief" in slang. The fiercest attack Quevedo made against the *moriscos* is found in his brief but devastating "Confesión de los moriscos" ("Confession of the Moriscos"), which is replete with puns. (O.C. I, 101) Practically every other word is a pun, and the entire "confession" is designed to demonstrate that the *morisco*, unable to speak good Castilian, unwittingly reveals his true heretical sentiments. Among the linguistic blunders are the use of *picador* (a mounted bullfighter who thrusts a goad into the bull) for *pecador*, "sinner"; the substitution of *herrado*, "shod" (what is done to a horse) for *errado*, "erred"; the utilization of *soneto*, "sonnet," for *santo*, "saint"; the perversion of the names of the saints *Pedro*, "Peter," and *Pablo*, "Paul," into *Perro*, "Dog," and *Palo*, "Stick"; and the employment of the words *pestilencia*, "pestilence," and *pescados*, "fish," for *penitencia*, "penitence," and *pecados*, "sins."

Quevedo effectively exposes the superficiality of hidalgos in his manipulation of the word *don* in the case of Don Toribio Rodríguez Vallejo Gómez de Ampuero y Jordán. *Don* has three meanings: it is the Spanish title used before masculine Christian names, which was originally given only to gentlemen; it means "gift" or "talent"; and it may be used to represent the sound made by a church bell. In portraying this parasitic person, Quevedo criticizes the indiscriminate use of the title *don* which, in this case, is used by a person who is devoid of the qualities one would expect of a true hidalgo. Moreover, he associates Don Toribio with a bell—when the first and last syllables of this fellow's long name are pronounced over and over, the resulting *don-dan* resembles the ringing of a bell. In other words, Don Toribio is as "hollow" inside as a church bell but does "sound off" to give the impression of being a noble individual. (BAC, 145)

Several other puns in *The Swindler* come to mind. When Pablos was the "king" in the game he played with the other children, he was pelted by *nabos*, "turnips," and other vegetables. (BAC, 29) Consequently, he felt that he was engaged in a *batalla nabal*, "turnip battle." The equivoque arises when one understands that the word *nabal* is pronounced exactly the same as *naval*, "naval." Thus he remarks that he was fighting a *batalla nabal* despite the fact that he was mounted on a horse. Cabra's nose is described as being a cross between the Roman and French varieties. (BAC, 33) This means that it was flattened (*romo* is translated as "Roman" and "flat-nosed") and disfigured by syphilitic sores. Syphilis was commonly called the "French disease" by Spaniards during Quevedo's time. When Pablos became a cardsharp at the end of *The Swindler,* he informed the reader that he would reveal the *flores* ("flowers" and also "tricks") that he practiced. (BAC, 258)

The *Visions* naturally contain a profusion of plays on words. A prime example is the ubiquitous pun on *pluma* ("feather," "pen," "wing"), which is not uncommonly linked with the verb *volar* ("to fly," "to steal"). The *escribano,* "notary," is always accompanied by his *pluma* which is not only a writing instrument, but also a weapon with which he helps to condemn people by writing lies. In Chapter 19 of *The Swindler* we find the notary "unsheathing" his *pluma* to write down a series of distortions. (BAC, 202) One of the prophesies of Pero Grullo in the "Vision of Death" concerns the notary who will "fly with his feather." (O.C. I, 108) Quevedo explains that notaries are wont to steal money right in front of one's face. In the satirical poem "*Yo, que nunca sé callar*" ("I, who never know how to keep quiet"), Blecua, 716-18, the notary is characterized as writing so fast with his pen—this image is found several times in the *Visions*— that he becomes invisible. At the beginning of *Vida de San Pablo Apóstol* (*Life of the Apostle St. Paul*), the word *pluma* denotes the pen with which St. Paul wrote, and also the wings with which his writings soared through the heavens. (O.C. I, 1462) In "¡Oh, corvas almas, oh facinorosos," ("Oh, twisted souls, oh criminal [spirits]"), *pluma* means pen, wing, and also the legendary Icarus. (Blecua, 130-40)

Quevedo creates a play on the homonymous words *sí son,* "yes, they are," and *sisón,* "thief" in the "Vision of Final Judgment." (O.C. I, 129) When some of the denizens of hell deny that certain persons are *despenseros,* "stewards," others contradict this by saying *sisón.* The *despensero* is usually represented as stealing provisions from the larder which he manages for his master. The stolen goods are then sold by the steward to obtain money. In the *Visions,* Judas is considered the prototype of *despenseros* because he betrayed Christ for money. When Pablos becomes Don Diego's steward in Alcalá, he calls himself a Judas since he has acquired the penchant for stealing.

Three meanings of the verb *guardar* ("to protect," "to observe" or "fulfill," and "to save") are exploited in the "Vision of Final Judgment." (O.C. I, 129) When a miser approaches a door in hell he finds that the Ten Commandments are guarding a door to prevent the entry of those who have not observed them in life. In his defense, the miser unwittingly condemns himself by saying that he kept the Ten Commandments, motivated by a desire to save or amass money. He declares that he loved God above all things since he wanted to obtain all things in order to love God above them, he confesses he uttered God's name, not in vain but rather out of "interest" and, he did not fornicate since this activity cost money. When a devil informs him that he is condemned, the miser quickly resigns himself to his fate and asks the devil to admit him quickly to hell since he does not wish to *gastar* ("to spend," "to waste") time in the process. In the "Vision of Hell," (O.C. I, 147), *pasteleros,* "pastry cooks," are condemned for carnal sin despite their disclaimer that they had sinned with women. However, their carnal sin stemmed from having included all sorts of flesh—meat from dogs, horses, and other animals not fit for human consumption—in their meat pies. Furthermore, their pies bark and whinny!

Other equivoques in the *Visions* are formed with such words as *gracia,* "grace" and "joke"; *bote,* "small jar" (used by apothecaries), and "thrust" (of lance or pike), O.C. I, 146; *dieta,* "diet" (to reduce) and "diet" (the general assembly of Germany), O.C. I, 256; the combining of Philip III and Philip IV to arrive at three-quarters of an hour (O.C. I, 183); and *tiro,* "shot" and "deceit." (O.C. I, 135)

The illustration of Quevedo's punning in his poetry will necessarily be brief because of limitations in space. Indeed, an exhaustive study of his equivoques in poetry alone would fill a large tome. A good number of his puns in poetry are the same as those found in his prose—Quevedo often repeats himself ideologically and stylistically—and, therefore, I shall mainly use examples different from the ones previously given.

Quevedo relentlessly and severely critizes physicians in his poetry also. Since he considers them to be assassins, by an extension of meaning the eyes of a girl who causes her sweetheart to suffer pangs of death are called "doctors." (Blecua, 613 and 867) In the poem "Los médicos han de errar" ("Doctors must err"), Blecua, 1024-29, there is a play on the verbs *errar,* "to err," and *herrar,* "to shoe" (an animal). Thus, physicians, who always make mistakes in their cures, do not heal the sick any better than the shod mules on which they travel. In addition, they are pictured as waging war on the sick with their *erre*—the letter R they wrote on their prescriptions which is the same as the Rx that physicians use today.

In "Llorando está Manzanares" ("Manzanares is weeping"), Blecua, 1072, there is a play on the word *gota*, ("drop" [of water], "gout"). The river Manzanares is pictured as being without a drop of water, its stream is motionless. It is compared to a person paralyzed with gout, but the condition of the dried-up river is contrary to that of a gouty person since the latter's joints were thought to be inflamed from an excessive secretion of fluids.

Early in the "Poema heroico de las necedades y locuras de Orlando el enamorado" we come across two equivoques. (Blecua, 1334) In addressing the Muses, Quevedo plays with the word *infundir*, "to inspire," which he purposely confuses with *enfundar*, "to stuff a pillow [*funda*] into a pillowcase," and also puns with the words *embocadas*, "swallowed up," and *invocadas*, "invoked." He tells the Muses not to inspire him since he is not a pillow and, furthermore, he wants them to be swallowed up and not invoked. The satirical *letrilla* ("rondelet") "Prenderánte, si te tapas" ("They will seize you if you hide your face"), Blecua, 715-16, presents the case of a shrewd woman who leads her husband by a halter (*cabestro*) and her lover by a chain fastened around his neck (*cabestrillo*). In addition, she will turn her *novio*, "sweetheart," into a *novillo*, "young bull," "cuckold," and thus will till the ground with him.

In his poem dedicated to a pretty woman in tatters and patches (Blecua, 640-42), Quevedo uses the verb *romper* ("to break," "to tear") with varied meanings. Not only is this lady *rota*, "in tatters," but she also has her conscience *rota*, "destroyed." Her celebrated pretty eyes are described as *rasgados*, literally "torn," but also "large," when referring to a lady's eyes. Just as a torn flag gives evidence of victory and glory in the case of the warrior who has borne it through battle, so the more tattered the clothes of this woman—each rent in her clothing reveals a bit of her beautiful body—the more glorious she appears. In strophe 5 the word *romper* is used with the meanings "to plow," "to break down one's resistance," and "to burst into flower." He compares the plowing of a field to making the earth bring forth fruit with love's conquering of the lady's resistance so that she may blossom forth. Finally, poverty did her a great service in causing her to wear tattered garments since her beauty is no longer hidden. In the first strophe of this poem, the poet declares that these thoughts originated in Rota, a town in southwest Spain.

VI *Accumulation*

We have seen examples of Quevedo's habit of returning over and over again to certain themes and for repeated lampooning of the types he most despised. Stock epithets, similes, and metaphors reappear in all his works. There is no doubt that this obsessive repetition serves to reinforce his criticism of the abuses and abusers that plagued Spain. Quevedo probably felt at times that the cumulative effect of such repetition did not sufficiently impress or convince the reader and, consequently, he frequently paused to produced intensified accumulations. Thus, the portrait of Cabra, his most masterful attack on misers, impresses the reader more than the cumulative effect of all the short potshots levelled against niggards throughout his writings. In this section, we shall show examples of the effect achieved by a piling up of evidence in concentrated doses.

Quevedo frequently employs anaphora, a technique used by classical and medieval writers, to string together a number of observations, with the purpose of etching his theme on the reader's mind.[6] The anaphorical word or words are equivalent to a series of numbers used to catalogue a collection of related items in some inventory. This is clearly illustrated in the repeated use of *¡oh!* at the beginning of ten short sentences that describe Don Diego de Noche in the "Vision of Death" (O.C. I, 191): *¡Oh estómago aventurero! ¡Oh gaznate de rapiña! ¡Oh panza al trote! ¡Oh susto de los banquetes! ¡Oh mosca de los platos!* . . ("Oh adventurous stomach! Oh plundering gullet! Oh belly that trots about! Oh dread of banquets! Oh fly that plagues dishes of food! . . .) Quevedo simply is listing here a number of attributes which unmistakably identify the character of this sponger who always seeks to satisfy his hunger at the expense of others. This procedure is certainly more effective than reeling off these traits in a list using numbers or letters as a student might do in making an outline.

Quevedo isolates what he considers Marcus Brutus' folly in assassinating Julius Caesar in several paragraphs which begin with the two words *¿Qué necedad?*, "What foolishness?" (O.C. I, 868-69) In effect, he is pinpointing here all the events that precipitated and followed this crucial episode in Roman history, all of which he envisions as one stupidity heaped upon another.

In his satire of Juan Ruiz de Alarcón, Quevedo repeats the word *¿quién?*, "who?", at the beginning of each strophe, and usually once or twice more in each stanza as he rhetorically asks who can this monstrously ugly person be. (Blecua, 1211-15) And each strophe ends with the one-word verse *Corcovilla,* "the little hunchback." Rarely, if ever, does Quevedo surpass this ingenious and cruel gem in the many efforts he made to annihilate a person or type he detested. Each *¿Quién...Corcovilla* unit is a crushing indictment of Alarcón's physical appearance, but the sum total of all the units piled one atop the other produces a devastating result.

The verb *ser,* "to be," is used anaphorically in several poems to bind together and unify a series of definitions. A patent example of this is found in the celebrated poem that portrays in superb hyperboles a man with a long nose. (Blecua, 562) Practically every verse of this sonnet begins *érase,* "there once was." And we learn at the outset that this man "who once was," since his nose is his most dominant feature, can better be described as a man attached to his nose. In staccato fashion Quevedo proceeds to inform us that he is a badly bearded swordfish, a lopsided sundial, an elephant face up, the bowsprit of a galley, a pyramid of Egypt, etc.[7] In his "Comisión contra las viejas" ("Indictment of Old Women"), Quevedo launches a corrosive attack against one of his favorite targets. He begins his accusation of old women with the statement that they ought to be expelled from Spain just as heretical New Christian women. The detestable morals and physical appearance of these hags are highlighted in a series of eight strophes which commence with the word *vieja,* "old woman." (Blecua, 824)[8]

In one sonnet, the verb *es,* "is," introduces a succession of definitions of the chaotic effects love causes. One oxymoron follows another in the attempt to exhibit the contradictory emotions experienced by the lover. Love is scorching ice, frigid fire, a painful wound that one does not feel, a tiring short rest, a carefree state that leaves one troubled, an incarcerated freedom, and an illness that grows if it is tended to. (Blecua, 387-88) A concatenation of similar contradictory emotions experienced by a lover occurs in the burlesque ballad "A la sarna" ("To the Itch"). Blecua, 1113 The emotion-draining effects of love are revealed in the poem "¿Qué verdadero dolor?" ("What a veritable suffering!"). (Blecua, 544-45) The repeated anaphoric use of the exclamatory *¡qué!,* "what a," presents a picture of a man whose innards are seared by the chaotic effects of love, more so than if the poet had used the declarative *es* or *érase.* In addition, each

¡qué! that pours forth from his pained soul is followed by a
modified noun or an infinitive used substantively. The last verse
of alternate strophes always ends *¡Qué puro morir de amor!*
("What a sheer dying of love!") Quevedo purposely dispenses
with verbs in these frenetic exclamations in order to concentrate
on the series of sentiment-charged utterances which confused
emotion has created; the utilization of the copulatives *es,* a manifestation of normal grammatical logic, would have lessened the
impact of the emotional outbursts of the suffering lover.

Quevedo effectively uses anaphora to demonstrate life's transi-
toriness and vanity. This is evident in his Psalm XXVI in which
después de tantos(as), "after so many," is repeated several times.
The poet tells us that after so many sleepless nights and after
so much pain and suffering he ends up with illusion and cold
hope. (Blecua, 38-39) One of his love sonnets uses anaphorically
tras, "after," and, as an occasional substitute, the synonymous
después de. Notice also that the second hemistich of each verse
of the first octave begins with *nunca,* "never," *jamás,* "never,"
or just plain *no.* Thus every line of the octave patently negates or
nullifies the poet's suffering in his zealous pursuit of his beloved:

> *Tras arder siempre, nunca consumirme;*
> *y tras siempre llorar, nunca acabarme;*
> *tras tanto caminar, nunca cansarme;*
> *y tras siempre vivir, jamás morirme;*
>
> *después de tanto mal, no arrepentirme;*
> *tras tanto engaño, no desengañarme;*
> *después de tantas penas, no alegrarme;*
> *y tras tanto dolor, nunca reírme;* (Blecua, 385)
>
> (After burning always, never to be consumed;
> and after ever crying, never to finish;
> after so much travelling, never to tire;
> and after ever living, never to die;
>
> after so much misfortune, not to repent;
> after so much deceit, not to be undeceived;
> after so many tribulations, not to be happy;
> and after so much pain, never to laugh;)

Quevedo's marked penchant for the repetitive use of a single
word or phrase is by no means restricted to anaphora. At any
time he may pause to isolate a salient characteristic of some

theme, some person, some event, or some place. One of the most memorable examples of this is the recurrent use of the phrase *por no gastar,* "in order not to waste," which epitomizes Cabra's essential miserliness. To avoid waste, he goes to absurd extremes in saving food, bedclothes, time, doctor's fees, and medicine. In the *Visions,* Quevedo becomes so obsessed with traits that are dominant in certain types that the epithets used to characterize them become their names. The people who regret having failed to fulfill certain obligations while alive are called the *¡Oh, quién hubiera!,* "If I had only!"—the phrase they repeatedly use in their wails of repentance; those who ingenuously believed that things should have turned out differently from the way they did are termed the *penséque,* "I thought that," because of the expression with which they introduce their series of laments.

In the sonnet "Verdugo fue el temor, en cuyas manos" ("Fear was an executioner, in whose hands"), Blecua, 104, Quevedo recalls how a number of spectators died in a Madrid bullring when a false alarm of fire caused them to panic. He repeats the word *nada,* "nothing," "nothingness," "meaninglessness," to show the utter folly of this occurrence. Nothing could allay the fears of the spectators whose fright arose from nothingness. And it is entirely meaningless that nothingness was the instrument of death of so many.

The ingenious ballad "Boda de negros" ("Wedding of Negroes"), Blecua, 850-52, is reminiscent of Góngora's remarkable tour de force "Por una negra señora" ("For a black lady") in the repeated use of *negro* with different meanings. In addition, Quevedo's more ambitious poem cleverly exploits many other words which convey the meaning of blackness or darkness. Quevedo recounts that he witnessed a gloomy wedding which seemed hellish since the bride and groom and their retinue were all black. The wedding couple seemed and smelled like black crows. The bride's makeup consisted of soot and coal. The wedding ceremony took place in a dark room off a somber patio. The whole retinue was excited for they were *perrengues* —this word colloquially means Negro, and also refers to a person who easily gets angry. Black was the color of the tablecloth and dishes on the wedding table and the wedding party ate black food. Since the food was the color of the skin of the participants, they sometimes chewed their fingers instead of the food. After the feast they washed their hands with water from a black kettle and then dried themselves with towels of black baize customarily used to cover coffins. The water in which they washed became black from their skin. They sang funereal songs as they sat on their black chairs. Finally, Quevedo predicts a gloomy future for the newly married couple since their dowry is *en blanco*, "blank," or nonexistent.[9]

The word *cornudo*, "horned," "cuckold"—it was a commonplace to picture cuckolds with horns on their heads—and variations on it are repeatedly used adjectively and substantively in the sonnet "Cuando tu madre te parió cornudo" ("When your mother gave birth to you as a cuckold"), Blecua, 624, and again in another sonnet "A las bodas que hicieron Diego y Juana" ("At the wedding between Diego and Juana"). Blecua, 635-36 In the first poem, everything associated with the cuckold has some relationship with horns: his cradle was made of horns, he was weaned by milk from a horned animal—a *cabra* "goat"— his coat of arms has a bull on it, his feet are made of horns, and a horned star is his constant companion. In the second sonnet, a series of nouns that have the root *corn* or *cuern* are employed. Wedding flowers are displayed in the horn of plenty of Amalthea, the mythical goat that nursed Jupiter, a *corneta*, "cornet," supplies the music, and they all eat out of a *cuerna*, "a vessel made out of a horn." Then the bride and groom urinated in horns and the *corneja*, "morning owl," sang to them from the *cornija*, "cornice," of the chimney. The priest *Cornejo*, "dogwood tree," married them for only a *cornado*, "old copper coin." Finally, all signs pointed to the inevitable conclusion that Diego would become a *cornudo*, "cuckold."

In Chapter 10 of the *Política de Dios* (*Politics of God*), Quevedo wishes to emphasize the king's obligation to establish peace throughout his realms, and the word *paz*, "peace" is constantly repeated. He reiterates the basic notion that Christ's whole life denoted peace, and that peace was his legacy to mankind. Since kings are Christ's vicars on earth, their first lesson is the promotion of peace.

VII *Enumeration*

In effecting his obsessive urge to impress upon the reader his jaundiced views of life, Quevedo often resorts to the medieval technique of enumeration. In Quevedo's writings enumeration is customarily used to undermine execrable types or customs, but occasionally it is employed for constructive purposes.

Chaotic enumeration is exemplified in the "Vision of
Final Judgment." Using the verbs *ver*, "to see," and *notar*, "to
note," Quevedo magnificently imparts a succession of apparently
disconnected impressions of what he sees about him. His observations are rendered more vivid by the use of the first person
singular in the narration. The reader is constantly kept off
balance as he is guided swiftly and abruptly from one hellish
type to another. His mind reels before this bewildering pano-
rama, which is precisely what Quevedo set out to accomplish.

The "Vision of Hell" contains two catalogues of historical
figures in which their names and qualifying remarks pertaining
to their activities are listed. The first series incorporates a host
of alchemists, astrologers, palmists, and other pseudoscientists
who are thrown together with no discernible order. The second
series comprises a twofold list of heretics: those who existed
before the birth of Christ, and those who came after Christ.[10]
These two catalogues stress Quevedo's aversion to false ideas
and his devout Catholicism. He remarks at the conclusion of
this vision that those who wish to avoid damnation in hell
should learn from the experience of those who now inhabit it.

Quevedo effectively inventories the topsy-turvy ideas of people
found on Hypocrisy Street in the "The World from Within."
(O.C. I, 166) The old men want to recapture their youth by
dyeing their hair, young men think they are wise, the shoemaker
and the wineskin maker put on airs, the groom calls himself a
gentleman, the hangman becomes a minister of justice, the
whorehouse is an innocent house and whores are called ladies,
bawds pretend to be puritanical, cuckolds pass for honorable
gentlemen, lust is friendship, usury is thrift, cheating is joking,
lying is wit, malice is cleverness, cowardice is meekness of
nature, the tramp is a courtier, the medical student is a full-
fledged physician, etc. This is a good example of chaotic enumeration in which disparate elements are thrown together with no
apparent organization. Evidently it was Quevedo's intention to
assemble his thoughts without any definite order to represent
the absurd chaos of the world about him.

In the "Vision of Death" enumeration enables Quevedo to
achieve successful satirical inroads against physicians, druggists,
and surgeons. These men are made to appear like soldiers of
conquering armies laying waste to the territories they have
invaded. Their instruments and drugs become weapons of war:
the druggists' spatulas become swords, their syringes are pistols,

and their pills are bullets. Quevedo makes a list of long Latin terms, the stock-in-trade of these charlatans, and demonstrates that they are simply fancy names for common vegetables. The surgeons parade by, laden with pincers, probes, catheters, scissors, knives, saws, files and lancets, and a mournful voice is heard to say: "Cut, tear, open, saw, flay, pierce, mince, slice, rip the flesh, and burn." (O.C. I, 176)[11] Very few descriptions can rival the corrosive nature of this savage excoriation of those associated with medicine.

Although Quevedo frequently uses enumeration to convince the reader of society's absurd mores, at times this technique also serves to reinforce and render more credible the causes he espouses. In *La España defendida* (*Spain Defended*) there are several examples of accumulation of evidence designed to demonstrate Spanish glory. He claims that omnipotent God supported Spanish armies as shown in the several historical episodes he adduces from the time of the Cid to the bold actions of Cortez. (O.C. I, 523-24) His chauvinism impels him to inventory outstanding Spanish writers who do not yield in quality to the greats of classical antiquity. Among the works and literary figures he considers exceptional in Spanish literary history are Fray Luis de Léon's *Nombres de Cristo* (*Names of Christ*), the *Celestina* of Francisco de Rojas, the anonymous *Lazarillo*, the *Coplas* (*Verses*), of Jorge Manrique, Luis de Granada, Pedro Mejía, Fernando de Herrera, Bartolomé Torres Naharro, Garcilaso de la Vega, Juan Boscán, Juan de Mena, and Juan Huarte de San Juan. (O.C. I, 514-15) These works and writers have admirably survived the test of time.

At the beginning of *La Vida de San Pablo apóstol* (*The Life of the Apostle St. Paul*), Quevedo lists the different peoples to whom St. Paul brought the Christian doctrine. (O.C. I, 1463) In the fifth chapter of *Su espada por Santiago* (*His Sword for St. James*), Quevedo lists a series of "truths" in support of his arguments that St. James should be the one and only patron saint of Spain. (O.C. I, 429-30) The Christian responsibilities and activities of kings are concatenated in a passage of *Virtud militante* (*Militant Virtue*). O.C. I, 1247-48 However, the enumerative technique occurs more often and has greater impact on the reader when Quevedo uses it as a weapon to harass and to destroy.

IX *Neologisms*

Quevedo's effective use of neologisms has been extensively studied by Alarcos García and Mas.[12] In this section some examples will be given to show the affective force of the words and phrases invented by our author.

Quevedo frequently coins a new word by parodying a particular word. From the word *quintaesencia,* "quintessence," he derives *quintainfamia,* "the embodiment of infamy," *quintacuerna,* "the quintessence of cuckoldry," and *quintademonia,* "the quintessence of the infernal world." He creates the word *marivinos* to describe mosquitoes that drown themselves in wine. This word is derived from *mari-* (this root means "sea" in Latin), the first element of *mariposa,* "butterfly," and *vino,* "wine." Thus Quevedo's mosquito is drawn to wine and drowns in it just as a butterfly is fatally attracted to a flame. By using the second element of *mariposa*—this time Quevedo is thinking of the prettiness of a butterfly—the word *diabliposa* is coined with the meaning "devil of pleasant appearance." By analogy with the word *sacamuelas,* "tooth puller," or "quack"—derived from *saca,* "remove," and *muelas,* "molars"—*saca-agüelas* is formed in a burlesque sonnet. The word *agüela* is a form of *abuela,* "grandmother," and by extending the meaning we arrive at a "woman who is many years old" and the final meaning "many years." The advice given to this toothless old hag is that she does not need a dentist—it is already too late for that—but someone who can remove the years from her.

Neologisms are also created by utilizing established linguistic patterns as a point of departure. First, we shall illustrate this with newly-coined words that are fabricated in imitation of legitimate Spanish words with affixes. Quevedo uses the prefixes *proto-* and *archi-,* which denote preeminence or superiority in such words as *protomédico,* "eminent physician," and *archiduque,* "archduke," and concocts *protocornudo,* "master cuckold," *protomiseria,* "highest degree of misery," *archipobre,* "exceedingly poor," and *archidiablo,* "archdevil." Analogizing with words *contraveneno,* "antidote," and *contrapeste,* "remedy for the pest," Quevedo contrives *contraculto,* "contra-affectation" (in speech or writing), *contrasayón,* "pug nose," and *contracorito,* "humpback." Using the suffix *-ario,* as in the word *vocabulario,* "vocabulary" (i.e., a collection of words), Quevedo devises *disparatario,* "a collection of absurdities." The words *dinerismo,* "religious sect that worships money" and *dinerano,* "a follower of *diner-*

ismo," are spawned following the examples of *judaísmo,* "Judaism" and *luterano,* "Lutheran." Mocking forms of address (*divinidad,* "divinity," *excelencia,* "excellency") and titles of dignity (*deanazgo,* "deanship"), Quevedo contrives several variations on the word *diablo,* "devil": *diablazgo, diabledad, diablencia.* New nouns are fashioned with the suffixes *-ia* ("y" in English) or *-ería* ("ery" in English): *tigresía,* "science of knowing about tigers," *cornudería,* "district of cuckolds," and *zurdería,* "condition of lefthandedness."

This technique of creating new words by imitating established linguistic phenomena is found in two other areas, namely, the formulation of compound words and the generation of infinitives. The word *putidoncella,* "a girl who pretends to be a respectable maiden but is really a prostitute," derives from *puta,* "prostitute," and *doncella,* "maiden." The neologism *calvi-casadas,* "women married to bald men," originates from *calvo,* "bald," combined with *casadas,* "married women." The word *latiniparla,* "a woman who speaks Latin," is created from *latín,* "Latin," and *parla,* "chatters." Some infinitives invented by Quevedo are: *bodar,* "to marry," from *boda,* "marriage"; *condar,* "to be a count," from *conde,* "count"; *cabellar,* "to put on false hair," from *cabello,* "hair"; *cornudar,* "to cuckold," from *cornudo,* "cuckold"; *jordanar,* "to bathe someone in the (rejuvenating) waters of the Jordan river," from the name of the river; *encalvar,* "to marry a bald man," from *calvo,* "bald"; *despicarar,* "to clear rogues out of a place," from *pícaro,* "rogue"; *desmujerar,* "to lose one's wife," from *mujer,* "wife"; and, *desnacerse,* "to deny one's heritage," from *nacer,* "to be born."

Quevedo also parodies set expressions. In the sentence *no sabe lo que se hace,* "he does not know what is being done," *se hace* is converted into *se diabla,* "what devilish work is being done." The well-known *olla podrida,* "Spanish stew" (made of meat, fowl, sausage, vegetables, etc.)—literally "rotten stew"—becomes *cara podrida,* "face that looks like a stew" when Quevedo describes a woman's ugly face which appears to incorporate the heterogeneous ingredients of a stew. A book written by Pérez de Montalbán is characterized as a *libro podrido* because of the large number of absurd and disparate thoughts included in it. In lampooning poetasters, he applies the expression *mujeres públicas y cantoneras,* "prostitutes and streetwalkers," to poets— *poetas públicos y cantoneros* he calls them—in order to show how base and degrading their poetry is. Using the expression *alma en pena,* "a soul suffering in purgatory," as a base, he creates such expressions as *marido en pena, soldados en pena, alcalde en pena,* etc., to describe the hellish sufferings of husbands, soldiers, and mayors.

Quevedo often accomplishes the burlesque imitation of common expressions which consist of verb plus noun or adverbial phrase. He refines the idiom *dar perro a uno,* "to deceive"—*perro* means "dog"—by substituting *gozque,* "little dog," or *alano,* "mastiff," for *perro* in this expression. Thus *dar gozque a uno* means "to effect a deceit of little consequence," and *dar alano a uno* means "to perpetrate a great deceit." Using *darse a,* "to give oneself over to," as a model, Quevedo invents *darse a médicos,* "to put oneself at the mercy of physicians." The expressions *condenar a galeras,* "to condemn to the galleys," or *condenar a las penas eternas,* "to condemn to eternal suffering," yield *condenar a dueña,* "to condemn one to the suffering inflicted by a duenna," and *condenar a privado,* "to condemn one to the mercy of an (unscrupulous) favorite of the king." The phrase *tomarse uno del vino,* "to become drunk"—literally "to come under the influence of wine"—serves as a model for other expressions: *tomarse del arbitrio,* "to fall prey to the wild schemes of politicians"; *tomarse de los años,* "to become drunk with old age"—used in connection with old women who are disturbed by their advancing age; and, *tomarse de las necedades,* "to have one's mind reel with stupidities." The common expression *llover a cántaros,* "to rain pitchforks," is the model for *llorar a cántaros,* "to cry pitchforks," *hablar a cántaros,* "to speak unendingly," and *escribir a cántaros,* "to write reams."

It is curious that the first dictionary published by the Spanish Royal Academy, the *Diccionario de Autoridades* (1726-1739), included many of Quevedo's neologisms, usually appending notes indicating they were invented words designed to achieve a humorous effect. However, starting with the second edition (1780), neologisms created by Quevedo, Lope, Calderón, and other writers were excluded from this dictionary.

X *Sensorial and Motive Stimuli*

Quevedo frequently appeals to the senses in the *Visions* and *The Swindler.* Usually this stimulation of the senses and emotions is calculated to offend or disgust the reader with the ultimate goal of shocking him into an awareness of the duplicity and nefarious actions of the types who inhabit the author's topsy-turvy world.

In order to persuade the reader of the validity of all that he sees in the *Visions,* Quevedo relies heavily on the verb *ver,* "to see," which he nearly always uses in the first person singular. As an example, the first seven paragraphs of the "Vision of Final Judgment" contain fourteen cases of a form of the verb "to see" and the related noun *vista,* "sight." By repeatedly telling the reader "I saw this" or "I saw a person doing this and that," Quevedo lends more of a sense of reality to his hellish scenes. The vividness of these images is frequently heightened by the spirited dialogues he has with the devils and their victims.

Quevedo has a penchant for offending the reader's olfactories. In *The Swindler,* certain episodes readily come to mind: the time when Pablos fell into the open privy and "martyred" the noses of all who came near him; the hazing adventure when Pablos smelled like a chamber pot from having lain in excrement; and the occasion when Pablos slept next to the stinking chamber pot while in jail. The *Visions* also provides fertile ground to commit offense against the sense of smell: the world vomits tailors into hell, shoemakers emit a bedbug stench, coachmen and apothecaries are malodorous, and a foul sepulchral smell emanates from Doña Quintañona's nose. ("Vision of Death") Quevedo revolts the reader's sense of taste with his descriptions of the meat pies concocted by pastry cooks in *The Swindler* and the *Visions,* the starvation of Cabra's pupils, the excrement-filled sandwich that the old man eats in *The Swindler,* and the tactics of such characters as Pablos, the starving hidalgo, (*Swindler*), and the parasitical Don Diego de Noche ("Vision of Death"), who obtain food by guile.

Auditory stimulation abounds in the *Visions.* Quevedo often informs the reader of the sounds he heard during his peregrinations through the infernal regions. At the outset of the first vision, "Vision of Final Judgment," a youth floating through the air blew so hard on a trumpet that he deformed his face. The piercing sound of the trumpet was sufficient to command the obedience of the marble tombstones and the ears of the dead, and the earth began to open and free the bones to go in search of one another. Throughout the *Visions* there are jarring noises: clanking of chains, thunder, shouts, groans, laments, howls, cracking of whips, raging of fires, singing, laughing, and crying.[13] Whenever barbers appear on the scene they are loudly strumming lively marches, sarabands, and chaconnes on their guitars.

Tactile sensations seem to be less in evidence than those of the other senses. Usually they are found when money is involved. Pablos fingers the same coins over and over to impress his landlady and her daughter that he is wealthy. In the "Vision of Final Judgment" we have the image of the corrupt judge who is endlessly washing his hands to remove the stain of bribery from them.

Quevedo evinces a chaotic view of the world in *The Swindler*. However, the absurdity and utter confusion which inform his society are more sharply revealed in the *Visions* in which he obviously contrasts world disorder with the ideal, harmonious kingdom of God. Scenes rapidly follow each other. All of hell is in constant movement. People are jumping, running, fleeing, sliding, falling, fighting, and bumping into one another. Quevedo is ever on the move: ascending, descending, turning, coming, and going. Hell is turmoil and is boiling over with curses and the unspeakable activities of those who populate it—especially women.

CHAPTER 6

Quevedo's Poetry

I Editions of His Poetry

TWO of Quevedo's earliest printed poems were sonnets, one in praise of Lucas Rodríguez (1599), and one lauding Lope de Vega's *El peregrino en su patria* (*The Pilgrim in His Native Country*), 1604. His reputation as a poet was apparently established by 1605, the years in which some of his poems were published in the anthology *Flores de poetas ilustres de España* (*Flowers of Illustrious Poets of Spain*) of Pedro Espinosa, and several of his ballads were included in the *Romancero general* (*General Collection of Ballads*) of Miguel de Madrigal. Quevedo's ballads appeared in many *romanceros* during his lifetime, but our poet never took the time to collect his original verses in his own anthology. In 1648 the humanist José González de Salas published in Madrid *El Parnaso español, monte en dos cumbres dividido, con las nueve musas castellanas* (*Spanish Parnassus, Mount Divided into Two Summits, with the Nine Castilian Muses*), which contains about two-thirds of the poetry attributed to Quevedo. In the prologue to this edition, the editor tells us that Quevedo kept putting off preparing an edition of his poems until the time he would have sufficient leisure for this task, a time which never materialized.

The title of González de Salas' edition indicates that he intended to use all nine Muses, but, probably for reasons of space, only six appeared in print. He probably would have published the remaining three Muses himself had he not died in 1661. Quevedo's nephew, Pedro Aldrete, having inherited his uncle's papers and those of González de Salas, decided to publish additional poems in the volume *Las tres musas últimas castellanas* (*The Last Three Castilian Muses*), 1670. However, both collections contain errors and, furthermore, some of Quevedo's poetry is missing while apocryphal poems are attributed to him. Of the many editions of Quevedo's poetry that have been published through the years, the most scholarly and reliable is

José Manuel Blecua's *Francisco de Quevedo: Poesía original* (Barcelona, 1963).

Quevedo also translated, recreated, and imitated the poetry of other writers: *Lágrimas de Hieremías* (*Tears of Jeremiah*), a commentary and translation in prose and poetry of the twenty-two verses of the first chapter of the lamentations of the Hebrew prophet;[1] *Epicteto y Focílides en español* (*Epictetus and Phocylides in Spanish*) on the philosophy of these Greek stoics;[2] *Anacreón castellano* (*Spanish Anacreon*), containing all the known anacreontics;[3] and translations of Martial and Ausias March.

My discussion of Quevedo's poetry will have three divisions that demonstrate once more his well-known dichotomous posture vis-à-vis the people and customs of his day and the meaning of life. The first encompasses his satirical and burlesque poetry which comprises the major part of his poetic writings. The second category embraces his serious poetry which can be sub-divided into: (1) metaphysical, moral and religious poetry, and (2) love poetry, especially the collection of poems dedicated to Lisi. Finally, I shall deal with Quevedo's severe criticism of Góngora and the *culteranistas* upon whom he showers corrosive invectives despite the fact that his own poetry at times follows *culteranista* custom.

II *Satirical and Burlesque Poetry*

Quevedo's poetic outpourings reveal his endless pursuit of authentic truth, the sempiternal quest for *desengaño*. The types lampooned, the themes, and the style of the *Visions* and the *Swindler* are echoed in Quevedo's satirical and burlesque poetry, and in order to avoid needless repetition, I shall only touch briefly on the salient features of the poetry to be discussed in this section. His satirical poetry abounds with sanguinary physicians, dentists who pull teeth indiscriminately, venal judges, corrupt notaries, ignorant bearded lawyers, pastry cooks who adulterate their meat pies, guitar-strumming barbers, Genoese bankers, thieves, constables, rogues, and cuckolds. Hypocrisy, self-interest, envy, deceit, and discord are rampant. However, the nefarious actions of women and the evils of money are the two themes of most frequent occurrence. Both are often found inextricably intertwined.

The satire directed against women in Quevedo's poetry shows more crudity and prurience than in the corresponding prose works. A great obsession in his devastating incrimination of female types seems to be old women. They are portrayed as impious, lewd, malodorous, and decaying inhuman figures. The *dueña* is as mercilessly slandered in his poetry as in the *Visions*. Deceitful women of all types abound: whores, courtesans, fake virgins, adulteresses, sorceresses, bawds, scullery maids, and nuns. And then there are the golddigging women who appear throughout the satirical poetry. In the famous poem "Poderoso caballero es don Dinero ("A Powerful Knight is Sir Money"), the narrator is a girl who tells her mother at the outset: *Madre, yo al oro me humillo;/ él es mi amante y mi amado* ("Mother, I humble myself before gold;/ he is my lover and my beloved"). Blecua, 734 When a suitor repeatedly offers his soul to a girl in a burlesque song, she replies over and over that he is talking nonsense and that money will be a better gift. (Blecua, 741-42) A recurring theme is the tug of war between the *pedigüeña*, "demanding woman," "gold digger," and the man who is a *tenaza*, "tightwad"; the *tenaza* always promises but never gives anything of value. For Quevedo, money is the usual corruptor of female morals, but it is also pictured as an instrument to pervert the behavior of most other types.[4] Indeed, in Quevedo's satirical poetry, as well as in the *Visions* and *The Swindler*, money is the prime motivator of man's actions. Quevedo's custom is to view negatively the influence of money on the world. It is at the root of vice and sin; it is the cause of man's *engaño*.

Quevedo's penchant for caricaturizing is boundless in his satirical poetry. By effective use of hyperbole, anaphora, and accumulation of epithets, he creates monstrous people as in the celebrated sonnet describing a large-nosed person whose appearance is as fantastic as that of Cabra:

> *Érase un hombre a una nariz pegado,*
> *érase una nariz superlativa,*
> *érase una alquitara medio viva,*
> *érase un peje espada mal barbado;*
>
> *era un reloj de sol mal encarado,*
> *érase un elefante boca arriba,*
> *érase una nariz sayón y escriba,*
> *un Ovidio Nasón mal narigado.*
>
> *Érase el espolón de una galera,*
> *érase una pirámide de Egito,*
> *las doce tribus de narices era;*

érase un narcísimo infinito,
frisón archinariz, caratulera,
sabañón garrafal, morado y frito.

(Blecua, 562)

(Once there was a man stuck to a nose. It was a superlative nose, it was a half-alive alembic, it was a badly bearded swordfish; it was a poorly positioned sundial, it was an elephant face up, it was a nose fit for executioners and scribes, a badly-nosed Ovidius Naso. It was the bowsprit of a galley, it was a pyramid of Egypt, it was the twelve tribes of noses; it was an infinite hulk of a nose, a huge archnose, a mask-mold, a prodigious swelling, dark purple and fried.)

Quevedo and other baroque writers sought to destroy the mythological world of Antiquity and the medieval world of legend and chivalry since the fanciful beauty they represented clashed with their own anguished view of reality. Thus, Quevedo's annihilation of the anachronistic chivalresque world in his longest poem, "Poema heroico de las necedades y locuras de Orlando el enamorado" ("Heroic Poem of the Follies and the Madness of the Lover Orlando"), is reminiscent of Góngora's parody which obliterated the beautiful love story of Pyramus and Thisbe inherited from classical Antiquity. In the Orlando poem Quevedo seems compelled to obliterate the absurd medieval world of romantic chivalry captured by the fifteenth-century Italian writer Matteo Boiardo in his *Orlando Innamorato* (*Roland in Love*). Quevedo follows Boiardo's plot, but his boundless imagination gives rise to new points of view. His burlesque alternately reveals seriousness, irony, and crude realism. In his extensive study of Quevedo's Orlando poem, Alarcos has called attention to the poet's two antithetical styles that inform it; the idealistic, which embodies perfections and beauty, and the realistic, or infrarealistic, which contains ugliness, filth, and foul odors. He further declares that Quevedo's picaresque and refined styles fuse together to constitute an organic unity.[5] Burlesque treatment is accorded an episode from the monumental twelfth-century epic on the Cid, the recounting of the cruelty of Nero and the King Don Pedro of Castile, and the actions of mythological gods and goddesses.

We shall now see further evidence of Quevedo's apparently contradictory temperament which impelled him to swing from pole to opposing pole. His ribaldry in the satirical poetry is but one manifestation of his thought and style; by no means can we understand the whole of Quevedo without consideration of the complementary serious poetry. Quevedo sought to find truth, goodness, and beauty in the world. The satirical poetry and prose deny the attainment of success in this search; the serious poetry offers hope of fulfilling his goals, in the other world if not in this one.

III *Serious Poetry: Metaphysical, Moral, and Religious*

The commonplace idea of the brevity of life permeates the poetry that will be examined in this section. Quevedo begins one sonnet with the verse *Vivir es caminar breve jornada* ("Life is a short day's journey"). (Blecua, 11) In other poems the span of life is characterized as a brief battle of a persistent war, a brief year, and a short period of time that may pass slowly and imperceptibly or flee rapidly. In Psalm XIX of the "Heráclito cristiano" ("Christian Heraclitus"), the poet takes cognizance of the inexorable march of time with an anguished outcry:

> *¡Cómo de entre mis manos te resbalas!*
> *¡Oh, cómo te deslizas, edad mía!* (Blecua, 33)

> (How you slip from between my hands!
> Oh, how you slide away, my life!)

Besides being so transient, life deceives us since it nullifies all that one has accomplished and longed for during his lifetime. The recurring theme of life's frailty and vanity is concisely expressed in the last stanza of the sonnet mentioned above:

> *Cualquier instante de la vida humana*
> *es nueva ejecución, con que me advierte*
> *cuán frágil es, cuán mísera, cuán vana.*

> (Every moment of human life
> is a new decree which warns me
> how fragile, how wretched, how vain it is.)

For Quevedo *la trágica guadaña de la muerte*, "the tragic scythe of death," (Blecua, 26), constantly hangs over man's head. Death is the inevitable patrimony of mankind. In the famous sonnet "Miré los muros de la patria mía" ("I looked at the walls of my native land"), Blecua, 31-32, Quevedo sees the pall of death over everything. He continually warns the reader in a

number of poems that he should be aware of death's imminence
and prudently accept this inescapable fact.

Man has already set out on the road to death right after birth.
To emphasize this concept, Quevedo frequently calls life a *muerte
viva*, "living death." In one of his metaphysical sonnets he epitomizes the proximity of life to death by condensing the short span
of time between them so that one coincides with the other:

> *En el hoy y mañana y ayer, junto*
> *pañales y mortaja, y he quedado*
> *presentes sucesiones de difunto.* (Blecua, 4)

(In my today and tomorrow and yesterday, I join together
swaddling clothes and shroud, and I pass
as a dead man through the succession of events now occurring.)

Life is viewed as a meaningless illusion obliterated by death:

> *¡Fue sueño ayer; mañana será tierra!*
> *¡Poco antes, nada; y poco después, humo!*
> . . . .
>
> *Ya no es ayer; mañana no ha llegado;*
> *hoy pasa, y es, y fue, con movimiento*
> *que a la muerte me lleva despeñado.*

(Yesterday was a dream; tomorrow will be earth!
A little while ago, nothing; and a little later, smoke!
. . . .

It is no longer yesterday; tomorrow has not arrived;
today passes, and is, and was, with a movement
which hurls me off a cliff to death.)

Quevedo overcomes the natural fears man harbors in the face
of death and welcomes it as a liberation from the pain and
suffering he has undergone in the prison of life. (Blecua, 15)
Death is the true *desengaño*, so ardently sought after in his
writings, since it permits his soul to escape the ignorance and
corruption of the world. In accordance with Catholic dogma,
he believes that authentic life begins at the moment of death
when the soul attains God's kingdom. Life is simply a transitory
stage between birth and the eternal divine state. Life is death or
the negation of true existence because of the deceit, the base-
ness and the chaos that obtain during the soul's terrestrial period.
Death is authentic life since it elevates the spirit to Christ's

domain where truth, goodness, peace, and harmony hold sway
everlastingly.

The "Christian Heraclitus" is a confession of the repentant
Quevedo as he tells us in the introductory remarks written June
3, 1613. Recognizing the errors of his past, he seeks to rehabilitate
his life along true Christian paths with the assistance of a
ubiquitous and omniscient God. He welcomes death, for it will
put an end to his suffering on this earth. He begins Psalm XVI
with the verse *Ven ya, miedo de fuertes y de sabios* ("Come now,
terror of the strong and the wise"), Blecua, 30, and ends the
second strophe with the words *trae con mi vida fin a mis agravios*
("take away my suffering as well as my life"). Psalm XXVIII
sums up the poet's complete acceptance of God:

> *Corrido estoy de los pasados años,*
> *que reducir pudiera mejor uso*
> *buscando paz, y no siguiendo engaños.*
>
> *Y así, mi Dios, a Ti vuelvo confuso,*
> *cierto que has de librarme destos daños,*
> *pues conozco mi culpa y no la excuso.* (Blecua, 40)
>
> (I am sated with my past life,
> which I could have used more wisely
> in seeking peace, and not following illusions.
>
> And so, my God, confused, I turn to Thee,
> certain that Thou willst free me from sinful acts,
> since I recognize my guilt and do not excuse it.)

The moral poems evince typical Quevedesque strictures against
misers, gluttons, usurers, adulterous women, hypocrites, adulators, the venal, the lascivious, the intemperate, the covetous,
the conceited, the arrogant, and the corrupt. One can frequently
detect in many of them the message that "all that glitters is
not gold." Moreover, the pursuit of gold is seen as the motive
that perverts human behavior, causing mankind to abandon true
Christian ethics. One of his finest compositions in the group of
moral poems is the extensive "Sermón estoico de censura moral"
("Stoical Sermon of Moral Censure"), in which he reproves a
whole gamut of human vices and, in particular, excoriates merchants and tyrants. As Antonio de Guevara had done a century
before, he praises the simple, pure life of the country, and condemns the evils of city life and especially that of the Court.

Several years before his death he wrote the celebrated sonnet
"Retirado en la paz de estos desiertos" ("Withdrawn unto the
Peace of this Deserted Place"), Blecua, 105, in which he expresses
his enjoyment of solitude amid the great books contained in his
library.

Quevedo's deep concern for Spain manifests itself in the
"Epístola satírica y censoria contra las costumbres presentes de
los castellanos" ("Satirical Epistle, Censuring the Present Customs
of Spaniards"), written to Don Gaspar de Guzmán, Count-Duke
of Olivares, around 1624. Seeking to lay bare the naked truth of
his country's corroding customs, in the first strophe the poet
says to Olivares that regardless of the risk involved, he must
unburden himself of his grief:

> No he de callar, por más que con el dedo,
> ya tocando la boca, o ya la frente,
> silencio avises, o amenaces miedo. (Blecua, 140)

(I will not keep silent, no matter how much your finger alternately
touches your mouth and your forehead to warn me to be silent or to
threaten fear.)

He laments the passing of the time when Spain was a virtuous,
valiant and prosperous nation. Now honor scorns the man who
works, whereas formerly work was one's patent of nobility.
Now the spirited youth shows his prowess in bullfighting rather
than fighting for Spain on the battlefield. He beseeches the
Count-Duke to follow the example of his glorious ancestors and,
as an influential prime minister, to restore Spanish military might
more than Pelayo did.

Among Quevedo's religious poems, there are many devoted to
Christ's life, his death on the cross, his resurrection, and what
he symbolizes for mankind. His "Poema heroico a Cristo resuci-
tado" ("Heroic Poem to the Resurrected Christ") mystically
exalts the glory of Christ in one hundred *octavas reales* (strophes
comprising eight hendecasyllabic verses). He dedicated poems
to the Virgin Mary, the lives of saints, and figures from the Old
Testament. His gloss on the Pater Noster synthesizes his moral,
metaphysical, and religious ideas. His beautiful version of
Solomon's Song of Songs rivals those of the ascetics and mystics
of the Spanish Golden Age. In his religious poems, as well as in
the others studied in this section, he communicates his perfervid
adherence to traditional Spanish Catholicism.

IV *Serious Poetry: Love Poems*

In Quevedo's love poetry, we can discern three currents which were the common heritage of Spanish baroque poets: Petrarchism, courtly love, and platonic love. It is generally agreed that his conception of these literary tendencies arose from sixteenth-century Spanish poets' interpretation of them rather than from the original sources.

Otis Green has pointed out that "in the general conception and in the poetic treatment of the poet's love in the sequence to Lisi there is an unquestionable Petrarchan lament."[6] Dámaso Alonso, who has amply indicated Petrarchan influence in Spanish Golden Age poetry, has demonstrated that Quevedo's poetry follows Petrarchan formulas.[7] Some of its characteristics that Dámaso Alonso analyzes in Quevedo's poetry are: the varied, elaborate descriptions of beauty, the insatiable analysis of the feelings of love, the repeated metaphors, the conceits, the sumptuous, colorful images, and the antithetical dualism.

According to Green, courtly love is the central theme in Quevedo's love poetry. He defines courtly love as "a love consciously cultivated and an ever-repressed desire which denies its own fulfillment and makes a cult of suffering. . ."[8] This definition is somewhat limited if we were to take into account Father Denomy's three basic elements which set courtly love apart from all other conceptions of love: one, love as an ever un-satiated, ever increasing desire; two, the ennobling force of love; and, three, the cult of the beloved, in which the beloved is elevated to a place of superiority above the lover.[9] Mas has utilized Father Denomy's basic elements of courtly love in an attack upon Green's view of the preeminence of courtly love in Quevedo's amatory lyrics. He has stated that Quevedo's silence regarding the ennobling power of love by itself is sufficient to nullify Green's thesis.[10] However, Mas agrees that vestiges of courtly love can be found in Quevedo, but maintains that chivalric love should be considered as just one of the various Quevedesque themes.

The presence of platonic love in Quevedo's amatory poetry is generally recognized by literary critics. Whereas in courtly love poems the lover is apparently content to contemplate the beauty of his beloved, and to express his desire for her, knowing full well that physical possession will always be denied him, in platonic love the poet's love transcends the feelings he has for

his beloved, and soars to celestial heights seeking to encounter
absolute beauty and eternal love. In a number of Quevedo's
poems, and especially in those devoted to Lisi, we find the
fusion of elements from both courtly love and platonic love.

The following sonnet exhibits the coalesence of these two
type of love and probably typifies the love Quevedo felt for Lisi:[11]

> *Que vos me permitáis sólo pretendo*
> *y saber ser cortés y ser amante;*
> *esquivo los deseos, y constante,*
> *sin pretensión, a sólo amar atiendo.*
>
> *Ni con intento de gozar ofendo*
> *las deidades del garbo y del semblante,*
> *no fuera lo que vi causa bastante,*
> *si no se le añadiera lo que entiendo.*
>
> *Llamáronme los ojos las facciones;*
> *prendiéronlos eternas jerarquías*
> *de virtudes y heroicas perfecciones.*
>
> *No verán de mi amor el fin los días:*
> *la eternidad ofrece sus blasones*
> *a la pureza de las ansias mías.* (Blecua, 501)

(I only strive to have you inform me how to be a courteous and to be a
lover; I shun desires and in the constancy of my love which seeks no
reward, I only give heed to loving you. I do not offend the deities of
grace and countenance with an attempt to possess you; what I saw
would be insufficient cause to love you if what I understand were not
added. My eyes were attracted to the features of your face; eternal
hierarchies of virtue and noble perfection have been instilled in them.
My life will not see the end of my love: eternity offers its blazon to
the purity of my yearning.)

The two quatrains of this sonnet are expressed in the usual
manner of courtly love poems. The poet, ever constant in his
love, simply wishes to continue loving his beloved without any
thought of climaxing it by possessing her. His reason helps him to
temper the effect his beloved's extreme beauty has upon him. The
first tercet represents a transitional stage in which the poet leaves
the terrestrial region and starts ascending the "platonic ladder"
to the celestial realm. Lisi's virtue and beauty are idealized.
Finally, in the second tercet, the poet's love, having completely
transcended mundane limitations, becomes an eternal, spiritual
love.

I have pointed out in my discussion of Quevedo's meta-physical poetry, as well as in my analysis of the *Visions,* the recurrent leitmotif that absolute truth is attained in death. Although the lethal powers of love and the imminence of death are Petrarchan—indeed universal—commonplaces, Quevedo harps on the love-death theme more than any other Spanish love poet.[12] Platonism is an appropriate vehicle to lead Quevedo from wordly suffering and deceit that inform his concept of life to spiritual paradise. In a number of sonnets to Lisi, he repeatedly exclaims that his pure, ardent love for his beloved will endure beyond the tomb. This thought is beautifully captured in Quevedo's famous love sonnet which is perhaps the greatest in Spanish literature.[13]

Amor constante más allá de la muerte

Cerrar podrá mis ojos la postrera
sombra que me llevare el blanco día,
y podrá desatar esta alma mía
hora a su afán ansioso lisonjera;

mas no, de esotra parte, en la ribera,
dejará la memoria, en donde ardía;
nadar sabe mi llama la agua fría,
y perder el respeto a ley severa

Alma a quien todo un dios prisión ha sido,
venas que humor a tanto fuego dado,
medulas que han gloriosamente ardido,

su cuerpo dejará, no su cuidado;
serán ceniza, mas tendrá sentido;
polvo serán, mas polvo enamorado. (Blecua, 511)

(A Love Constant Beyond Death

The last shadow which will take the white day from me may close my eyes, and shortly release this soul of mine pleasing its anxious zeal; but it will not, on the further shore, leave the memory of where it used to burn; my fiery passion can swim the cold water and lose its respect for stern law. A soul which has been imprisoned by a complete god, veins which have supplied liquid sustenance to so great a fire, marrow which has gloriously burned: it [the soul] will leave its body but not its passion; they [the blood and marrow] will be ashes, but it will retain its feelings; they will be dust but dust in love.)

There are differing opinions concerning Lisi's identity. Some say that Quevedo, devoid of sincere emotion, was indulging in a poetic exercise in the Petrarchan or courtly mode; others maintain that she was a composite of several ladies he knew at Court; others assert that she was a specific woman whom he truly loved during a period of twenty-two years. A rather recent article contends, with a good deal of supportive evidence, that Lisi was the French Queen Isabel de Borbón, daughter of Henry IV, and wife of Philip IV.[14] Conclusive proof to substantiate one viewpoint or another will probably never be forthcoming. Dámaso Alonso has sagaciously observed: ¿Pero quién aquilataría los mil matices posibles entre servidumbre social y literaria, puro amor y deseo del sentido? ("But who would assay the thousand possible shades encompassing compliance with social and literary custom, pure love and sensuous desire?")[15]

It should not surprise us to learn that many of Quevedo's amatory poems are happy and playful. Among the sonnets to Aminta are two in which the poet recounts that on one occasion she burned a lock of her hair when she brought a candle close to her hair to reveal its color, and, on another occasion, she bit her lips while holding a carnation in her mouth. There is a madrigal dedicated to Floris' yawn. One sonnet is devoted to a cross-eyed woman who is pretty and another to a woman, blind in one eye, who is also pretty. And even some of the poems to Lisi are far removed from the desperate anguish that usually characterize them, as in the sonnet in which he tries to allay her fear of thunder.

The varying interpretations concerning the influences on Quevedo's love poetry, the speculation revolving about the sincerity of his feeling for Lisi, the hypothesis that he is a lineal ancestor of Unamuno and other modern existentialist poets, cannot detract from the consensus of modern criticism which esteems him as one of the greatest Spanish lyricists.

V Quevedo's Anti-Culteranismo

Time after time Quevedo deprecated the poetry of the culteranistas or cultistas for the obscurity and affectation of their style. In Chapter X of The Swindler he inserted a proclamation disabusing the public of addle-brained, insipid, and worthless poets. (BAC, 112-19) He calls them disgusting vermin and devils, who, with their perpetual nonsensical conceits and fracturing of the language, have inflicted the madness of poetry on women. In the Discourse of All Devils, poets are exposed as composers

of absurd, mad verse, and, because of the incomprehensibility
of his affected style, the *culto*, "euphuistic writer," is dubbed the
prince of darkness. (O.C. I, 213-14)

Three short prose works are specifically designed to satirize
most ingeniously the affectation that Quevedo observed in the
speech and writing of his day. In *La culta latiniparla* (*The
Macaronic Speech of a Pedantic Woman*), he ridicules the
deliberate effort of the female practitioners of mannered speech
to avoid saying what they mean in clear, simple terms. Examples
are calling chicken eggs "globes of the rooster's wife" and describing one's toothless condition as "having a boneless voice." The
"Cuento de cuentos" ("Story of Stories") effectively lampoons the
solecisms and barbarisms that plagued the speech of Spaniards.
It is so replete with idioms piled one upon the other that ample
commentary on the meanings of the expressions used is necessary
to comprehend the simple story Quevedo narrates. Finally, he
wrote the very brief satire "Aguja de navegar cultos" ("Compass
to Navigate as Pedantics") expressly directed against Góngora,
the dean of Spanish *culteranistas*. This opuscule is best known for
the poem found at the beginning, a *receta*, "recipe," for learning to
write poetry like Góngora's "in one day." Many of the words
Quevedo isolates as examples of *culteranista* gibberish have
survived in good repute to the present day.

Quevedo sustained one of the bitterest literary feuds of the
seventeenth century with Góngora. Their exchange of poetic
invectives began in 1603, and Quevedo did not desist until
Góngora's death in 1627. However, even after the passing of
Góngora, Quevedo continued to attack the *cultistas*—also frequently called *gongoristas*—for their obscurity stemming from
their neologisms and novel images. In 1631 Quevedo published
the works of Fray Luis de León and Francisco de la Torre
to oppose their clarity and purity of language to what he considered the affected and unintelligible poetry of those who wrote
like Góngora.

Yet despite the stream of venom directed at the *cultistas*,
Quevedo could not achieve a complete insulation from the influence of their technique. Eunice Joiner Gates has pointed out
the close similarity in imagery between the first line of Góngora's *Soledades* (*Solitudes*) and Quevedo's *silva* (a poem
combining hendecasyllables and seven-syllable verses) celebrat-
ing the killing of a wild boar by the Infanta María on May
6, 1625:[16]

> *Tú, blasón de los bosques,*
> *erizada amenaza de los cerros,*
> *temeroso escarmiento de los perros,*
> *que con las medias lunas espumosas*
> *de marfil belicoso y delincuente,*
> . . . .
>
> *al cáñamo burlaste las cautelas;*
> . . . .
>
> *Y el Toro, que, con piel y frente de oro,*
> *rumia en el campo azul pasto luciente,*
> *gastando en remolinos un tesoro,*
> *cuando mayo es corona de su frente,*
> *te dio lugar en el eterno coro* . . . (Blecua, 242-45)

(You, blazon of the woods, bristly menace of the hills, dreaded warning for the dogs, who, with your foaming half moons of bellicose and delinquent ivory . . . escaped the trickery of the nets . . . And Taurus, who, with his golden hide and head, ruminates the lucent grass in the blue field, whirling about a treasure, when May is the crown of his head, made a place for you in the eternal chorus . . .)

Gongorine imagery is also evident in other *silvas* such as his "Himno a las estrellas" ("Hymn to the Stars"). There are several poetic passages describing birds as flowers and musical instruments in good *culteranista* style such as the following poem addressed to a nightingale:

> *Flor con voz, volante flor,*
> *silbo alado, voz pintada,*
> *lira de pluma animada*
> *y ramillete cantor;*
> *di, átomo volador,*
> *florido acento de pluma,*
> *bella organizada suma*
> *de lo hermoso y lo süave,*
> *¿cómo cabe en sola un ave*
> *cuanto el contrapunto suma?* (Blecua, 238)

(Vocal flower, flying flower, winged whistle, painted voice, lyre of animated plumage and singing bouquet; tell me, flying atom, flowery, plumed melody, beautifully proportioned aggregate so lovely and gentle, how can there be contained in a single bird the sum total of its polyphony?)

María E. Malfatti has revealed in ample detail the many similarities in language, structure and imagery between Quevedo's *Orlando el enamorado* and Góngora's *Polifemo*.[17] However, Quevedo, in using the themes and formal techniques of the Italian-inspired baroque style characteristic of the *culteranistas,* did not attain Góngora's intensified stylistic luxuriance.

CHAPTER 7

Apologist of Christian Politics

QUEVEDO'S corrosive satire of the Spanish people and their mores ensued from his love of Spain and a yearning to have authentic Catholicism prevail. These two factors underlie also his works on theoretical and practical politics, and his religious writings. It is essential to probe Quevedo's ideas on religion before undertaking an examination of his political theory.

I   Quevedo's Christian Stoicism

Quevedo's advocacy of the resigned acceptance of the inevitability of death which swiftly overtakes man is often found within his works, and especially in the ascetic and philosophical writings. The chief source for this stoical attitude is Seneca—*mi Séneca*, "my Seneca," he calls him (O.C. I, 1307)—whose philosophy helped Quevedo to formulate his rationale of life. In addition, Quevedo felt a close kinship with Seneca who was born in Córdoba, a city in Southern Spain. Seneca's philosophy had had a continuous tradition in Spain from the Middle Ages through Quevedo's time.

Seneca's mark is evident throughout Quevedo's works. Quevedo translated the Cordoban philosopher's writings, he incorporated Senecan thought in his prose and poetry, he dedicated a sonnet to him, and in a letter to Justus Lipsius he indicated the great contribution Seneca made to Spain.

In 1633 Quevedo finished writing his translation with commentaries of a book which has been attributed to Seneca without substantiation. This work, *De los remedios de cualquier fortuna* (*On the Remedies of Any Fortune*), constitutes one of the clearest and most straightforward statements among the many that Quevedo made urging man to prepare himself for imminent death. In the first segment of this opuscule the word *morirás*, "you will die," is repeated over and over both in Seneca's statement and in Quevedo's commentary. According to Seneca, man

134

is a rational mortal who must not complain of his demise, a natural phenomenon of man's existence. Quevedo, in his commentary, adhering to Seneca's non-complaining attitude, repeats the commonplace idea that man begins to die at birth. However, he goes beyond the thought that death is the inescapable return of dust to dust which rational man should accept without mental anguish; it is an event which he fearlessly longs for since it brings true life. Throughout this short work Quevedo also presents Seneca's and his own recommendations that man must accept with calm fortitude all the misfortunes that may befall him in life, such as illness, poverty, pain, blindness, exile, and loss of children, friends, and wife.

Further espousal of Stoic teachings is found in *Nombre, origen, intento, recomendación y descendencia de la dotrina estoica* (*Name, Origin, Purpose, Recommendation and Descent of the Stoic Doctrine*), written around the same time as the work mentioned in the previous paragraph. He sees a close relationship between Stoic doctrine—he describes it as serious, virile, and robust philosophy—and Christian fortitude, but criticizes Stoicism for its insensitivity. What Quevedo is saying here is that he cannot wholeheartedly endorse Stoicism without including Christ's teachings as an integral part of this doctrine. He is proposing then a Christian stoic ideal in opposition to Seneca's pagan outlook. It is Job of the Hebrew Bible who is Quevedo's model of Christian stoicism. The example of Job's stoicism is examined at length in the work under discussion and the more extensive treatise written in the last years of Quevedo's life, *La constancia y paciencia del Santo Job* (*The Constancy and Patience of St. Job*).

Job was not self-sufficient; he relied for support on God, who tested him through Satan. God let Satan cause Job to lose his children, his fortune, his home, and suffer a disease of painful boils. Job, oblivious of the reason for his ill fortune, refuses to complain while enduring these tribulations. His faith in the blessed Lord is complete. Mental anguish is added to his physical trials. Three friends come to offer solace and to attempt to raise doubts in his mind about the justice of the situation. But Job still believes that God is righteous. Although he is not aware of having sinned, he continues to believe that God has not abandoned him. Pagan Seneca had to rely on his own resources in the face of natural phenomena, but the Christian stoic must have unconditional faith in God no matter how illogical and

unjust His workings may seem. This unquestioning trust in
God's will is an essential feature of Quevedo's political thought
also. We shall see that in the *Politics of God* he recommends that
a tyrant be endured because this punishment inflicted upon a
nation originates with God to fulfill some purpose that is unknown and unknowable.

Quevedo's Christian stoicism would require man to bear
patiently the harshest punishment that God can visit upon him.
God controls man's destiny and releases him from the misery
of his worldly existence only when He pleases. In other words,
man cannot take his own life, for, in doing so, he would usurp
God's power. Accordingly, Quevedo can never accept the Stoic
belief that permits man to commit suicide when life is no longer
worth living. The suicides of Socrates and Seneca are unjustifi-
able; in Seneca's case, not even the fact that he was a Spaniard
and an illustrious writer could erase the cowardice of his act
in Quevedo's eyes. Quevedo seeks to salve his wounded spirit
by turning to the words of another of his favorite Stoics,
Epictetus, who urged man to endure God's will on earth and
wait for God to snuff out human life.

Quevedo's Christian stoicism constantly reappears in other
religious works, which he wrote mainly in the last dozen years
of his life. The theme of the imminence of death and the necessity to prepare oneself for it from the moment of birth is cogently
synthesized in *La cuna y la sepultura* (*The Cradle and the
Grave*), written in 1633 and published the following year.
Quevedo informs the reader in his prologue to this book that
he has used the writings of the Stoics and the text of Job to
demonstrate the illusion and vanity of worldly affairs and to
convince man that God is the one and only truth. Man's wisdom
begins the day of his death, after his soul has left the darkness
and ignorance of the world. (O.C. I, 1208) He must resign
himself totally to the will of the Lord. *The Cradle and the Grave*
ends with a gloss on the Pater Noster.

In 1641 Quevedo wrote *Providencia de Dios* (*Providence of
God*) while incarcerated in San Marcos de León. Once more
it is the example of Job's patience—the teachings of Christ and
the saints are also adduced—that provides the key to the three
truths he conceives: that God exists, that Providence exists, and
that the soul is immortal. (O.C. I, 1398)

II *Defender of Spain's Traditional Values:*
Support of Santiago

The patriotic fervor of Quevedo is very evident in his *España defendida* (*Spain Defended*), written in 1609. In the dedication to Philip III, Quevedo states that he must rise to defend Spanish honor against the calumnies of foreigners. Seeking to demonstrate the greatness and antiquity of Spain, he delves into its origin, its glorious history, the richness of its language, and the excellence of its literature and humanistic studies. The *Celestina* and the *Lazarillo de Tormes* are praised, as well as the works of Luis de León, Garcilaso, Jorge Manrique, Juan de Mena, and Herrera. He immodestly extols his own translation of Anacreon's poetry which he claims is better than the original. However, in Chapter Five of this work, the eulogy ceases and Quevedo, forgetting the slander of foreigners, turns to his fellow countrymen, exhorting them to maintain their illustrious heritage. The Spaniards, under Philip III as their guide, must learn to dominate their vices and cowardice and serve God if they are to preserve and increase their country's grandeur. These serious, straightforward, and heartfelt observations offer a revealing glimpse into a fundamental aspect of his thought.

Quevedo's loyalty to Spanish tradition led him to defend vigorously the position of Santiago (St. James) as the patron saint of Spain. Toward the end of 1617, a movement was begun to bestow on Santa Teresa the glory of co-patronage with Santiago, the apostle who was the protector of Spaniards during the Crusades. Both Philip III and Philip IV supported the elevation of Santa Teresa to the eminence of patroness. Not long after Philip IV decreed, on July 31, 1627, that Santa Teresa become patroness of Spain with the proviso that this should not diminish Santiago's patronage in any way, Quevedo, a member of the Order of Santiago since 1618, published his famous *Memorial por el Patronato de Santiago* (*Memorial in Favor of the Patronage of Santiago*). His ardent defense of Santiago, published in February, 1628, brought on an avalanche of attacks and his exile from the Court until the end of that year. By early 1630 Pope Urban VIII decreed that Santiago should be the only patron saint of Spain.

In the *Memorial* and in its companion-piece, *Su espada por Santiago* (*His Sword for Santiago*), signed May 4, 1628 but not published until the nineteenth century, Quevedo maintains that Santiago's patronage was Christ's choice. Relying on biblical and

historical sources, Quevedo affirms that Santiago was the redeemer of Spaniards and the source of their true faith. Moreover,
Quevedo wonders how anybody can cast aside a tradition that
has been perpetuated by kings and nations during sixteen
hundred years.

III   *General Interest in Politics*

In the *Visions* there are several attacks against bad ministers
who undermine the king's rule and also against oppressive
tyrants. *The Hour of All Men* contains a satire of the ministers
of Philip IV, and that thinly-veiled incrimination of the Count-
Duke of Olivares and several secretaries, which was discussed
in a previous chapter. And in the *Discourse of All Devils*
none of the denizens of hell wanted the company of the
ministers or the monarchs who wound up tearing each other
to pieces. Between 1627 and 1628 Quevedo wrote the play *Cómo
ha de ser el privado* (*What the King's Favorite Should Be*),
which ostensibly praises the Count-Duke of Olivares, but, more
important, reveals Quevedo's ideas germane to the conduct of
a king's prime minister. The idea that an advisor to the king
should be capable, trustworthy, self-denying, and an adherent
of Christian ethics, always mindful that his role is to counsel
wisely the king with whom final authority rests, is more fully
developed in the *Política de Dios*.

Several short works are devoted to historico-political themes
such as: *Lince de Italia* (*Lynx of Italy*), 1628, on relations with
Italy; *Grandes anales de quince días* (*Great Annals of Fifteen
Days*), 1621, on the political situation in Spain when Philip IV
ascended the throne; and *El chitón de las tarabillas* (*The Bab-
bler's Stopper*), 1630, on the woeful financial condition of Spain.
In 1632 Quevedo published his translation of *Il Romulo* (*Romulus*), a work dealing with the founder of Rome written by the
Italian Virgilio Malvezzi who was Philip IV's ambassador to
London. Quevedo's *Marco Bruto* (1644) is a translation of what
Plutarch wrote on Marcus Brutus. Quevedo added his own commentaries which relate to the political situation of his own
time. In concise style he censures ineffectual princes, bad rulers,
unscrupulous ministers, and tyrants.

IV   *The* Política de Dios

Quevedo's greatest work on politics is his *Política de Dios*
(*The Politics of God*). In the balance of this chapter, I shall

study this book in detail since it encompasses the essence of his political thought. As we shall see, Quevedo's overriding purpose in this treatise was to set forth his ideal of a Spanish state—a powerful nation adhering to true Christian principles.[1]

Quevedo finished the first part of his book in 1621 and dedicated it to Olivares. However, it was not published until 1626 (Zaragoza), without Quevedo's authorization. Quevedo rejected this edition and decided to publish a new and enlarged version of this work which appeared in Madrid in the same year. The first part of the *Politics* went through nine separate editions—only two were authorized by Quevedo—an extraordinary publishing record for the Golden Age. The second part of this political treatise was first published in Madrid in 1655, in an edition which also contained the first part. After its initial success in 1626, the subject matter of this work undoubtedly prevented it from achieving the spectacular notoriety of the *Visions* and *The Swindler* either in Spain or abroad. A respectable number of Spanish editions have steadily appeared until the present day, but very few translations have been made. There exist a Polish translation of the first part (Warsaw, 1633), three Italian editions—Mantua, 1701; Venice, 1709; and an early eighteenth-century one published at Trent—and two in English —London, 1715, which is only the first part; and London, 1720, which is only the first eight chapters of the second part.

The *Politics of God* is one of the works that achieved prominence in the tidal wave of books on political theory, written in Spanish and Latin, that inundated the Iberian Peninsula during the sixteenth and seventeenth centuries. Critics have sought the sources of Quevedo's political thought in contemporary Spanish writers (Mariana and Suárez); works of Italians (Peruta, Campanella, Boccalini and Botero); in the *Utopia* of Thomas Moore; in French political philosophers (Bodin, Languet); and, in the Belgian, Justus Lipsius.[2] However, were one to peruse Spanish political treatises of the sixteenth century—and even before— he would most naturally uncover notable resemblances between these works and Quevedo's *Politics.* Furthermore, it is quite apparent that his political disquisitions stemmed from the common stockpile of western European political doctrine which, in turn, arose from the medieval heritage. This study will attempt to demonstrate that Quevedo's contributions in the realm of political theory constitute an iteration of principles that had been utilized by previous Spanish generations.[3]

V *Quevedo's Christian Monarch*

The full title of Quevedo's renowned work, *Política de Dios, Gobierno de Cristo Nuestro Señor* (*Politics of God, Government of Christ Our Lord*), indicates in sharp relief his immersion in the current of profoundly-imbedded religiosity characteristic of the Golden Age in Spain. The matrix of the political doctrine espoused in the *Politics* is founded upon the actions and words of Christ. The ruler depicted by Quevedo can only act in the manner of a Christian ruler; the government that controls the destiny of the Spanish Empire must exemplify noble Christian virtues. The pervasive nature of religious consciousness prior to the publication of Quevedo's book is particularly manifest in such works as Francisco de Monzón's *Libro primero del espejo del príncipe cristiano* (*First Book of the Mirror of the Christian Prince*), 1544; Felipe de la Torre's *Institución de un rey christiano colegida principalmente de la Santa Escritura y de sagrados doctores* (*Institution of a Christian King Derived Mainly from the Holy Scriptures and Sacred Doctors*), 1566; and Pedro de Rivadeneira's *Tratado de la religión* (*Treatise of Religion*), 1595. The fountain of the ethicopolitical structure envisioned by Spanish writers on the affairs of state invariably can be found in biblical passages and the commentaries of medieval theologians. Of the latter, the teachings of St. Thomas Aquinas undoubtedly constitute the most frequently utilized source.

Monarchy, the form of government espoused by Quevedo, was traditionally advocated in Spain. The author of the *Politics of God* accepts the basic medieval premise that oneness is a prime principle in Nature. The analogy he draws between the king-vassal relationship in social organization and the God-man relationship in the religious sphere recalls the numerous attempts to rationalize the existence of monarchy. In the fifteenth century Rodrigo Sánchez de Arévalo, in his *Suma de la Política* (*Summa of Politics*), c. 1454, proffered the customary arguments for the defense of monarchy: (1) it effectuates peace, unity, and agreement; (2) the princedom of one is more powerful than that of many in a single kingdom; (3) monarchy conforms most naturally to the phenomena in Nature; (4) terrestrial monarchy is a reflection of divine monarchy; and (5) strife is rampant in cities where there is no monarchy.[4] A century and a half later, Juan de Mariana, one of the foremost Spanish proponents of monarchy, chose this form of government because it conformed to the laws of nature, and also because it promoted internal peace and fostered more efficient administration in government.

The ruler portrayed in the *Politics of God* is absolute in his authority, which is of divine origin. This adherence to the divine right of kings existed widely in medieval times; during the Spanish Golden Age, this doctrine had vigorous backing from many writers. The oft-repeated words, *Per me reges regnant,* "Kings rule through me" (St. Paul to Romans, XIII), formed the catchphrase that helped lend credence to the concept that the terrestrial king is the immediate servant, vicar, or lieutenant of God. Since the prince or king acted in God's stead on earth, he must, in the words of Quevedo, perform his duties in strict accordance with the Lord's wishes.[5]

It was only natural that Quevedo should select Christ as the ideal king. Christ was frequently looked upon as the model for action during the Middle Ages, and also in the sixteenth century. The Erasmists, in particular, advocated the return to the original works of Christ in their attempt to establish a true Christian society. One of them, Felipe de la Torre, clearly indicated that Christ's mission on earth was that of a teacher whose word should be law for all, and especially for Christian kings; see the dedicatory epistle of his *Institución de un rey cristiano* (*Institution of a Christian King*), Antwerp, 1556.

Quevedo's king is considered a public person who has to give his all for the public good. Here Quevedo is repeating the medieval and Renaissance view that recognized the dual personality of a ruler, in whom the public side predominated over the private. Gierke clearly explained the existence of this phenomenon in the Middle Ages: "The person of the King is the organ and instrument of an 'intellectual and public person'; and it is this intellectual and public person that must be regarded as the principal, for the law pays more regard to the power of the principal than to the power of the organ."[6] In the middle of the sixteenth century, the practical Fadrique Furió Ceriol represented one of the many who put great stress on the fitness of the prince and his councillors as public persons; cf. Chapter I of his *El concejo i consejeros del príncipe* (*The Council and Councillors of the Prince*), Antwerp, 1559. In the pursuance of his regal public task, Quevedo's ruler had to learn obedience, just as Christ in his day. (PDC, 231)[7]

Spanish political philosophers of the sixteenth and seventeenth centuries universally felt that the ruler should emulate those who governed well in the past. For Quevedo, Christ was the sole king who ever existed, and only the one who imitated him could aspire to be a true king. In like manner, the prince portrayed by Quevedo was typically the prototype of his subjects in every phase of their life. The king had to be like Jesus, who said to Thomas: "I am the way, the truth, and the life." (St. John, 14-6) Quevedo considered the mission of the ruler divine; thus, by aping the ways of the good king, the subjects reflected also the divine will. The bad king brought destruction and death. A century before, Erasmus had expressed the well-known belief that the prince is imitated by all those who follow him:

The common people imitate nothing with more pleasure than what they see their prince do. Under a gambler, gambling is rife; under a warrior, everyone is embroiled; under an epicure, all disport is wasteful luxury; under a debauch, license is rampant ... No comet, no dreadful power affects the progress of human affairs as the life of the prince grips and transforms the morals and characteristics of his subjects.[8]

The statement *qual es el Rey tal es el Reyno,* "the kingdom is a reflection of the king," was frequently utilized during the Golden Age to illustrate the exemplary role of the monarch.[9]

The traits of Quevedo's good prince were the standard ones taken over from the Middle Ages.[10] In keeping the common good uppermost in his mind, the king has to rule firmly, vigilantly, carefully, and sagely. He is likened to the physician who brings medicine to alleviate the pains of the state. The true king avoids adulators and flatterers, and grants important posts to those deserving of such honors; he is born to aid the unprotected. Although the ruler relies upon the advice of others, he must not be forced into decisions by his councillors. The authentic king is a good king who imitates Jesus in everything, and provides his subjects with life, health, and freedom.

VI *The Function of the King's Advisors*

A large body of political literature on the role of advisors to the king came into being during the Golden Age.[11] This stemmed from the realization of the incompleteness and fallibility of man, a salient theological concept generally held by political thinkers of that period. Undoubtedly, the increasingly complex task of governing the extended territories of the Spanish Empire highlighted the need for competent councillors in the various government councils. The Bible itself furnished abundant examples demonstrating the need for counsel. Two of the most frequently quoted maxims concerning the indispensability of counsel prior to action were Proverb XII ("A fool is sure that his own way is right: sensible men will listen to advice") and Ecclesiasticus XXXII ("My son, do not do anything without counsel"). In the early part of the sixteenth century, Antonio de Guevara urged that rulers surround themselves with virtuous and experienced counsellors since there is no one so wise in the world that he does not need to rely on the advice of others.[12]

Quevedo, too, was vitally concerned with the function of advisors to the king. In discussing this problem, he deduces his ideas about the nature and duties of the prince's advisors principally from the relationship that existed between Christ and his disciples. He would require the king's ministers to play a role subordinate to the head of the state; their obligation to the king is to keep the king well informed.(PDC, 203) The prince constitutes the supreme terrestrial authority who, with the assistance of ministers, stirs the waters of the pool which represents the earth. (PDC, 108) Of course, the king always must seek the advice of his councillors, but the ruler is admonished not to follow their council slavishly. Quevedo is undoubtedly thinking of the insidious *privados*, "court favorites," usurpers of the monarch's power, when he declares that a faithful advisor may propose all that he wants, but it is the king's responsibility to make decisions on the governing of his dominions. (PDC, 114-16) When Quevedo discusses the recurring Golden Age problem as to whether it is better for the republic to have a good king and bad ministers or a bad king and good ministers, he subscribes to the latter situation.

Many of the characteristics attributed to the king are also applied to the minister. The latter's love for the prince and the people is to guide his every thought and action. Quevedo considers the good minister as one who looks out for the needy. The mission of the king's advisor is divinely chosen; he is to be the path, truth, and life of the people, just like the ruler. Quevedo would destroy the bad ministers, the first of whom was Satan. He would mete out punishment for those who advise badly, a recommendation generally supported by sixteenth- and seventeenth-century writers on politics.

VII   *The Role of Justice*

Justice goes hand in hand with religion in the foundation of
Quevedo's political theory, just as it does for many other Golden
Age writers, whether they were ecclesiastics or not. The king's
personal administration of justice as a keystone of his duties
is clearly expressed by the author of *The Politics of God.* (PDC,
250) Every writer of a political treatise during the sixteenth and
seventeenth centuries dwelt briefly or at length upon the
establishment of justice. Sánchez de Arévalo had quoted St.
Augustine to the effect that no republic could exist without justice
(*op. cit.,* p. 118); Alonso de Castrillo, at the beginning of the
sixteenth century, opined that without justice the entire world
would be corrupt (*op. cit.,* Chapter 29). The outstanding Renaissance humanist, Juan Luis Vives, ascribed to justice a fundamental place in human society when he said that justice is a
fundamental bond of all human societies.[13] Felipe de la Torre
had a Council of Justice as one of his five councils of state.
So important did Furió Ceriol deem the reign of justice in the
structure of the state that he proposed the organization of two
royal councils—the *Concejo de Pena,* "Council of Punishment,"
and the *Concejo de Mercedes,* "Council of Rewards"—to dole out
punishment for crimes and to grant rewards for good deeds.
At the close of the sixteenth century, Pedro de Rivadeneira
expressed very vividly that without justice society would
completely disintegrate.[14]

Quevedo demonstrates his adherence to distributive justice
in advocating that each person should receive what he deserves.
Plato, in the *Laws,* had shown the way for the institution of
distributive justice, later elaborated upon by Aristotle in the
Ethics.[15] Fox Morcillo, who so often followed Plato's line of
reasoning, extolled the virtues of distributive justice in the·whole
republic, proposing that everyone should be the recipient of what
is rightfully due him.[16] In the vein of other commentators on
justice, Quevedo proposes the selection of honest judges to
insure the equitable administration of rewards and punishments.
When there is a matter that pertains particularly to justice in his
own house, the king is exhorted to accord justice by his own hand,
punishing and rewarding in the manner of Christ. A just king
is deemed a true king; when the king did not fulfill his obligations
justly, he might be considered a tyrant.

VIII   *Quevedo Rejects Tyrannicide*

For Quevedo, tyranny is intimately associated with Satan. His conception of a tyrant is that of a person who has ceased to exist and deprives others of existence. Quevedo and many of his contemporaries believed that the extent to which a ruler evidences his desire to foster the public welfare constitutes a fundamental criterion for differentiating between a just prince and a tyrant.

Spanish writers of the sixteenth and seventeenth centuries conceived of two major ways in which a people could react to the tyrannical abuse of regal power: the oppressed people could either accept the government by tyranny, or kill the usurper. Such ecclesiastics as Molina, Soto, Suárez, and Mariana were the outstanding proponents of tyrannicide. Towards the end of the sixteenth century, the famous Jesuit, Mariana, did much to revitalize the medieval adherence to regicide expounded in the *Policraticus* of John of Salisbury (twelfth century). Especially significant in Mariana's *De rege* is the classic Chapter VI, entitled "¿Es lícito matar al tirano?" ("Is It Right to Kill the Tyrant?"), in which he unequivocally declared the affirmative. In wielding the medieval doctrine which taught that tyrannicide is justifiable, or at least excusable, in the event a king ceases to rule well, Mariana concomitantly pushed forward the cause of the people's sovereignty. Furthermore, it is quite probable that his purpose was to limit royal power—which was achieving great ascendancy in western Europe—and to increase, in inverse proportion, that of the papacy.

Quevedo, in an Erasmian attempt to return to the original teachings of the Christians, exemplified primarily in the New Testament, takes a stand diametrically opposed to that of the *monarchomachi*. However, much as he dislikes tyrannical rule, he still naturally allies himself with the majority of Spanish political writers who considered the emergence of a despot as the expression of God's will. It was commonly believed that non-resistance and passive obedience are enjoined by God; consequently, resistance to the divinely ordained king constituted transgression. In the middle of the sixteenth century, this idea was unequivocally expressed by Felipe de la Torre on the first page of his treatise. Juan Ginés de Sepúlveda followed the Thomistic concept that God permits the rise of a tyrant for the chastisement of the people's sins. As a result, the people must patiently bear the *publicus hostis*, "public enemy," until such time as the punishment is ended. Quevedo views tyrants as monsters who incarnate punishment for kingdoms that have abandoned evangelical law.

IX Can War Be Justified?

Most writers on political themes during the Golden Age decried the existence of war, but it was felt, for the most part, that war was inevitable. The theologian's concept that war was brought about by God as the direct chastisement of man's transgressions found fertile soil in the writings of the lay political theorists also. Quevedo avers that war is God's instrument of vengeance for his enemies. He believes that the military precepts of God, exemplified in the Bible, could very well serve in temporal matters. In all affairs of state and in times of war, he opines that everything would fail without the backing of religion and the Scriptures. Not only did God bring war but he also determined whether victory or disaster should result. Quevedo follows the well-established pattern of advocating adequate military education for the prince and his vassals. The author of the *Politics of God* considers it the monarch's function to lead his men personally into battle, even if the leader of the people is a woman!

Quevedo was aware of the problems inherent in justifying war. Yet so strong was his desire to insure religious peace and preserve his country that he even sanctioned war to attain these aims. (PDC, 198) The recommendation that war be used as an instrument to achieve peace was not uncommon among Quevedo's precursors. Mariana proposed this, and other writers echoed these sentiments: Juan Ginés de Sepúlveda in his *De regno (On Kingship)* 1570; and Pedro López de Montoya in his *Libro de buena educación y enseñanza de los nobles (Book of Good Rearing and Education of Nobles)*, 1595. It is pertinent to note that Quevedo's desire for *paz en la religión,* "peace in religion," unquestionably meant the extirpation of heretics from Spain. This is elucidated most vividly in the last chapter of the *Politics* where he states that war is just and holy. He proffers the example of the first war which was that of the angels against heretics. (PDC, 305)

For many of the Spanish writers of the sixteenth and seventeenth centuries, there was only one religion to be tolerated— Catholicism. It was generally believed that diversity of religious

beliefs would cause unrest and internal strife. Quevedo's assaults
in the *Visions* against the "accursed" Lutheranism and other
heresies are no more vitriolic than the incriminations of heretics
authored by many theologians and political theorists. In his
discussion of the royal councils, Bartolomé Felipe considered it
highly important to maintain a body of *Censura,* "Censure," to
watch over the customs of the people and another of *Religión* or
of the *Sancta Inquisición,* "Holy Inquisition," that would keep
the country free from heresy. (*op. cit.,* fol. 16v.) Of all the firm
defenses of Catholicism found in Spanish political treatises of
the Golden Age, perhaps the most fervent was that of Pedro de
Rivadeneira. The following words from this priest demonstrate
his intense desire for unity in religion: *Nuestra santa religión
es como una reina hermosísima y de grande majestad, venida del
cielo, que no admite fealdad, ni diversidad de opiniones . . . así
es imposible que en el mundo espiritual de la Iglesia haya más
de una fe y de una religión. . .* ("Our holy religion is like a very
pretty queen and of great majesty, originating from heaven, which
does not permit ugliness or diversity of opinions . . . thus it is
impossible that in the spiritual world of the Church there be
more than one faith and one belief . . ."). (*op. cit.,* pp. 491-92)

X *Evaluation of the* Política de Dios

The only references made to Spanish Golden Age political
writers found in the *Politics* are to Fadrique Furió Ceriol and
Bartolomé Felipe. Quevedo differs radically from these two men
in his approach to politics. His *Politics* constitutes a superb
example of the highly moral tone intrinsic in political writings
of that time. In the formulation of his concepts on the affairs of
government, Quevedo followed patterns that had been traced
by such men as Francisco de Monzón, Felipe de la Torre, and
Pedro de Rivadeneira, who laid great stress on religio-ethical
themes almost to the exclusion of practical realities of the contemporary scene. Quevedo perceived and attacked the existence
of unwholesome political situations; nevertheless, he rarely
offered tangible, workable advice designed to exterminate abuses
and corruption. A vivid contrast is obtained when Quevedo is
compared to Furió Ceriol, who, while sincerely advocating the
ubiquitous reign of Christian ethics and ideals, set forth a body
of practical recommendations to insure the amelioration of state
affairs. In the matter of offering concrete proposals for achieving

a more efficient operation of governmental processes, Quevedo's treatise certainly must yield to those of Furió and Felipe.

Quevedo's *Politics of God* cannot be regarded as comprising a systematic approach to the study of politics. The author of this work continually discoursed upon the moral behavior of the state's leaders and the ethical foundations of governmental institutions. In his constant endeavor to implant a Christian republic modeled upon the words and actions of Christ and the apostles, he did not treat specific political themes debated throughout the Golden Age. Indeed, a good many ecclesiastics of that period rehearsed numerous concepts—the social nature of man, the reason why monarchy is the best form of government, the location and fortification of the state, the function of the individual royal councils, etc.—which Quevedo completely shunned or mentioned only incidentally. Quevedo could not envision a state without the bedrock of religion revealed in the Scriptures.

The *Politics of God* harmonizes splendidly with most of the Spanish political literature written during the sixteenth and seventeenth centuries. If judged simply according to the nature of its contents, it may be asserted that this treatise could have seen the light of day almost a century before its original appearance. The rhetorical genius of Quevedo, his incisive aphoristic statements, his brilliant knack of varied treatment of a theme with minute analysis, the pervading trenchancy of his style, all contribute to enhance the importance of the *Politics of God* which might have been relegated to the ranks of forgotten books if it had had to rely upon its contents alone.

CHAPTER 8

Quevedo's Theater

QUEVEDO'S theatrical works complement in theme and
style his other writings. Thus, his only surviving full-length
play, *Cómo ha de ser el privado,* contains political and
religious ideas more fully developed in *The Politics of God* and
and the *entremeses,* short satirical plays or interludes that lam-
poon women and marriage, physicians, notaries, dandies, cuckolds, innkeepers, and other types found in the *Visions* and in
The Swindler. Quevedo was more successful as an *entremesista,*
"composer of interludes," than as a writer of *comedias,* "full-
length plays," since the short satirical pieces allowed him the
unbridled freedom to display his *conceptismo* and to permit his
imagination to run riot over a variety of themes in a spontaneous
manner as he did in the *Visions* and *The Hour of All Men.*

I Cómo ha de ser el privado

*Cómo ha de ser el privado (What the King's Favorite Should
Be)* was written between 1627 and 1628. It is essentially a
political play which has the aim of expressing the hopes of
Quevedo and his fellow Spaniards for an improvement in Spain's
political fortunes at the time that Philip IV ascended the throne
and selected the Count-Duke of Olivares to govern his realms.
The historical allusions were unmistakenly clear to the audience
for which it was intended. They could easily see through the
thin disguise of locale and characters: the Court of Naples really
represented that of Madrid, King Ferdinand was really the
monarch of Spain, and the Marquis of Valisero was really the
Count-Duke of Olivares—the anagram is obvious.

The play largely deals with the character and duties of a perfect
privado, "Court favorite," his relationship with the king, and,
to some extent, the conduct of a true Christian monarch. The
two subplots serve to highlight the functions of the *privado* and
his king. In one of the minor plots, the king realizes his public
role overshadows his private life in his relationship to Serafina,

149

a lady-in-waiting at the Court. He loved her before ascending the throne, and is still in love with her; but the necessity of protecting his public image dictates that he conquer his passion for her. In addition, he is reluctant to hurt Serafina's feelings. The *privado's* wise counsel aids the king in arriving at his decision. The second subplot, more significant than the first, revolves about the choice of a husband for the *Infanta,* Doña Margarita, who represents Doña María, the sister of Philip IV. After seeking the advice of his *privado,* the king decides that his sister should marry the King of Transylvania—in reality Ferdinand III of Hungary whom the *Infanta* married in 1626—because he is a Catholic, whereas the other suitor, the Prince of Denmark, is not. This choice is mandatory in view of the legion of Spanish political treatises which almost invariably required that the Spanish monarch be a Catholic king. The outcome of the play is already evident toward the end of the first act. The Marquis tells the king that he should extend the utmost hospitality to the Prince of Denmark, (historically the Prince of Wales) but he cannot approve the marriage between the king's sister and a heretic. Immediately thereafter the *Infanta* declares that she cannot consider becoming the wife of a man who espouses another religion.

As we have seen in the chapter on politics, political theorists of the Golden Age generally supported the idea that the king, no matter how powerful, wise and just he might be, always had need of good advisors. The *privado* or *valido* "prime minister," serving as the most trusted of all the king's counsellors, was to possess the most sterling characteristics. He must honestly and frankly advise the king, always keeping in mind that the king is the supreme ruler of the land. He must be completely selfless in aiding the king to achieve greatness. In the play, the *valido* stoically receives the news that his only son has died, and declares that his service to the king must take precedence over mourning for the loss. When the king wishes to reward the *valido* handsomely for his services, the latter says that his financial needs are very small especially in view of the loss of his only heir, and adds that his faithful service to the king is sufficient to sustain him.

This glorification of the Count-Duke of Olivares as a model *privado* is deficient in dramatic interest and is undoubtedly more appropriate for reading than for production on the stage. Quevedo's attempts to expose the psychological conflicts of the characters fail to convince. Unlike the popular plays of the time, action is kept at a minimum, and there is a lot of talk concerning the motives and feelings of the characters, all of which would undoubtedly fail to interest an audience fond of plays written by Lope de Vega and his contemporaries.

It appears that Quevedo wrote only the beginning of the first act of a projected full-length play, *Pedro Vázquez de Escamillas*. Escamillas is apparently an obstreperous, defiant fellow from Seville whom Don Juan of Austria freed from the galleys as a reward for his gallant service during the Battle of Lepanto. He bursts upon the scene with his sword in his mouth and naked except for his soaking pantaloons. He has just swum across the Guadalquivir River, hotly pursued by the police for having killed two men in Triana. Without taking any time to rest, he arrogantly subdues a fight among four men who cower before Escamillas on hearing his name. The truncated first act ends with the brief exchange of flowery speeches between the typical young noble and his sweetheart.

There also remains the fragment of a play which Quevedo wrote on the reverse side of a letter. All that we can glean from this fragment is that it was possibly intended to criticize marriage.

II   *The* entremeses

As a playwright Quevedo achieved notable success in his short dramatic pieces, the popular *entremeses*. The word *entremés* comes from the French *entremets,* "a dish served at dinner between the principal courses," and denoted festal pieces accompanied by singing. We know that *entremeses* already were performed in the early fifteenth century, and it is very probable that they were of Valencian origin. By the second half of the sixteenth century, every short dramatic piece, whether in verse or in prose, was called an *entremés* which may be translated as "interlude." In the first half of the sixteenth century, Lope de Rueda (d. 1565), one of the founders of Spanish drama, popularized his own brand of interlude, the *paso* in prose. The *paso* was comic in nature, and its main characters were popular types such as the fool, the shepherd, the farmer, and the Basque. They were practically devoid of plot, and their interest for the audience stemmed from the lively dialogue and the picturesque charm of their rustic scenes. The *pasos* were staged at the beginning of plays or between the acts, or sometimes were inserted in the main action of the play.

The *entremeses,* utilized in a manner similar to that of the *pasos,* served to relieve the boredom that might affect the audience between acts of a play. They varied in length and character. Usually two *entremeses* were represented with a play, but at times there was only one and sometimes there were three. In his youth, Lope de Vega wrote *entremeses,* usually three, to insert between the acts of his full-length plays.[1] It is generally accepted that Cervantes surpassed all other writers of the genre. His interludes, in part modeled after Lope de Rueda's *pasos* which he admired, are notable for their realistic, lively dialogue, true-to-life characters, and benevolent humor that never becomes bitter even when it is satirical.

There was a proliferation of *entremeses* in the seventeenth century. The most prolific writer of them was Luis Quiñones de Benavente (d. 1651) who is supposed to have written as many as nine hundred short dramatic pieces. Endowed with a polished satirical style, Quiñones de Benavente was able to dramatize the customs, the social types, and the actions of the society of his time, and usually censured the morals of the characters he created. Quevedo does not lag behind Lope de Rueda, Cervantes, and Quiñones de Benavente as an *entremesista.* His short, satirical, dramatic scenes vividly recall his other comic works and especially the *Visions* in wit, style, and in the types and situations lampooned. Perfidious, golddigging women who usually triumph over man play the most significant roles in his interludes as we shall see in our discussion. His *entremeses* are typically of varying length and some are written in prose and some in poetry.

Most if not all of Quevedo's *entremeses* were probably written in the second and third decades of the seventeenth century. Of the eleven *entremeses* included in the Aguilar edition of Quevedo's *Obras completas,* edited by Felicidad Buendía, I have rejected two as being apocryphal in view of Armando Cotarelo Valledor's evaluation of them.[2] To this we shall add the five *entremeses* recently published by Eugenio Asensio: the two parts of the *Entremés de Diego Moreno,* the *Entremés de la vieja Muñatones,* the *Entremés de la destreza, La polilla de Madrid,* and the two parts of the *Entremés de Bárbara.*[3]

My discussion of Quevedo's *entremeses* will be divided according to the characters who dominate their action: (A) importunate women, (B) effeminate men and cuckolds, (C) bawds like Celestina, (D) female delinquents, and (E) other types.

A. *Importunate women*

El caballero de la Tenaza (*Sir Tightwad*), first published in 1657, represents the familiar struggle between a golddigging woman and a man who is loath to part with his money. Sir Tightwad was a character in an early prose work by Quevedo and is also mentioned in the preface to *The Swindler*. In this very short piece, Anzuelo (literally meaning "fishhook") unsuccessfully tries to wheedle money from Tenaza and he foils her effort to pull a ring off his finger. The interlude ends in song and dance as is the case in many *entremeses* of the time. A group of female dancers chorus Anzuelo's demands for money, and another group of male dancers support Tenaza's refusal to submit. The play ends in a stalemate.

El niño y Peralvillo de Madrid (*The Child and Peralvillo*[4] *of Madrid*) is the story of a young boy, Perico, whose mother cautions him about the dangers of Madrid prior to his departure for that city. In Madrid, he meets the knife sharpener, Juan Francés, who introduces Perico to five victims of women's wiles. In their efforts to satisfy the demands of women for clothing, jewelry, fancy meals, entertainment, and gifts, these men were destroyed just as the criminals were tortured by the Holy Office of the Inquisition in the true Peralvillo. Three women accost him in Madrid, but he has learned his lesson well and refuses to give them anything. At the end of the interlude, Perico promises to give the girls something if they sing. When one asks what it can be, he replies that he will gladly give all his attention to their singing and playing on their stringed instruments.

El marido fantasma (*The Ghost Husband*) is a satire against marriage and more particularly a criticism of mothers-in-law and relatives of the wife. The dandy, Muñoz, would like to get married to a woman who has no mother, no female relatives, no girl friends or maids. Muñoz falls asleep, and while dreaming he hears and sees his friend Lobón who has married and is suffering at the hands of his in-laws, his marriage broker, and a *dueña*. Lobón disappears and Muñoz awakes to find Doña Oromasia de Brimbronques who is extremely eager to get married. But she is a frightening creature with the air of death about her, and Muñoz promptly refuses to marry her or anybody else. Lobón reappears, this time as a widower. He advises Muñoz to marry just to have the pleasure of becoming a widower also. Muñoz accepts his advice and prepares to marry Doña Oromasia, certain that his wife will last less than a year. The wedding takes place amid singing and dancing.

B. *Effeminate men and cuckolds*

The main character of the two-part *entremés* entitled *El marión* (*The Sissy*), first published in 1646, is Constanzo, an effeminate dandy who is pursued by three ladies who serenade him and even propose to fight over him. This is a complete reversal of the customary Golden Age plays in which only males vie with each other in duels, and is reminiscent of what occurs in *The Hour of All Men*. In the topsy-turvy situation depicted in the first part of the interlude, the father of Constanzo is as deeply concerned over the tarnishing of his son's honor as if Constanzo were a girl. Constanzo gets married in the second part, and his wife mistreats him verbally and physically. Neighbors intervene to remedy the situation, but to no avail. Finally, musicians enter and Constanzo begins to dance as the play ends. This interlude seems to have been a source for Quiñones de Benavente's *Los mariones*, which develops the theme more but softens the grotesque exaggerations of Quevedo's version.

The complaisant husband was evidently one of the types Quevedo enjoyed lampooning. The last of the legendary types parodied in "The Vision of Death" was Diego Moreno, the permissive husband, who claims that an *entremés* was made of his life. Asensio has revealed that the sixteenth-century Spanish dramatist Fernán Gonzáles de Eslava inserted an *entremés* of Diego Moreno and Teresa in his work *Coloquio séptimo de Jonás Profeta*.[5] He has also shown that Diego Moreno was a popular figure in the ballads of the sixteenth century. The cuckold appears in Quevedo's *Premáticas y aranceles generales*, in "El mundo por de dentro," and in a satirical ballad[6] in which the cuckold coughs loudly and announces that he has just entered the house so that the wife might know what to do in case she is entertaining a male guest in her boudoir. Poetic justice prevails in this two-part *entremés* which is perhaps the best written by Quevedo.

In the first scene of *Diego Moreno*, Don Beltrán and his friend, the captain, are evidently on their way to visit Doña Justa. Beltrán informs the captain, who has just returned from service in Flanders, that the beautiful, golddigging Justa is unfaithful to her husband, Diego Moreno, who is resigned to his wife's infidelities. His acceptance of cuckoldry occurred a month after he married Doña Justa. When he arrived home unexpectedly and saw his wife in an embrace with her lover, he was not piqued in the least and surprisingly invited the other man to embrace him also since he considered himself a friend of the intruder. From that time on, he would always make loud noises when entering the house, just in case his wife was entertaining, and he would never ask his wife questions which might embarrass her. When Diego Moreno returns home near the end of the first part of the *entremés*, he finds his wife entertaining four male visitors: Beltrán, the captain, a doctor, and an ecclesiastic with whom she had made love the night before. Alerted to Diego Moreno's arrival home, Justa feigns illness related to her pregnancy, and the four visitors crowd around her pretending to help in alleviating her suffering. The distressed husband cannot penetrate the circle of suitors in his attempt to get close to his wife, and he assumes the blame for his wife's feigned condition.

In the second part of the play, Diego Moreno has already died, and Justa does not wish to endure widowhood longer than necessary. Consequently, she marries her former lover, Diego Berdugo (*verdugo* means executioner) who is the complete opposite of the complaisant Diego Moreno. Berdugo opposes every whim of Justa. During the wedding celebration Justa pretends to faint in order to embrace a lover, and the clever Berdugo promptly cures her of her illness by placing a lighted candle near her hand. The lyrics of the songs that terminate the *entremés* indicate that Berdugo will try to keep close vigil over his wife, but Justa's ever-smoldering desire to deceive is implicit in the repeated verses of the chorus: "To seek constancy during one's absence/ is to seek pears on an elm tree."[7]

In *Los refranes del viejo celoso* (*The Proverbs of the Jealous Old Man*), Quevedo makes use of a traditional theme in literature. The plot of an old man who marries a pretty young girl can be found in one of the medieval tales collected by Pero Alfonso in which the young wife's lover is concealed behind a leather hanging. In the fifteenth century, the Archpriest of Talavera used this trick in *El corbacho*, and Cervantes resorted to it in his interlude, *El viejo celoso* (*The Jealous Old Man*). In addition, *The Jealous Extremaduran*, one of his *Exemplary Novels*, is based on the same theme.

In Quevedo's *entremés*, a poor student makes love to the scatterbrained young wife of an old man. The student manages to

escape undetected while the wife pretends to remove a straw
from her old husband's eye. In the second part, a host of imaginary types that appear in "The Vision of Death" appear as the
old man names each one in a proverb. Some of the proverbial
characters who appear are: Calaínos, dressed as a Frenchman,
who is the teller of insignificant tales; Juan del Encina, who
is known for his absurd statements; the fool, Perico; Maricastaña,
the ancient *dueña*; the decrepit *dueña*, Quintañona; and Pero
Grullo, who always makes gratuitous remarks. The proverbial
figures vigorously rain blows upon the old man as the interlude
ends. The appearance of proverbial figures is found in another
entremés, Las sombras (*The Shades*), which was formerly attributed to Quevedo, and also in *Las carnestolendas* (*The Carnival
of Shrovetide*), an interlude written by Calderón de la Barca.

C. *The Celestinesque female*

The Celestinesque figure has had a rich tradition in Spanish
literature. The most famous example of this type plays a prom-
inent role in *La Celestina* (1499), the only work of Fernando de
Rojas. Celestina's servant Pármeno relates in Act I the several
talents of Celestina: she is a seamstress, a perfumer, an expert
in preparing cosmetics, a mender of maidenheads, a procuress,
and a bit of a witch. This bawd appeared as Trotaconventos in
the Archpriest of Hita's poetic work, *The Book of Good Love*, and
her characteristics are found in women who appear in the
Archpriest of Talavera's anti-feminist writing. This type appeared
in the Spanish Golden Age theater and novel, especially in Lope
de Vega's *La Dorotea* and *El caballero de Olmedo*. Quevedo
satirizes this type in his *Visions,* and Pablo de Segovia's mother
and the bawd Mary in Chapter 8 of *The Swindler* have Celestinesque traits.

In *La vieja Muñatones* (*Old Muñatones*), the procuress who
provides the title for the *entremés* tenders sage advice to the
prostitutes in her establishment on how to wheedle from their
clients the most amount of money for their services. The devilish
Muñatones provides her girls with implements for weaving to
veil their true trade in case the police raid the house. When
the sheriff and his notary come to investigate what is going on in
Muñatones' domicile, they are confused on seeing the girls
weaving. Muñatones tells the girls to take a rest from their
"labors" and suggests that they dance with their gentlemen

callers. The interlude ends in the customary dance and song in which allusion is made to extracting money from men.

La destreza (*Skill*), a work probably written in 1624, returns to the theme of the bawd who gives her pupils a lesson in verse on how to beguile men into loosening their purse strings, using metaphors taken from the art of fencing.[8] When the sheriff and his notary come to investigate the activities in Mother Monda's house, she informs them that she is teaching her girls to use the castanets. The playlet ends amid dancing and singing, with lyrics reminiscent of those in the previous interlude.

The final play to be discussed in this section is *La ropavejera* (*The Remnant Lady*), which was first published in 1670. She rejuvenates people by cleverly covering up gray hair, by restoring a youthful appearance to wrinkled old hands, by changing hairdos, by providing false teeth, by using depilatories on hairy women, and by plastic surgery. We see Ropavejera using a cloth to wipe the faces of all the characters who perform the expected song and dance routine at the end of the *entremés*.

D. Female Delinquents

The heroines of the two interludes in this section—Bárbara of the *entremés* of the same name, and Elena of *La polilla de Madrid* (*The Swindler of Madrid*)—exhibit traits of the female rogue. Both are attractive women who perpetrate tricks on their suitors. This calls to mind the deceits of such female delinquents as Justina, especially in the fourth book of *La pícara Justina* (1605), written by Francisco López de Ubeda, and Elena in *La hija de Celestina* (*The Daughter of Celestina*), by Alonso de Salas Barbadillo, published in 1612 and republished in 1614 in an enlarged version with the title *La ingeniosa Elena* (*The Ingenious Helen*).

The subterfuge employed by Bárbara is mentioned in Chapter 2 of the first part of *Guzmán de Alfarache*, and is also found in a prose interlude, *La mamola* (*The Female Deceiver*). Bárbara, the concubine of Hartacho, is an irresistible, strong-willed woman who believes that men should satisfy her every whim. At the outset of the first part of the interlude, Bárbara tells Hartacho that anyone who wishes to enjoy her must give a lot of himself in return. If a suitor should come to her house while she is with another, he must either return on some other occasion or hide his presence. When she is sad, the suitor should make her happy; when she is cheerful, he should caress her; when she is offended, he should take revenge for her; when she is cold, he should put a cloak around her shoulders; and when she is hot, he should fan her. Bárbara schemes to obtain money and jewels from a number of her suitors at once by informing each one that he is the father of a child to whom she has just given birth. In reality, a new baby has been hired to carry out her trick. She plans to use these contributions from her suitors as a dowry for her impending marriage to an innocent young Italian from Gelves. In the final dance of the first part of the interlude, Hartacho and three suitors attend the wedding and hear Bárbara say that women must not keep faith with anybody.

In the second part, we learn that Bárbara has become a widow not too long after her marriage. Her husband had sailed to the New World with all Bárbara's jewels and reportedly drowned near the shores of Florida. Once again she is besieged by the former suitors who bring valuable gifts. Just as she is about to marry the jealous Ascanio, Octavio, her "dead" husband, returns. He had feigned death in order to test his wife's fidelity. Unperturbed by this trick played upon her, Bárbara welcomes her resuscitated husband. As the playlet ends, the musicians sing of the primacy of the first love. Asensio has pointed out several elements which demonstrate this interlude's affinity with the Italian *Commedia dell'arte*: the chance events, the novelistic ingredients of travels and resuscitated husbands, the final triumph of the woman in love, the vertiginous effect of excessive action within the framework of a short play, and the deliberate repetition in triplicate found in the dialogue and in the action of the interlude.[9]

Elena of *The Swindler of Madrid* is the typical Quevedesque female, expert in coaxing money from male friends. She manages to cajole a number of gallants into contributing jewels and finery for an amateur play in which she, her mother, her sister, and her pander will act. For this purpose she has hired a rehearsal hall from an actor. When the boyfriends arrive to witness the play, they find that the hall is completely empty.

E. *Types or* figuras.

The central theme that runs through the three interludes in this section is the hypocrisy of various types whom Quevedo often disparaged in his satirical writings. The attitudes and actions of these *figuras* and the witty style utilized to caricaturize them will offer no novelty to the reader who is already familiar with the *Visions, The Hour of All Men* and *The Swindler.*

El zurdo alanceador (*The Left-Handed Picador*) was first published in 1628. It appears to be a *sueño* in miniature: a magistrate sits in judgment of four people and obliges them to confess their true motives in life. Don González appears before the judge and portrays himself as a would-be gentleman whose exaggerated public behavior reveals that he is a mockery of all that a true gentleman should represent. When he rides into the bullring, he is always the last of the *picadores* and is so frightened of the bull that he tells his horse to stay clear of that animal. But like the hidalgo Don Toribio in *The Swindler,* he must keep up with false appearance. He blames his horse for cowardly conduct and shouts insults at him, but when they return home, he begs forgiveness of the horse.

Zaraza is another annoying type who at first supplies the judge with information on the hypocritical practices of the people of Madrid. Ostensibly an hidalgo, he is in reality a sponger and an inveterate rogue at heart. Two female types are exposed: the sempiternal importunate woman, in the figure of Luisa; and the prostitute, represented by Doña Lorenza who prides herself on enhancing Spain's reputation by providing inexpensive remade "virgins" for visiting foreigners.

In the interlude *El hospital de los malcasados* (*The Hospital for Mismated People*), Quevedo once again assails doctors. The charlatan, Escaramujo, prescribes nonsensical cures for four people who seek his advice: the wife of a profligate poet; a young girl married to a seventy-year-old man; a man who has been widowed twelve times and is now married to a young woman; and a man married to a jealous old woman. When the sheriff arrives to raid the hospital, they all pretend to be acting in a play. Finally, in *La venta* (*The Inn*), first published in 1627, Quevedo satirizes the innkeepers who steal from the guests, water the wine, and serve abominable food.

III Bailes *and* Jácaras

Music, dancing, and singing usually accompany the plays of the seventeenth century. Quevedo followed custom in having his *entremeses* end in a *baile,* "dance."[10] When actors were contracted for a theatrical company, it was generally required that they sing and dance in addition to act. The *bailes* are found inserted in plays, at the end of *entremeses,* and also as separate entities. The satirical and burlesque *bailes* were sung or recited in monologue or dialogue form, and some were performed totally in pantomime. Almost all the writers of *entremeses,* especially Quiñones de Benavente, composed *bailes.* They became so coarse and licentious—in particular the *zarabanda,* the *chacona,* and the *escarramán*—that many theatergoers were scandalized and the authorities had to suppress them.

Quevedo's *bailes* display the stylistic virtuosity which we have seen in other works. His *bailes* typically represent people from the lowest stratum of society and admirably capture their argot. All of them are in ballad form and are recited. Thieves, importunate women, pimps, galley slaves, beggars, hypocritical types of the Court, drunkards, and swindlers take part in the scintillating *bailes.*

Quevedo also wrote a considerable number of *jácaras,* short burlesque or satirical pieces sung between the acts of a full-length play. These boisterous ballads, sung in the dialect of the criminals, received their name from the *jaques,* the bullies who sang them. These lively and witty songs rarely lasted more than ten or fifteen minutes. Quevedo's *jácaras* were evidently very successful. In his exemplary tale, *El rufián viudo,* Cervantes considered as divine Quevedo's famous *jácara* of *Escarramán.*

CHAPTER 9

Conclusion

A cursory examination of the bibliography of Quevedo's writings found in Felicidad Buendía's edition of his complete works (4th edition, Madrid: Aguilar, 1960, II, 1272-1357) reveals his continued appeal to the present day. Spanish editions have appeared throughout the Spanish-speaking world and translations of his best-known works have been published in English and in all Western-European tongues. In recent years, *The Swindler* has even been translated twice into Russian (1950 and 1956) and once into Serbo-Croatian (1951). Alejandro Casona's last play, *El caballero de las espuelas de oro* (*The Gentleman with the Golden Spurs*), 1965, is based on Quevedo's life. The publishing house Gredos has placed Quevedo's picture on the dust jacket of the voluminous second tome of Juan Luis Alborg's *Historia de la literatura española* (1967), which treats Spanish literature of the seventeenth century from Cervantes on.

Quevedo's writings have directly and obliquely left their mark on Hispanic writers. The patent influence of the *Visions* is observed in Luis Vélez de Guevara's *El diablo conjuelo* (*The Crippled Devil*), 1641, a social satire that has some resemblance to the picaresque novel. The Portuguese writer Francisco Manuel de Melo (1608-1666), who wrote poetry and prose works in Spanish as well as in Portuguese, openly admitted and revealed in his writings the influence of his friend Quevedo. Sor Juana Inés de la Cruz, the celebrated seventeenth-century Mexican writer, has been shown to have undergone the influence of Quevedo as well as that of Góngora. Seventeenth-century critics of Spanish mores, notably Francisco de Santos and Juan de Zabaleta, exhibit apparent stylistic and thematic influence of Quevedo. Diego de Torres y Villarroel's imitation of Quevedo was so overt that he was commonly called the eighteenth-century Quevedo; his deliberate efforts to follow in Quevedo's footsteps are manifest in his poetry as well as in prose works such as *Sueños morales* (*Moral Visions*), 1727-1751, in which the author, guided by Quevedo, passes through the streets of Madrid

161

satirizing the types and customs of his day. Quevedo is one of the main sources of inspiration for José Cadalso, an eighteenth-century Spanish poet. In the nineteenth century, Mariano José de Larra's mordant satire of the Spanish people and their customs, motivated by a strong feeling of patriotism, seems to be in consonance with Quevedo's spirit.

Dámaso Alonso has graphically pointed out Quevedo's attraction for himself and other twentieth-century Spanish writers: a searing anguish of which Unamuno's literary output is the best example.[1] Indeed, we do find in twentieth-century Spanish poets and prose writers a predilection for Quevedo and other Golden Age writers. Quevedo's style and world view can be traced to other Spaniards besides Unamuno and Dámaso Alonso —for example, Juan José Domenchina, Ramón del Valle-Inclán, Ramón Gómez de la Serna, José Bergamín, Rafael Alberti, Miguel Hernández, and Blas de Otero. In Spanish America, Quevedo has been a source of inspiration for the Chilean poet Pablo Neruda. Jorge Luis Borges, an Argentine writer who is one of the finest literary figures in modern Latin America, has declared his admiration for Quevedo's writings, and there exists some affinity between his style and that of Quevedo, especially in *Inquisitions* (1925).

In all of Spanish literature, few writers have possessed Quevedo's talent for understanding so profoundly and disclosing so cogently the essential genius of the Spaniards. His literary production has gripped the minds of many generations and will undoubtedly continue to endure.

Notes and References

Preface

1. *Poesía española: Ensayo de métodos y límites estilísticos,* 3rd ed. (Madrid: Gredos, 1962), pp. 518-19.
2. *Historia de la lengua española* (Madrid: Escelicer, 1942), p. 181.
3. *El valle de Josafat* (Buenos Aires: Austral, 1944), pp. 35-36.
4. *Otras inquisiciones* (Buenos Aires: Emecé, 1960), p. 64. This statement was originally written in 1945, on the three hundredth anniversary of Quevedo's death.

Chapter Two

1. This libel against Quevedo was reprinted in Luis Astrana Marín's edition of Quevedo's *Obras completas* (Madrid: Aguilar, 1943), II, 1091-1159. The quote above is from the long title of the work, p. 1091.
2. José Manuel Blecua, in the introduction to his edition of Quevedo's *Obras completas* (Barcelona: Editorial Planeta, 1963), p. LV.
3. Quevedo, *Obras completas* (Madrid: Aguilar, 1961), pp. 1352-53. This work on Job was finished by the end of 1641 and first published in 1713.
4. Quevedo, *Obras completas* (Madrid: Aguilar, 1960), II, 975.
5. Tarsia's life of Quevedo is found in Luis Astrana Marín's edition of Quevedo's *Obras completas* (Madrid: Aguilar, 1943), II, 741-79. Tarsia's biography is replete with factual errors. He did not know Quevedo personally and he supposedly drew his material from people who knew Quevedo and also from numerous documents.
6. *La vida turbulenta de Quevedo* (Madrid: Editorial Gran Capitán, 1945), p. 575.

Chapter Three

1. "The Dream" in *Lucian* (London and New York: W. Heineman and Macmillan, 1921), III, 231, translated by A. M. Harmon.
2. *Obras completas de Francisco de Quevedo* (Madrid: Aguilar, 1961), edited by Felicidad Buendía. From this note on, all references to this edition will appear as O.C. in the text proper.
3. *Nueva Biblioteca de Autores Españoles* (1907), VII, 119b.

4. Act II, Scene 19 of *La vida es sueño* by Pedro Calderón de la Barca. The life-is-a-dream theme is repeated in the *auto sacramental, La vida es sueño,* and seven other plays by Calderón. See Ludwig Pfandl, *Historia de la literatura nacional española en la edad de oro* (Barcelona: Sucesores de Juan Gili, 1933), p. 247.

5. For a detailed analysis comparing thematically and stylistically the paintings of Bosch and the visions of Quevedo see Margarita Levisi, "Hieronymus Bosch y los *Sueños* de Francisco de Quevedo," *Filología,* IX, (1963), 163-200.

6. José López-Rey, *Goya's Caprichos* (Princeton: Princeton University Press, 1953), I, 78, 200.

7. See Quevedo, *Obras completas,* ed. of Luis Astrana Marín (Madrid: Aguilar, 1943), II, 1375-1455, for a long list of the Spanish editions and translations of the *Visions.*

8. The titles of three other *sueños* were altered also: "El alguacil endemoniado" ("The Bedevilled Constable"), written in 1607, became "El alguacil alguacilado" ("The Outwitted Constable"); "El sueño del infierno" ("The Vision of Hell"), written in 1608, became "Las zahurdas de Plutón" ("Pluto's Pigsties"); and "El sueño de la muerte" ("The Vision of Death'), written in 1622, became "La visita de los chistes" ("The Visit Filled with Jokes"). Only "El mundo por de dentro" ("The World from Within") did not require a new title for obvious reasons.

9. Angel Valbuena Prat, *Historia de la literatura española* (Barcelona: Editorial Gustavo Gili, 1946), I, 1001.

10. This word is derived from the Greek *mónos,* "one," and *pantos,* "all," meaning "the one of all people" or "omnipotent."

11. In order to glimpse Quevedo's *conceptismo* here, it should be noted that one of the peddlers sold combs and the other was a scissors grinder.

12. Cejador y Frauca states in his edition of the *Sueños* (Madrid: Ediciones "La Lectura," 1916-1917), I, 57-58, that he found an edition of Psellus' *Dialogus de energia, seu operatione daemonum* (Venice, 1516) which was possibly annotated by Quevedo himself. Psellus was a famous Byzantine writer of the eleventh century. Coleridge referred his reader to Psellus' work according to Maximilian Rudwin, *The Devil in Legend and Literature* (Chicago: Open Court Publishing Co., 1931), p. 18. Rudwin also shows in his work (p. 24) that Luther's followers believed in all sorts of devils, such as the devil of blasphemy, the dance-devil, the servant's devil, the drink devil, etc.

13. According to superstitious belief, left-handed people were considered sinister.

14. See Rudwin, *op. cit., pp.* 45-46.

15. Cf. the machinations of the *dueña* in *El celoso extremeño* by Cervantes.

16. Amédée Mas, *La caricature de la femme, du mariage et de*

l'amour dans l'oeuvre de Quevedo (Paris: Ediciones Hispano-Americanas, 1957), p. 11.

17. *Día y noche de Madrid* (1663), reprinted in BAE, XXXIII (1924), 401b. "You are worse than the devil who, in order to establish sin in the world, used your face and called you his lawyer, since you are the principal instrument that caused sin to enter nature."

18. See José Goyanes Capdevilla, *Sátira contra los médicos y la medicina en los libros de Quevedo* (Madrid, 1934), pp. 11-14.

19. Amédée Mas in his edition of *Las zahurdas de Plutón* (Poitiers, 1955), p. 95.

20. See his article "La sociedad española según Quevedo y las Cortes de Castilla" in *Abside,* XVI (1952), 321-43. Berumen's study covers only the transactions of the Cortes included in Volumes 18 through 32.

21. In his edition of *Las zahurdas de Plutón,* p. 94.

22. José López-Rey in *Goya's Caprichos,* pp. 71-72.

23. J. H. Elliott, *Imperial Spain* (London: Edward Arnold, Ltd., 1963), p. 295.

24. Américo Castro, *The Structure of Spanish History* (Princeton: Princeton University Press, 1954), p. 193.

25. Baltasar Gracián, *El criticón,* Part II, crisis xi, in *Obras completas* (Madrid: Aguilar, 1944), pp. 659-60.

26. This is found in *Poesía original,* Volume I of *Obras completas,* edited by José Manuel Blecua (Barcelona: Editorial Planeta, 1963), p. 734.

27. See Julio Cejador y Frauca's edition of the *Sueños,* I, 170, 175, and Raúl A. Del Piero, "Algunas fuentes de Quevedo," *Nueva Revista de Filología Hispánica,* XX (1958), 36-52. It is shown that Quevedo used principally the book of a fourteenth-century bishop, Philastrius, entitled *Philastrii episcopi brixiensis haereseon catalogus* (Basle, 1528) and also the catalogues of Juan Ravisio Textor, *Joannis Ravissi Textoris Officinae* (Leyden, 1585).

28. See John A. Crow, *Spain: The Root and the Flower* (New York: Harper and Row, 1963), for other examples of presumptive proofs used to determine if a person was a Judaizer. Among other things, a person was accused of being a Jew if he wore better clothes on the Jewish Sabbath, if he ate with Jews, or if he gave Hebrew names to his children (p. 146).

29. Guillermo Díaz Plaja, *El espíritu del barroco* (Barcelona: Apolo, 1940), pp. 74-75.

Chapter Four

1. Critics have generally vacillated between 1603 and 1608 for the termination of the *Buscón* manuscript. All my references to the *Buscón* are from Américo Castro's revised Clásicos Castellanos edition

(Madrid, 1927) in which Castro uses a manuscript extant in the Biblioteca de Menéndez y Pelayo of Santander to correct his earlier edition of 1911 which was based on the first printed version (Zaragoza, 1626). The title of the manuscript in the Biblioteca de Menéndez y Pelayo is *La vida del Buscavida, por otro nombre don Pablos* (*The Life of the Swindler, Known as Paul*) and that of the Zaragoza edition is *Historia de la vida del Buscón, llamado don Pablos, ejemplo de vagamundos y espejo de tacaños* (*The Life Story of the Great Rascal Paul, an Exemplary Vagabond and an Ideal Sharper*). Hereafter, BAC will designate Castro's 1927 edition (1960 printing).

2. The most authoritative and complete study of *pícaro* is found in Juan Corominas, *Diccionario crítico etimológico de la lengua castellana* (Madrid: Gredos, 1954), III, 768-71.

3. This promise of a second part appears only in the manuscript which Castro uses for his 1927 edition of the *Buscón*. Castro informs us that in the eighteenth century a *Tercera parte del Gran Tacaño* was published, but this work, which deals with life in the Philippine Islands, has not even the slightest connection with Quevedo's *Buscón* (BAC, 270).

4. Américo Castro (BAC, 247, note for line 2) informs us that the wooing of nuns was an ancient custom, and especially prevalent during the sixteenth and seventeenth centuries.

5. I am indebted to Gerald Wade who first suggested this avenue of analysis to me.

6. Norman O. Brown, in *Life against Death* (New York: Vintage Books, 1961), after observing that Freudian theory views the anal product as a child's symbol of self-gratification, gift-giving to obtain love, the assertion of independence, and the expression of aggression, states: "When infantile sexuality comes to its catastrophic end, nonbodily cultural objects inherit the symbolism originally attached to the anal product, but only as second-best substitutes for the original (sublimations). Sublimations are thus symbols of symbols. The category of property is most simply transferred from feces to money; on the contrary, money is feces, because the anal erotism continues in the unconscious. The anal erotism has not been renounced or abandoned but repressed." (p. 191)

7. Notice that Quevedo uses *hijo de algo* (literally "son of something") from which "hidalgo" is derived. He undoubtedly does this to contrast *algo*, "something," with *nada*, "nothing." For a discussion of the origin of the word "hidalgo" see Américo Castro, *The Structure of Spanish History* (Princeton: Princeton University Press, 1954), pp. 100-101, note 34.

8. See BAC, pp. 247-48, note 3, for a discussion of this practice at the time when many women lived in the large number of convents in Spain. Santa Teresa was scandalized by the immorality in the convents, and several other writers of the time censured this custom.

Castro ascribes the courting of nuns to *discreteo y juego sentimental,* "a display of wit and a sentimental game."

9. In *The Structure of Spanish History,* Castro states: "And this polemical dualism between consciousness and conduct is precisely the premise from which derives the permanent and universal quality of Spanish civilization—*vivir desviviéndose*—one of whose expressions is the literature of the Golden Age." (p. 94)

Chapter Five

1. The use of artifice in style is probably as old as literature itself. Ernst R. Curtius in his *European Literature and Latin Middle Ages* (New York: Pantheon, 1953) has shown that Spanish baroque writers utilized medieval Latin theory and practice (pp. 273-301). Spanish Renaissance treatises on rhetoric and letter writing emphasize style as do the medieval works, and frequent attention is paid to the achievement of unusual stylistic effects.

2. My discussion of this *sueño* takes into account the material added to it in the *Juguetes,* which is found in Cejador y Frauca's Clásicos Castellanos edition (1916-1917), II, 49-56.

3. Found in José Manuel Blecua's edition of Quevedo's *Poesías originales* (Barcelona: Editorial Planeta, 1963), pp. 972-75. Unless otherwise noted, future references to Quevedo's poetry will be from this edition and so indicated in the text proper.

4. Other examples of cold scorn returned for the poet's burning love are found on pages 342, 344, 363, 372, and 471 of the Blecua edition.

5. A similar pun on Ponce occurs in the *jácara,* "merry ballad," *En casa de las sardinas* (*In the home of the sardines*). Blecua, 1249

6. For an excellent study of the use of anaphora in Quevedo's poetry, see Ernesto Veres D'Ocón's "La anáfora en la lírica de Quevedo," *Boletín de la Sociedad Castellonense de Cultura,* XXXV (Oct.-Dec. 1949), 289-303.

7. Elias Rivers has made an excellent translation of this poem in his anthology *Renaissance and Baroque Poetry of Spain* (New York: Dell Publishing Co., 1966), pp. 288-89.

8. In the second stanza of this series, *vieja* is the second word, but this in no way nullifies the effect of the repeated use of the word.

9. Notice Quevedo's superb utilization of antithesis in the felicitous expression *en blanco* whose second word means not only "blank" but also "white."

10. Cf. the list of rabbis who attended the conference on the island of the Monopanti in *The Hour of All Men.* (O.C. I, 266) Apparently Quevedo believes that by cataloguing the names of heretical persons the reader will give more credence to the dangers he points out.

11. Cf. the description of the fierce battle in Canto II of the "Poema heroico de las necedades y locuras de Orlando el enamorado"

in which a long series of verbs expressing violence are heaped one upon the other. (Blecua, 1373)

12. See Emilio Alarcos García, "Quevedo y la parodia idiomática," in *Archivum* (Oviedo), V (1955), 1, 3-38, and Amédée Mas, *La caricature de la femme, du mariage et de l'amour dans l'oeuvre de Quevedo* (Paris: Ediciones Hispano-Americanas, 1957), pp. 259-88.

13. Also described are the many unpleasant emotions which the author and the people he meets undergo—pain, disgust, fear, sorrow, pity, shock, and horror.

Chapter Six

1. The only complete edition of this work was done by Edward M. Wilson and José Manuel Blecua (Madrid: Consejo Superior de Investigaciones Científicas, 1953).

2. See Crosby's chapter "La historia del texto de la traducción de Focílides" in *En torno a la poesía de Quevedo* (Madrid: Castalia, 1967,) pp. 175-204.

3. For a study of Quevedo's lack of erudition in Greek, see Sylvia Benichoud-Roubaud, "Quevedo helenista: el *Anacreón castellano*," *Nueva Revista de Filología Hispánica*, xiv (1960), 51-72.

4. For detailed analyses of the themes of women and money in Quevedo, see Amédée Mas, *La caricature de la femme, du mariage et de l'amour dans l'oeuvre de Quevedo* (Paris: Ediciones Hispano-Americanas, 1957), and Emilio Alarcos García, *El dinero en las obras de Quevedo* (Valladolid, 1942).

5. Emilio Alarcos García, "El poema heroico de las necedades y locuras de Orlando el enamorado," in *Mediterráneo*, 13-15 (Valencia, 1946), 57-59.

6. *Courtly Love in Quevedo* (Boulder: University of Colorado Press, 1952), p. 32. For further evidence on Quevedo's Petrarchism, see Carlos Consiglio, "El 'poema a Lisi' y su petrarquismo," *Mediterráneo*, 13-15 (Valencia, 1946), 76-94, and Joseph C. Fucilla, *Estudios sobre el petrarquismo en España* (Madrid: Consejo Superior de Investigaciones Científicas, 1960).

7. See especially pp. 502-22 in the chapter "El desgarrón afectivo en la poesía de Quevedo," in *Poesía española*, (Madrid: Gredos, 1962, 4th ed.).

8. *Courtly Love in Quevedo*, p. 9.

9. Alexander J. Denomy, *The Heresy of Courtly Love* (New York: D. X. McMullen Co., 1947), pp. 20-21. Green refers to this book in his footnotes but ignores these three fundamental characteristics of courtly love.

10. Amédée Mas, *La caricature de la femme*, p. 303. It is interesting to note that Green indicated the ennobling nature of love for Quevedo and all courtly lovers in the concluding remarks of his study (p. 81) but did not go into this in his exposition.

11. We are indebted to Dámaso Alonso who has pointed this out in his *Poesía española*, pp. 514-16.

12. For further study of the love-death theme in Quevedo's amatory poetry see: Otis Green, *op. cit.*, pp. 62-69; Pedro Laín Entralgo, "La vida del hombre en la poesía de Quevedo," in *Vestigios* (Madrid: Ediciones y Publicaciones Españolas, 1948), pp. 17-48; and Blecua, pp. xcvii-cii.

13. This is Dámaso Alonso's opinion expressed in his *Poesía española*, p. 526.

14. Fernando Valera, "Reinvención de Don Francisco de Quevedo," *Cuadernos*, 34, (1959), 65-74.

15. *Op. cit.*, p. 515.

16. *The Metaphors of Luis de Góngora* (Philadelphia: University of Pennsylvania Press, 1933), pp. 139-40.

17. In her edition of this poem (Barcelona, 1964), pp. 35-44.

Chapter Seven

1. This analysis of the *Politics of God* is based on my article "*La Política de Dios* de Quevedo y el pensamiento político en el Siglo de Oro," *Nueva Revista de Filología Hispánica*, IX (1955), 385-94.

2. See Pedro Pérez Clotet, *La "Política de Dios" de Quevedo* (Madrid: Reus, 1928), pp. 27-29.

3. More recent criticism has departed considerably from the idea that Quevedo manifested great originality in the *Politics of God*. Mérimée's superb study, *Vie et oeuvres de Quevedo*, (Paris: Picard, 1886), was one of the first to indicate the true merit of Quevedo's political thought. Pedro Pérez Clotet, *op. cit.*, a recent dissenting voice, highly lauded the *sistema de Quevedo tan original*. (p. 191) Osvaldo Lira in *Visión política de Quevedo* (Madrid: Editorial Cultura Hispánica, 1947), and Emilio Carilla in *Quevedo* (Tucumán: Universidad Nacional, 1949), point out the lack of originality and system in the *Politics of God*.

4. Rodrigo Sánchez de Arévalo, *Suma de la política*, ed. by Juan Beneyto Pérez (Madrid: Consejo Superior de Investigaciones Científicas, 1944), pp. 89-90.

5. *Política de Dios* (Madrid: Castalia, 1966), edition of James O. Crosby, p. 252. This is undoubtedly the most reliable edition extant. All further quotes to this work will appear in parentheses in the text proper, e.g. (PDC, 252).

6. Otto Friedrich von Gierke, *Political Theories of the Middle Age*, translated with introduction by Frederic Wm. Maitland (Cambridge: Cambridge University Press, 1913), p. 69.

7. Cf. Alonso de Castrillo, *Tractado de república con otras historias y repúblicas* (Burgos, 1521), Chapter VI, who stated that

170 QUEVEDO

obedience is due the king in the way in which the queen bee is
obeyed by all the rest.

8. Desiderius Erasmus, *The Education of a Christian Prince,* translation and introduction by Lester K. Born (New York: Columbia University Press, 1936), pp. 156-57.

9. Bartolomé Felipe, *Tractado de conseio y de los conseieros de
los príncipes,* 2nd ed. (Turin, 1589), cited Plato as the author of this
dictum (fol. 72); Thomas Cerdán de Tallada, *Verdadero gouierno
desta monarchía* (Valencia, 1581), reproduced exactly the same
phrase (fol. 100v).

10. This can be readily discerned in such outstanding Spanish
medieval political treatises as the following: Raimuno Lulio's *Libro
de los proverbios* (1296), Alvaro Pelayo's *Speculum* (1341-1344),
Juan Manuel's *Libro de los estados* (1330), López de Ayala's *Rimado
de palacio* (1385), and Rodrigo Sánchez de Arévalo's *Suma de la
política* (1454). See also Helen J. Pierce, "Aspectos de la personalidad
del rey español en la literatura hispano-arábiga," *Smith College
Studies in Modern Languages* Vol. X, No. 2 (Jan., 1929), for a discussion of the nature of the king and his councillors.

11. Fadrique Furió Ceriol set off a whole series of treatises on the
role of the king's advisors with his work of reference of 1559: *El
concejo y consejeros del príncipe.* Others that followed were: Juan
Costa, *El regidor* (Salamanca, 1578); Bartolomé Felipe, *Tractado de
conseio* (Coimbra, 1584); Jerónimo Castillo de Bodadilla, *Política
para corregidores y señores de vassallos* (Madrid, 1597); Juan Már-
quez, *El gobernador christiano* (Salamanca, 1612); Juan de Mada-
riaga, *Del senado y de su príncipe* (Valencia, 1617); Lorenzo Ramírez
de Prado, *Consejo i consejero de príncipes* (Madrid, 1617); and José
Laynez, *El privado christiano* (Madrid, 1641).

12. Antonio de Guevara, *Epístolas familiares,* selection by Augusto
Cortina (Buenos Aires: Espasa Calpe, 1942), p. 72. This is taken from
an undated letter addressed to Count Pedro de Acuña. See the similar
reasoning of Felipe de la Torre, *Institución de un rey christiano*
(Antwerp, 1556), fol. 54.

13. Juan Luis Vives, *Obras Completas,* tr. from Latin by Lorenzo
Riber (Madrid, Aguilar, 1947), II, 268. Our statement is from Vives'
pedagogical work *De disciplinis* (1531).

14. Pedro de Rivadeneira, *Tratado de la religión* (Madrid, 1854),
BAE, LX, p. 526.

15. Plato, *Dialogues* (New York: Random House, 1937) II, 519.
This is Jowett's translation. For Aristotle's development of this, see
Ernest Barker's translation of the *Politics* (Oxford: Clarendon Press,
1946), p. 362.

16. Sebastián Fox Morcillo, *De regni regisque institutione* (Antwerp, 1556), folio after M5.

Chapter Eight

1. *Arte nuevo de hacer comedias* (Madrid, 1609), fol. 206.

2. See his *El teatro de Quevedo* (Madrid: S. Aguirre, 1945), p. 49, in which he claims that *El médico* and *Entremés de Pan Durico* are not Quevedo's mainly because their style is inferior to that of our writer.

3. These are published in his *Itinerario del entremés: Desde Lope de Rueda a Quiñones de Benavente* (Madrid: Gredos, 1965), pp. 259-364.

4. The Peralvillo was a district near Ciudad Real where the Inquisition tortured criminals with arrows. See Sebastián de Covarrubias, *Tesoro de la lengua castellana o española* (Barcelona: S. A. Horta, 1943, reprint of the Madrid, 1611 edition), pp. 862-63.

5. *Itinerario del entremés*, p. 207.

6. Quevedo, *Poesías originales* (Madrid: Editorial Planeta, 1963), p. 1031.

7. Asensio, *Itinerario del entremés*, p. 285.

8. Asensio in his *Itinerario del entremés* (p. 218) suggests that Quevedo intended to ridicule Luis Pacheco de Narváez, the fencing master who was caricaturized by Quevedo in several works.

9. *Ibid.*, p. 203.

10. There were two kinds of dances in Quevedo's time: the *baile*, which was a lively, spontaneous, and boisterous dance accompanied by spicy lyrics, and the *danza*, the stately, aristocratic dance usually performed in the palaces.

Chapter Nine

1. *Poesía española* (Madrid: Gredos, 1962), p. 576.

Selected Bibliography

PRIMARY SOURCES

1. Modern Editions

El Buscón. Edition of Américo Castro (Madrid: Ediciones de "La Lectura," 1911). First Clásicos Castellanos edition.

El Buscón. Edition of Américo Castro (Madrid: Ediciones de "La Lectura," 1927). New Clásicos Castellanos edition based on a manuscript of the Biblioteca Menéndez y Pelayo. Best extant edition of this work.

Espistolario completo de Quevedo. Edited by Luis Astrana Marín (Madrid: Reus, 1946). Good collection of his letters.

España defendida y los tiempos de ahora, de las calumnias de los noveleros y sediciosos. Edition of R. Selden Rose (Madrid: Imprenta Fontanet, 1916). Fine edition.

Ideario de don Francisco de Quevedo. Edition of Luis Astrana Marín (Madrid: Biblioteca Nueva, 1940). Popular collection of passages from Quevedo's works.

Lágrimas de Hieremías castellanas. Edition of Edward M. Wilson and José M. Blecua (Madrid: Consejo Superior de Investigaciones Científicas, 1953). First edition of this work.

Obras completas. Edition of Luis Astrana Marín (Madrid: Aguilar, 1943). Two volumes. Contains some of Quevedo's works published for the first time together with useful bibliography and Tarsia's biography of Quevedo.

Obras completas. Edition of Felicidad Buendía (Madrid: Aguilar, 1961). Two volumes. Probably best edition of his complete works.

Obras completas. Edited by Aureliano Fernández-Guerra y Orbe (Madrid: Sucesores de Hernando, 1910-1923). Two volumes. Good edition.

Obras satíricas y festivas. Edition of José Bergua (Madrid: Ediciones Ibéricas, 1958-1959). Popular edition with notes.

Obras satíricas y festivas. Edition of José María Salaverría (Madrid: Espasa-Calpe, 1924). Fair edition with sparse notes.

Poema heroico de las necedades y locuras de Orlando el enamorado. Edition of María E. Malfatti (Barcelona, 1964). Very fine edition with useful introduction and notes.

Poesía original. Critical edition of José Manuel Blecua (Barcelona: Editorial Planeta, 1963). Best extant edition of Quevedo's poetry.

Política de Dios. Edition of James O. Crosby (Madrid: Castalia, 1966). Excellent scholarly edition of this work.

Sueños. Edited by Julio Cejador y Frauca. (Madrid: Ediciones "La Lectura," 1916-1917). A well-annotated edition.

Teatro inédito. Edition of Miguel Artigas (Madrid: Real Academia Española, 1927). Useful mainly for *Cómo ha de ser el privado.*

Vida de Marco Bruto. Edition of Ana María Barrenechea (Buenos Aires: Estrada, 1943). Has prologue by Ramón Gómez de la Serna.

Las zahurdas de Plutón (El sueño del infierno). Edition of Amédée Mas (Poitiers, 1955). Very fine edition.

2. Translations

COHEN, J. M. *Visions* (Carbondale: Southern Illinois Press, 1963). The editor uses Sir Roger L'Estrange's translation.

DUFF, CHARLES. *Quevedo: The Choice Humorous and Satirical Works.* (New York: E. P. Dutton and Co., 1926). Contains the *Buscón* and the *Sueños.* Duff uses basically the seventeenth-century translation of Sir Roger L'Estrange and John Stevens.

HARTER, HUGH A. *The Scavenger.* (New York: Las Américas, 1962). Translation of the *Buscón.*

RIVERS, ELIAS. *Renaissance and Baroque Poetry of Spain* (New York: Dell Publishing Co., 1966), pp. 250-305. Very good prose translations of many important poems of Quevedo.

SECONDARY SOURCES

1. Bibliographies

INSTITUTO NACIONAL DEL LIBRO ESPAÑOL. *Aportación a la bibliografía de Quevedo* (Madrid, 1945)

QUEVEDO, FRANCISCO DE, *Obras completas* (Madrid: Aguilar, 1960), II, 1115-1384. Edition of Felicidad Buendía which comprises the best extant general bibliography.

————. *Obras completas:* I, Poesía original (Barcelona: Planeta, 1963), cxxiii-cl. Edition of José Manuel Blecua which contains best extant bibliography on Quevedo's poetry.

RODRÍGUEZ MOÑINO, ANTONIO. "Los manuscritos del *Buscón* de Quevedo," *Nueva Revista de Filología Hispánica,* VII (1953), 657-72. Very useful list.

THOMAS, SIR HENRY. "The English Translations of Quevedo's *La vida del Buscón,*" *Revue Hispanique,* LXXXI (1933), 283-99. Valuable bibliography.

2. Biographical Studies

AGUADO, EMILIANO. *Francisco de Quevedo* (Madrid: Nuevas Editoriales Unidas, 1962). Biography and anthology.

ASTRANA MARÍN, LUIS. *La vida turbulenta de Quevedo* (Madrid: Colección histórica "Gran Capitán," 1945). Popular biography, not always factually reliable.

CAMPOAMOR, CLARA. *Vida y obra de Quevedo* (Buenos Aires: Ediciones Gay-Saber, 1945). Good general exposition of Quevedo's life and works.

CROSBY, JAMES O. "Noticias y documentos de Quevedo, 1616-1617," *Hispanófila*, II (1958), no. 4, 3-22. Reliable information as in the case of other articles and books by Crosby.

————. "Quevedo's Alleged Participation in the Conspiracy of Venice," *Hispanic Review*, XXIII (1955), 259-73. Shows that Quevedo was not in Venice during the famous conspiracy.

————."Quevedo and the Court of Philip III: Neglected Satirical Letters and New Bibliographical Data," *PMLA*, LXXI (1956), 1117-26.

ESPINA, ANTONIO. *Quevedo* (Madrid: Atlas, 1945). General study of his life and works.

FERNÁNDEZ Y GONZÁLEZ, MANUEL. *Amores y estocadas: Vida turbulenta de don Francisco de Quevedo*. Novela histórica (Madrid: Editorial Tesoro, 1950).

GÓMEZ DE LA SERNA, RAMÓN. *Quevedo* (Buenos Aires: Espasa-Calpe, 1953). Good personalized biography.

GONZÁLEZ DE AMEZÚA Y MAYO, AGUSTÍN. "Las almas de Quevedo," *Boletín de la Real Academia Española*, XXV (1946), 251-98. General biographical material.

PÉREZ BUSTAMENTE, CIRÍACO. "Quevedo, diplomático," *Revista de Estudios Políticos*, XIII (1945), 159-83. Quevedo in Italy.

PORRAS, ANTONIO. *Quevedo* (Madrid: Plutarco, 1930). Popular biography.

SERRANO PONCELA, SEGUNDO. "Quevedo, hombre político (Análisis de un resentimiento)," in *Formas de vida hispánica* (Madrid: Gredos, 1963), 64-123. Good insight into Quevedo's political life during 1613-1619.

3. Doctoral Dissertations

BASTERRA, R. "Contribution au lexique de 'germanía' de Francisco de Quevedo" (diss. University of Paris, 1961).

BERUMEN, ALFREDO. "The Satirical Art of Quevedo" (diss. University of Texas, 1950).

BIRCH, WILLIAM GRAYSON. "Politico-religious philosophy of Francisco de Quevedo" (diss. University of Chicago, 1951).

CROSBY, JAMES O. "Quevedo in Italy: A Satirist in Politics" (diss. Yale University, 1954).

DURÁN, MANUEL. "Motivación y valor de la expresión literaria en Quevedo" (diss. Princeton University, 1954). Very fine study of the style and thought of Quevedo.

FRANKEL, HANS HERMANN. "Figurative Language in the Serious Poetry of Quevedo" (diss. University of California, 1942). Penetrating study on Quevedo's style.

GOLDENBERG, BARBARA B. "Quevedo's *Sueños*: A Stylistic Analysis" (diss. Columbia University, 1963).

LEVISI, MARGARITA. "Los *Sueños* de Quevedo" (diss. Ohio State University, 1964).

4. Books

ALARCOS GARCÍA, EMILIO. *El dinero en las obras de Quevedo* (Valladolid: Universidad de Valladolid, 1942). Good study on this theme.

ASENSIO, EUGENIO. *Itinerario de entremés* (Madrid: Gredos, 1965). Includes and studies five new *entremeses* by Quevedo.

BOUVIER, RENÉ. *Quevedo, homme du diable, homme de Dieu* (Paris: Champion, 1929). Spanish edition: *Quevedo, hombre del diablo, hombre de Dios* (Buenos Aires: Losada, 1951). Good, suggestive study on life and works.

CARILLA, EMILIO. *Quevedo (entre dos centenarios)* (Tucumán: Universidad Nacional, 1949). Excellent analysis of his important works in prose and poetry.

COTARELO VALLEDOR, ARMANDO. *El teatro de Quevedo* (Madrid: S. Aguirre, 1945). Fine, short study.

CROSBY, JAMES O. *En torno a la poesía de Quevedo* (Madrid: Castalia, 1967). Useful textual studies on Quevedo's poetry.

DÍAZ PLAJA, GUILLERMO. *El espíritu del barroco* (Barcelona: Apolo, 1940). He claims that *La hora de todos* is the key work of the Spanish baroque period.

FERNÁNDEZ, SERGIO E. *Ideales sociales y políticos en el Infierno de Dante y en los Sueños de Quevedo* (Mexico: Universidad Nacional, 1950). Useful study.

GONZÁLEZ DE LA CALLE, PEDRO U. *Quevedo y los dos Sénecas* (Mexico: El Colegio de Mexico, 1965). A fine study on Quevedo's use of Senecan philosophy.

GOYANES CAPDEVILLA, JOSÉ. *La sátira contra los médicos y la medicina en los libros de Quevedo* (Madrid, 1934). A lecture by a physician that exhibits and justifies Quevedo's severe criticism of physicians.

GOYOAYA Y ESCARIO, JOSÉ LUIS DE. *Don Francisco de Quevedo y su significación en la literatura española* (Bilbao, 1942). General appreciation of Quevedo as a writer.

GREEN, OTIS H. *Courtly Love in Quevedo* (Boulder: University of Colorado Press, 1952). Spanish edition: *El amor cortés en Quevedo* (Zaragoza: Librería General, 1955). Very good, scholarly study.

JUDERÍAS, JULIÁN. *Don Francisco de Quevedo: La época, el hombre, las doctrinas* (Madrid: Establecimiento Tipográfico de Rates, 1922). Good general study.

LIRA, OSVALDO. *Visión política de Quevedo* (Madrid: Editorial Cultura Hispánica, 1948). Good analysis of Quevedo's political thought.

MANCINI, GUIDO. *Gli Entremeses nell'arte di Quevedo* (Roma: Facoltâ di Magistero dell' Università, 1955). Fine study on Quevedo's interludes.

MARTÍNEZ FERNÁNDEZ, JESÚS. *Quevedo y la medicina* (Asturias: Luarca, 1957). Useful.

MAS, AMÉDÉE. *La caricature de la femme, du mariage et de l'amour dans l'oeuvre de Quevedo* (Paris: Ediciones Hispano-Americanas, 1957). Excellent study. Also contains very good analysis of Quevedo's style.

MÉRIMÉE, ERNEST. *La vie et les oeuvres de Quevedo*. (Paris: Picard, 1886). Standard reference.

MILLER, STUART. *The Picaresque Novel* (Cleveland: Press of Case Western Reserve University, 1967). Studies *Buscón, Guzmán de Alfarache, Lazarillo de Tormes* and German, French, and English picaresque novels.

PAPELL, ANTONIO. *Quevedo* (Barcelona: Barna, 1947). Useful reference work on Quevedo's life and works.

PARKER, ALEXANDER A. *Literature and the Delinquent* (Edinburgh: University Press, 1967). The picaresque novel in Spain and Europe from *Lazarillo de Tormes* to 1753. Claims that the Spanish picaresque novel reaches its zenith with the *Buscón*.

PÉREZ CLOTET, PEDRO. *La "Politica de Dios" de Quevedo: Su contenido eticojurídico* (Madrid: Reus, 1928). Originally a doctoral dissertation which unduly lauds Quevedo as a political theorist.

YNDURÁIN, FRANCISCO. *El pensamiento de Quevedo* (Zaragoza: Universidad de Zaragoza, 1954). General appreciation of Quevedo's works.

ZAMORA VICENTE, ALONSO. *¿Qué es la novela picaresca?* (Buenos Aires: Editorial Columbia, 1962). Good, short, general exposition of this genre.

5. Articles in Journals and Books

ALARCOS GARCÍA, EMILIO. "Quevedo y la parodia idiomática," *Archivum* (Oviedo), V (1955), 3-38. Excellent study on Quevedo's creation of neologisms.

ALBERTI, RAFAEL. "Don Francisco de Quevedo: Poeta de la muerte," *Revista Nacional de Cultura*, XXII (1960) nos. 140-41, 6-23. Personal evaluation of theme of death in Quevedo's poetry.

ALONSO, DÁMASO. "El desgarrón afectivo en la poesìa de Quevedo," in *Poesía española* (Madrid: Gredos, 1952), pp. 531-618. One of the best studies on Quevedo's poetry.

ASENSIO, EUGENIO. "Hallazgo de 'Diego Moreno,' entremés de Quevedo, y vida de un tipo literario," *Hispanic Review*, XXVII (1959), 397-412. On a newly found *entremés* of Quevedo.

AYALA, FRANCISCO. "Observaciones sobre el *Buscón*," in *Experiencia e invención* (Madrid: Taurus, 1960), pp. 159-70. Good analysis.

BENICHOUD-ROUBAUD, SYLVIA. "Quevedo helenista: *El Anacreón Castellano*," *Nueva Revista de Filología Hispánica*, XIV (1960), 51-72. Reveals Quevedo's lack of erudition in Greek.

BERSHAS, HENRY N. "Cardenales: The Case History of a Pun," *Romance Philology*, IX (1955), 23-26. Worthwhile note on Quevedo's punning.

————. "Three Expressions of Cuckoldry in Quevedo." *Hispanic Review*, XXVIII (1960), 122-35. Good scholarly article.

BERUMEN, ALFREDO. "La sociedad española según Quevedo y las Cortes de Castilla," *Abside*, XVI (1952), 321-43. Useful material taken from his doctoral dissertation.

BLANCO AGUINAGA, CARLOS. "'Cerrar podrá mis ojos . . .': Tradición y originalidad," *Filología*, VIII (1962), 57-78. Excellent analysis of this poem.

BLEZNICK, DONALD W. "La *Política de Dios* de Quevedo y el pensamiento político en el Siglo de Oro," *Nueva Revista de Filología Hispánica*, IX (1955), 385-94. Comparison between Quevedo's ideas on politics and those of political theorists of the Golden Age.

BONET, CARMELO M. "Quevedo prosista," *Logos*. V (1946), 103-18. Short general analysis of Quevedo's prose writings.

CARAVAGGI, GIOVANNI. "Il poema eroico de *Las necedades y locuras de Orlando el enamorado* de Francisco de Quevedo y Villegas," *Letterature Moderne*, XI (1961), 325-42, 461-74. Fine study.

CARILLA, EMILIO. "Quevedo y *El Parnaso Español*," *Boletín de la Academia Argentina de Letras*, XVII (1948), 373-408. Very good analysis of Quevedo's poetry.

CASTRO, JOSÉ ANTONIO. "Estructura y estilo de los *Sueños* de Quevedo," *Anuario de Filología, Universidad de Zulia* (Venezuela), I (1962), 73-85. Good general analysis of the *Sueños*.

CHACÓN Y CLAVO, JOSÉ MARÍA. "Quevedo y la tradición senequista," *Realidad*, III (1948), 318-42. Good study on Quevedo's stoicism.

CONSIGLIO, CARLO. "El 'Poema a Lisi' y su petrarquismo," *Mediterráneo*, IV (1946), 76-94. Useful analysis.

COTARELO VALLEDOR, ARMANDO. "El teatro de Quevedo," *Boletín de la Real Academia Española* (January, 1945), pp. 41-104. Good overview.

DEL PIERO, RAÚL A. "Algunas fuentes de Quevedo," *Nueva Revista de Filología Hispánica*, XII (1958), 36-52. Good scholarly study on heretics in the "Sueño del infierno."

————. "Two Notes on Quevedo's Job," *Romanic Review*, L (1959), 9-24. Worthwhile analysis of Quevedo's stoicism.

DUNN, PETER N. "El individuo y la sociedad en la *Vida del Buscón*," *Bulletin Hispanique*, LII (1950), 375-96.

FERNÁNDEZ, SERGIO E. "El inmanentismo del Infierno de Quevedo," *Filosofía y Letras* (Mexico), XXIII (1952). 175-81. Fair study on the *Sueños*.

FRANK DE ANDREA, PETER. "El Ars Gubernandi de Quevedo," *Cuadernos Americanos*, IV (1945), 161-85. Good general study on Quevedo's politics.

FRANKEL, HANS H. "Quevedo's *letrilla* 'Flor que cantas, flor que vuelas,'" *Romance Philology*, VI (1953), 259-64. A model analysis of this poem.

GREGORES, EMMA. "El humanismo de Quevedo," *Anales de Filología Clásica*, VI (1953-1954), 91-105. Useful general interpretation of Quevedo's work.

IRACHETA, MANUEL CARDENAL. "Algunos rasgos estéticos y morales de Quevedo," *Revista de Ideas Estéticas*, V (1947), 31-51. A good study on Quevedo's suffering and resentment.

IVENTOSCH, HERMAN. "Onomastic Invention in the *Buscón*," *Hispanic Review*, XXIX (1961), 15-32. Useful analysis of names in the *Buscón*.

————. "Quevedo and the Defense of the Slandered," *Hispanic Review*, XXX (1962), 94-115, 173-93. Excellent scholarly study on maligned real and proverbial types in "Sueño de la muerte" and other works.

LAÍN ENTRALGO, PEDRO. "La vida del hombre en la poesía de Quevedo," *Cuadernos Hispanoamericanos*, I (1948), 63-101. Penetrating study of meaning of life, death, and love in Quevedo's poetry.

LASCARIS COMNENO, CONSTANTINO. "La epistemología en el pensamiento filosófico de Quevedo," *Bolívar*, XV (1955), 911-25. Good study on Quevedo's philosophy.

————. "La mostración de Dios en el pensamiento de Quevedo," *Crisis*, II, 7-8 (1955), 427-44. Useful analysis of Quevedo's religious ideas.

————. "Senequismo y augustinismo en Quevedo," *Revista de Filosofía*, XL (1950), 461-85. Very useful study.

LÁZARO CARRETER, FERNANDO. "La originalidad del *Buscón*," *Studia Philologica: Homenaje ofrecido a Dámaso Alonso* (Madrid: Gredos, 1961), II, 319-36. Good general study.

————. "Quevedo entre el amor y la muerte," *"Papeles de Son Armadans* (Palma), I, no. 2 (1956), 145-60. On the sonnet "Cerrar podrá mis ojos . . ."

LEVISI, MARGARITA. "Hieronymus Bosch y los *Sueños* de Francisco de Quevedo," *"Filología*, IX (1963), 163-200. On the affinity between the *Sueños* and Bosch's paintings, taken from her doctoral dissertation.

LIDA, MARÍA ROSA. "Para las fuentes de Quevedo," *Revista de Filología Hispánica*, I (1939), 369-75. Very useful study.

————. "La *España defendida* de Quevedo y la síntesis paganocristiana," *Imago Mundi*, II (Sept., 1955), 2-8. Brief but useful.

————. "Estilística: Un estudio sobre Quevedo," *Sur*, No. 4 (1931), 163-71. Review article on Spitzer's "Zur Kunst Quevedos in seinem *Buscón*."

————. "Quevedo y su España antigua," *Romance Philology*, XVII (1963), 253-71. A good study of Quevedo's views on early history of Spain.

LIDA, RAIMUNDO. "*Como ha de ser el privado*: De la comedia de Quevedo a su *Política de Dios*," *Libro jubilar de A. Reyes* (México, 1956), pp. 203-12. Keen analysis of this play.

MARCILLY, C. "L'angoisse du temps et de la mort chez Quevedo," *Revue de la Méditerranée* (Alger), XIX (1959), 365-84. Worthwhile study on themes of time and death.

MAY, T. E. "Good and Evil in the *Buscón*: a Survey," *Modern Language Review*, XLV (1950), 319-35. Very fine study.

MORREALE, MARGHERITA. "Luciano y Quevedo: La humanidad condenada," *Revista de Literatura*, VIII (1955), 213-27. Lucian's possible influence on Quevedo.

PARKER, ALEXANDER A. "La 'agudeza' en algunos sonetos de Quevedo," *Estudios dedicados a Menéndez Pidal* (Madrid, 1952), III, 345-60. Keen analysis of Quevedo's wit in poetry.

————. "The Psychology of the Pícaro in *El Buscón*," *Modern Language Review*, XLII (1947), 58-59. Penetrating study.

PENZOL, P. "Comentario al estilo de Quevedo," *Bulletin of Spanish Studies*, VIII (1931), 76-88. General study on Quevedo's style.

PRICE, R. M. "Quevedo's Satire on the Use of Words in the *Sueños*," *Modern Language Notes*, LXXIX (1964), 169-80. Noteworthy stylistic study.

ROSE, R. SELDEN. "The Patriotism of Quevedo," *Modern Language Journal*, IX (1925), 227-36. Informative scholarly article.

SÁNCHEZ ALONSO, BENITO. "Los satíricos latinos y la sátira de Quevedo," *Revista de Filología Española*, XI (1924) 33-62, 113-53. Useful study.

SCHALK, FRITZ. "Über Quevedo und *El Buscón*," *Romanische Forschungen*, LXXIV (1962), 11-30. Very good analysis.

SERRANO PONCELA, SEGUNDO. "Los *Sueños* de Quevedo," *Papeles de Son Armadans*. (Palina) XXIII (1961), 32-61. Good overview of the *Sueños*.

————. "Estratos afectivos de Quevedo," *Cuadernos*, no. 34 (1959), 75-82. On Quevedo's writings in general.

SOMERS, MELVINA. "Quevedo's Ideology in *Cómo ha de ser el privado,*" *Hispania,* XXXIX (1956), 261-74. Good analysis of this play.

SPITZER, LEO. "Zur Kunst Quevedos in seinem *Buscón,*" *Archivum Romanicum,* XI (1927), 511-80. Excellent study.

TAMAYO, JUAN ANTONIO. "El texto de los *Sueños* de Quevedo," *Boletín de la Biblioteca Menéndez Pelayo,* XXI (1945), 456-93. Classical influences on Quevedo's *Sueños.*

TERRY, ARTHUR. "Quevedo and the Metaphysical Conceit," *Bulletin of Hispanic Studies,* XXXV (1958), 211-22. Scholarly study on Quevedo's poetry.

VALERA, FERNANDO. "Reinvención de Don Francisco de Quevedo," *Cuadernos,* 34 (1959), 65-74. Claims that Lisi was Isabel de Borbón, wife of Philip IV.

VERES D'OCÓN, ERNESTO. "Notas sobre la enumeración descriptiva en Quevedo," *Saitabi,* VII (1949), 27-50. Excellent, well-documented article.

WAGNER DE REYNA, ALBERTO. "Quevedo ante la vida y la muerte," *Realidad* (1949), 154-76. Noteworthy study on the meaning of life and death in Quevedo's works.

WILSON, EDWARD M. "Quevedo for the Masses," *Atlante,* III (1955), 156-66. On Quevedo's popular appeal.

Index

Prison of Love, 71
Privado cristiano, (El), 170
Protestants, 16, 17, 21, 27, 63
Proverbs of the Jealous Old Man,
    (The), 155
Providence of God, (The), 38, 136
Providencia de Dios, (La), 38, 136
"Psalm XVI," 125
"Psalm XXVI," 109
"Psalm XXVIII," 125
Psellus, Michael, 51, 164
Puns, 94, 101-6

"¿Qué verdadero dolor?," 108
Quiñones de Benavente, Luis, 152,
    154, 160

Ramírez de Prado, Lorenzo, 170
Rattlesnake, (The), 42
Ravisio Textor, Juan, 165
Refranes del viejo celoso, (Los), 155
Regidor, (El), 170
Religious poetry, 123-26
Remnant Lady, (The), 157
"Retirado en la paz de estos desier-
    tos," 126
Riber, Lorenzo, 170
Richelieu, Duc de, 27
Rimado de palacio, 170
Rivadeneira, Pedro de, 140, 144,
    147, 170
Rivers, Elias, 167, 174
Roderick Random, 78
Rodríguez, Lucas, 119
Rodríguez Moñino, Antonio, 174
Rojas, Fernando de, 55, 113, 156
Roland in Love, 122
Romancero general, 119
Romulo, (Il), 138
Romulus, 138
Ropavejera, (La), 157
Rose, R. Selden, 173, 180
Rudwin, Maximilian, 164
Rueda, Lope de, 151, 152
Rufián viudo, (El), 160
Ruiz de Alarcón, Juan, 107-8

Salas Barbadillo, Alonso Jerónimo
    de, 78, 157
Salaverría, José María, 173

Salisbury, John of, 145
San Pedro, Diego de, 71
Sánchez Alonso, Benito, 180
Sánchez de Arévalo, Rodrigo, 140,
    141, 169, 170
Sandoval y Rojas, Don Francisco,
    see Duke of Lerma
Sandoval y Rojas, Isabel, 33
Sannazaro, Jacopo, 73
Santiago, Order of, 32, 35, 137
Santiago, patron saint of Spain, 35,
    137-38
Santibáñez, María de, 30
Santos, Francisco de, 55, 161
Satan, 135, 143, 145
Satira Menippea Somnium, 43
Satire, 32, 37, 41-44, 45, 57-59, 61,
    65, 68, 70, 76, 80, 93, 94, 112,
    120-23, 134, 149, 152-60, 161-62,
    175, 180
"Satirical Epistle, Censuring the
    Present Customs of Spaniards,"
    34, 126
Satirical poetry, 120-22
Scavenger, (The), 174
Schalk, Fritz, 180
Seneca, 48, 134-36, 179
Sensorial stimuli, 117-18
Sentimental novel, 71
"Sermón estoico de censura moral,"
    125
Serrano Poncela, Segundo, 175, 180
Shades, (The), 156
Simplicissimus, 78
Sir Tightwad, 153
Sissy, (The), 154
Smollett, George, 78
Socrates, 136
Soledades, 131
Solitudes, 131
Solon, 48
Sombras, (Las), 156
Somers, Melvina, 181
Soto, Domingo de, 145
Spain Defended, 31, 113, 137, 173
Spanish Anacreon, 120
Spanish Parnassus, Mount Divided
    into Two Summits, with the Nine
    Castilian Muses, 119
Speculum, 170